Best wishes

From

Subroto Shee
4·19-'15

Culture Can Kill

How Beliefs Blocked India's Advancement

By

S. Subodh

authorHOUSE™

1663 LIBERTY DRIVE, SUITE 200
BLOOMINGTON, INDIANA 47403
(800) 839-8640
WWW.AUTHORHOUSE.COM

First published by AuthorHouse 12/09/05

ISBN: 1-4208-8058-6 (sc)

Printed in the United States of America
Bloomington, Indiana

This book is printed on acid-free paper.

"You have to be strong enough to say: If the culture does not work, don't buy it. Create your own."
---Mitch Albom in 'Tuesdays with Morrie'—(Doubleday, NYK)

PROLOGUE
To the Ocean on a Raft

Why is India under-developed? Why is it so poor and backward? How was it that foreign invaders could defeat and enslave India continuously for 800 years before 1947? Before anybody grows intrepid enough to commit such a massive indiscretion as to attempt to answer such momentous questions, he needs to do a little bit of explaining.

A foreign traveler (let us call him John) driving down a country road saw a man being robbed at pistol point. Not wishing to miss the chance of a lifetime, he had started secretly recording the scene on his video when a police van appeared from nowhere and a police officer overpowered the criminal. Another officer then approached John and announced, 'You are under arrest.' 'But I did not do anything,' said John. 'Yes, exactly. That's why we are arresting you. Under our laws, if a witness does nothing to help a crime victim, he is to be prosecuted as an abettor in the crime,' explained the officer. In the courtroom, John produced the tape to show that he did indeed try to help the victim by nailing down the identity of the criminal through taping the scene. He was then held guilty of invasion of privacy through unlawful taping!

So you are damned if you do, damned if you don't. Writing anything on India is a similarly hazardous act. Apart from practical problems like accessing accurate data, and dodging stereotypes, there is a very real problem of the writer facing a two edged sword. If he writes something commendable, he is accused of being blind to the realities of everyday life in India today, which are pretty grim and appalling. On the other hand, if he ventures to mention anything even remotely critical, a million patriotic souls immediately spring to the defense of the country. "Don't you know what a great nation we have been?" they say. "We are the most ancient civilization, a nuclear power today, the largest democracy in the world."

Nobody likes criticism; it hurts the ego and it is not politically correct. Anything you say can be used against you. It is a Tar Baby. Everyone who touches it gets stuck, one way or the other. There is nothing more enraging than someone exposing your faults---and being right. It takes breathtaking indiscretion or a touching belief to chase the maze of such a sensitive subject, where the interdependence of micro and macro, cause and effect, constitute an intricate web of life.

Again, India is so difficult to understand completely. A genie, pleased with an Indian American, promised that he would grant him any one wish. "Build me a direct highway from Los Angeles to Calcutta so I can drive instead of flying to India every time," the Indian requested. The genie scratched his head. He said, "That would be crazy. Ask for something else." The Indian said, "OK, then, enlighten me with a complete understanding of India and its culture." The genie thought for a moment and said, "How many lanes did you say you needed?" It is that difficult. Even for a genie. Why then, this book?

Poet Milton said, 'They also serve who only stand and wait.' On the other hand, it was Dante who said: "Those who in a time of crisis maintain their neutrality have the hottest place in hell reserved for them." I am not exactly worried about heaven or hell at the moment, but my vote will go to Dante in such matters. I simply cannot stand and wait. Why?

"Do you want to be a writer? Where are your wounds?" said Hemingway. Well, I never planned to be a writer, but I do have my wounds. Still more important, my Mother has wounds. Deep wounds. Serious wounds. Festering wounds. Mother India is bleeding. How can a son----any son----look on and do nothing?

But doing something should not mean desiring to cross the ocean in a wooden raft, as Kalidasa, India's greatest poet, put it so well, almost 1500 years ago. Yet, that is exactly what I have set out to do. A gall so great does need some explaining. Presenting an unconventional viewpoint from a fresh perspective is a goal worthwhile in itself, but the following story may also help a little.

A Hindu ascetic was performing penance. A bull used to graze in the green pastures in front of his cottage. The animal looked great, and the pious man's thoughts strayed to watch and admire him. "What a fine animal! How strong! How healthy! Moreover, what beautiful round horns! Almost a perfect sphere like a human head! Perhaps my own size." He saw the horns everyday for several months and had an urge to check, but common sense stopped him. Finally, one day, he could hold back no more and decided to take the plunge, no, not a plunge exactly, but a leap. He held the bull by the horns to put his own head through them. With quite predictable results. Recovering on his hospital bed, body all wrapped up in bandages, he was asked by a well-wisher, "My good man, did you not think before carrying out such a hazardous act?" And the pious man flared up. "What do you think I am? A fool? I thought about this for six months!"

Well, dear reader, I have thought about this for sixteen years. And so, here it goes.

Table of Contents

ACKNOWLEDGEMENT

A large number of friends, too numerous to list fully, helped me with this book at the manuscript stage. I am deeply indebted to all of them. I would like to mention the following friends in particular: Ashok Vidwans, Dr. Vijay Joshi, Aba Gawande, Dr. Gopal Shroff, Laxman Phadke, Pramod Khanna, Dr. R.N. Tiwari, Shekhar Joglekar, Kishor Raval, Dr. Prabal Dey.

I owe a deep debt of gratitude to all the named and unnamed authors and publishers from whom I have freely adapted a lot of quotes, phrases and ideas. To acknowledge each one individually is almost an impossible task. A short list of principal authors will be found in the Bibliography at the end.

My publishers have been most helpful at every stage---I thank my friend and guide, J.R. Harris of Authorhouse and Matthew Monroe and his team from the bottom of my heart.

S. Subodh

East Windsor, New Jersey 08520
USA.
June 2005.

WHY THIS BOOK?

In the marathon race of life, how is it that certain societies advance and others fall behind? Is there any kind of discernible pattern behind this? Such issues are quite complex because they constitute a maze of networks---history, sociology, psychology, environment, culture and more. A penetrating look at one specific or typical case in detail can form a good starting point in such a complicated analysis.

India is one such case. There is no better example than that of this vast ancient culture to illustrate, analyze and examine in depth the multifarious issues involved. This great ancient civilization, a billion people strong, with tremendous resources, how did it fall so far behind in the human race? There are no easy answers. But they need to be asked, investigated and debated because they are of interest to such a great mass of humanity and typical of many other societies too.

1. Ever since the last Hindu king Prithviraj Chauhan was defeated in 1198 A.D., India had been ruled by alien invaders, first from Central Asia and then from Europe---until 1947. No other country in the world has such a long history of subjugation under foreign rule for almost 800 years at a stretch. A long line of invaders---Gizni, Timur, Changiz, Nadir---set fires to Delhi, destroyed temples and robbed India at will. Hindu pundits were sold as slaves in the streets of Gizni. Why were we so weak? And still are? 2. This country of tremendous natural and human resources today lies at the bottom rungs of the economic ladder. The glamour and glitz of a miniscule westernized minority and brave talks of reaching the moon cannot hide the ugly fact that vast populations think, act and live like those in the eighteenth century. Why are we so poor and backward?

Many Indians are deeply disturbed today by India's current and chronic problems. If you happen to be one of them and have the urge and the will to think out of the box, I invite you to share with me a few uncommon thoughts of a common Indian regarding what I call **the universal collapse of common sense in India** today. Open any Indian newspaper and you will find a lot of problems, complaints and heart-burns about the situation in India---corruption, pollution, maladministration, the dirt, the superstition, and so on and on. Well meaning people describe these in vivid impressive detail. Their opponents react with hurt pride. There is no dearth of dissatisfaction as well as of complacency. Is it not time to go beyond this verbal point-counter-point and inquire into the deeper issues? To go beyond a routine repetition of anecdotal, incidental, personal experience? Should we not connect the factual dots to form a conceptual pattern that can leverage opinions into meaningful conclusions? When we shall stop complaining and start analyzing, we shall graduate into a brave new world of mature adults from the current world of raging infants. Our old Tower of Babel needs a modern voice synthesizer software. This book will demonstrate (I hope) that these problems are only the outward manifestations of a deep-rooted malaise. Then, in a step by step procedure, **it will analyze causes and suggest remedies. It will question assumptions, challenge beliefs and tread a road less traveled.**

Arnold Toynbee is the most celebrated historian of modern times. In his magnum opus---'A Study of World History'---he described in elaborate detail the rise and fall of all major civilizations. His conclusion is that neither the lack of natural resources nor the problems of geography nor Determinism can explain the fall of major civilizations in the past. It is the way a society responds to its challenges that determines its ultimate fate. (We have little control over geography and natural resources in any case).

Prof. Jared Diamond of the University of California at LA wrote a book titled "Guns, Germs and Steel---The Fate of Human Societies" (Norton, NYK). He asks a question (Page 409) that we Indians should have asked ourselves long ago but never did: "Why---were European societies rather than those of China or India the ones that took the lead and became dominant in the modern world?" In other words: Why did proximate factors of progress (like capitalism, industrialization and critical empirical inquiry) arise in Europe rather than in Asia? Let me ask this: **Why did not an Indian discover Europe** rather than a Vasco-de-Gama discovering India? If tiny Taiwan and ancient Israel could become a force in the modern world, why didn't India become one?

There cannot be any simple, easy or brief answers to such broad questions because these are multi-causal and multi-consequential issues, complex and serious. But even more serious is the fact that most Indians, even intellectuals, are too proud, presumptive, polite, indifferent or complacent even to ask them. Everyone has a strong suspicion that he already knows. "What can a new book tell us?" they are apt to say. Many profess intellectuality when they are only voicing their bias. It is truly amazing how often writers on India---otherwise brilliant---can come so close to truth and yet may miss it. Surely, a country with lots of brilliant brains can do much better. **This book will ask unpleasant questions and attempt honest, if at times unpopular, answers**.

We are too casual. We all pine for truth in a hurry. To summarize such broad issues has its own risks; but in this busy age of instant everything, it needs to be done. So here it goes: This book will present the theory that neither fate nor foreigners nor genes nor sins caused our demise as a strong nation and our degradation to the depths of destitution. We ourselves are responsible for our fall. Our culture killed us. Since culture is closely aligned with and forms an indistinguishable part of our religion, our traditional beliefs, values and attitudes originating in religion lie at the root of our seemingly intractable problems. Which beliefs, values and attitudes? As they say, the devil is in the detail. But very briefly, they are: Fatalism, Contentment, Irrationality, Obsession with spirituality, considering Gurus as Gods, Elevation of poverty and renunciation as desirable values, and many more. It is easy to criticize religion but not so easy to reject it. Religion is vastly useful, influential and even indispensable to most people. So what is the way out? The way out is a realistic cost-benefit analysis of our culture and religion. They had their day; they block us today. We must make a revolutionary transformation in our religion-based value system. We must "ignore the lure of advertised values." We need new values, new frames of reference. This takes clarity, thinking out of the box, a fresh approach and unconventional ideas. These are things for which most of us Indians are not too famous.

We in India today are "a society in uneven transition, with mixed messages in uneven stereo". Imposition of a western culture on an ancient bedrock of tradition has created a kind of rootless elite. Those elite are always wondering about which direction to take, although they may have a compass; because its needle keeps flickering constantly, once to the east, once to the west. They are, so to say, strangers to themselves; yet they themselves may not always know it clearly. The same considerations apply to our younger generation in India today; and to the bright boys and girls in the world wide non-resident Indian community who are trying to find their bearings in a global context today. Any attempt to clear the cobwebs of conflicting ideas should be of immense help in this age of global interaction of cultures. I invite you to share with me this rewarding but challenging endeavor.

This humble effort by a man possessed by a book, by an idea, by a fire, is nothing if not an anguished Indian's cry for modernity. I have no axe to grind, no ideology to promote. I have much to lose and little to gain. But, as J.C. Beckett, a historian, wrote: "I am concerned only to disentangle a confused stream of events and make the present situation intelligible by showing how it arose" and suggest possible action. To ask for a fundamental transformation in the basic attitudes and beliefs of an entire population is to root for a veritable revolution in culture. It is not easy and it can turn unpleasant. It can burn. But surely, to light the flame of hope in the life of a billion people is an undertaking worth any kind of effort or risk.

The following synopsis will provide a quick overview of the chapters that follow. However, this is a broad and controversial subject on which all of us feel we have an opinion. But an opinion, however passionate, is not an argument. So I would like to encourage the reader to approach the core issues in stepwise detail in the body of the book itself in order to gain the right perspective. For, while brevity may be the soul of wit, detail is essential to gauge real dimension in a complex network of interconnected ideas. Snippets and summaries do not let us grasp the full import of an argument even if we want to disagree knowledgeably.

SYNOPSIS

This book is divided into four sections: Section One 'The Symptoms' enunciates the superficial manifestations of a deep disease underlying the problems that India faced in the past and continues to face today. Section Two describes 'The Disease' itself. Section Three analyzes the Causes. Section Four specifies 'The Cure', the proposed new direction.

Though things in India are certainly changing today, apart from a small, vocal, visible, educated and urbanized minority, huge numbers of Indians in this twenty-first century after Christ live and think in ancient modes. The opening chapter of **Section One** titled 'Scenes Unsightly' provides a window-view to such life in India. The two most basic problems of India have been: Socio-economic backwardness and Failure to live in dignity, as evidenced by eight centuries under subjugation. We are a third world country at the bottom rungs of the ladder in the comity of nations (Ch. 2), not only in material aspects but also in the intellectual world of ideas. Yet a huge majority of Indians today refuse even to acknowledge such obvious facts. A kind of willing amnesia, a mass denial, vanity and confused thinking grip the country. Ch. 3 provides data on comparable periods in world history to cure us of our exaggerated notions of past glory. People in India often blame politicians, foreigners, economic policies, overpopulation or immorality for their woes. I point out the fallacies in such popular perceptions (Ch.4). We, the people ourselves, are responsible for our chronic problems. In 'God Janus Incarnate' (Ch. 5) I summarize India's recent achievements and ascribe them to a highly visible minority of the western educated urban elite. We all know the uneasy juxtaposition of overwhelming orthodoxy and pockets of modernity in India today.

Section Two starts with the definition of the central theme and a few clarifications in Ch.6. History teaches us that when Europe was going through the Renaissance and the Reformation, India failed to graduate out of the Dark and Middle Ages into the Industrial age. This failure occurred because our traditionalist culture did not have the supporting groundwork necessary to nurture innovative ideas (Ch. 7). This is one of the principal roots of our backwardness. A comparison of the cultural traits of other advanced societies with those of ours is amply supportive of this conclusion (Ch. 8). Our social situation---particularly the position of women, the caste system, the educational deficiencies and our negative philosophy---contributed heavily to our backwardness and military defeats (Ch. 9). Our negative attitudes, unreal beliefs and romantic cultural predilections lie at the roots of our regression; and these were derived from our religion. Irrespective of anyone's personal beliefs, we must objectively scrutinize the positive as well as the negative sides of spirituality and what consequences flow from it, whether intended or not (Ch. 10). We need religion to promote ethics. But ethics is a separate discipline. Religion included everything--ethics, psychology, literature, science--in ancient ignorant times. Man, a weakling in unpredictable and cruel Nature, created God to promote group cooperation through ethics. Today man has alternatives (Ch.11) like: Law is a form of ethics; a budget balances our priorities and values.

Section Three: Our beliefs inject ideological issues of impractical morality in statecraft. Belief in Rebirth promotes fatalism, lack of motivation, contempt of the world and passivity. Constant harping on the evils of money glorifies poverty. Worshipping gurus as gods upholds faith in orthodoxy and old ideas. Hindu society has an obsession with soul and spirituality leading to the neglect of this world, diversion of resources to abstract pursuits, pessimism and negativity in worldly affairs (Ch.12). Our culture holds us back. Some of the Cultural Blocks that retard us are: lack of innovation and creativity, anti-modernism, narrow focus, verbosity, duality and hero worship (Ch. 13). Tradition, culture and religion are an inseparable triad in Hindu society. Even educated Hindus will not give up wrong traditions because they are firmly rooted in religion. India's cultural isolation resulted in such wrong attitudes. Because religion has an all-pervasive influence on all aspects of life in India, and it bears full responsibility for our regression, understanding of our spirituality is of critical importance to gaining a real understanding of India's problems (Ch.14). I list several reasons why we need God and religion. But the non-rational and conflicting nature of theosophical beliefs makes it difficult for modern man to accept them. Religions promote irrational assumptive thought processes (Ch. 15). Interpretation of our ancient texts is full of controversy. Accusation of misinterpretation is a two-edged sword and meaningless. The Hindu penchant for redefining common words makes confusion worse confounded. Hindu religious literature is replete with hyperbole, metaphor, ambivalence, myth, jargon and throw-ins. All these can be embellishments in poetry but are handicaps in clear and logical understanding of serious ideas (Ch.16).

Several Indian writers have often criticized this or that part of Hindu religion like ritual and idolatry. But (1) They have traditionally viewed religion and worldly progress as separate and unconnected subjects. (2) The preaching of Unbalanced values and Ill-defined principles of Hinduism (Ch.17) have not received due attention. None has clearly made the obvious connection yet between the country's problems and the rampant irrationality fostered by a mythical religion for centuries. On the other hand, India's spirituality has always been glorified and the so called materialism of the rest of the world has been denounced, not only by priests but also by the public and tradition bound intellectuals.

We must be aware of the strengths and drawbacks of both, Faith and Reason (Ch.18). I illustrate that the self-styled rational Indian personality actually has deep rooted irrational predilections. Devout Hindus play down the importance of Intelligence; demand excessive faith; and encourage beliefs in Myths and miracles. They are nurtured in a culture of non-reason. Their decisions are based on presumption and speculation rather than on hard facts (Ch. 19). Hindu Logic is circumlocutory, plastic, inconsistent and ambivalent. Scholars splitting hairs and brandishing faith as science are good examples (Ch.20).

While all religions have some of the faults listed here, Hinduism is critically different qualitatively and quantitatively from other religions. Hinduism revels in fantasy, is blind to its innate contradictions and espouses inequality among men and gods to a degree that none else has preached or practiced. It displays imbalanced unidirectional vision through its preaching of one virtue at the cost of another (Ch. 21). Centuries of compounded growth in irrational mental gymnastics have produced a state of arrested mass intelligence in our society (Ch. 22). Hindu society mistook poetry for philosophy, equated group ethics with personal ethics and extrapolated desirable individual selflessness into a damaging societal suicide. Some concepts of Hindu philosophy need a second look at the other side of this precious coin (Ch.23).

What should we do today? That is the last, **Section Four**, of the book. Complex cures needed for a chronic disease should not be oversimplified. Yet the age of fast foods and instant cures craves for quick fixes. I suggest several practical lines of action (Ch.24) to tackle our perennial problems. Since extreme obsession with orthodox cultural and spiritual ideas has caused our problems, the only way left for us is to flush out our myth-based religion with modern rational ideas, if we want to save it and us from being perished. I make an humble plea to The Good Believers in Hindu religion and to our Modern Bright Youth for genuine modernization and rejection of old myths, while they may or may not continue to personally believe in the basics of Hindu religion (Ch. 24). I describe how most attempts at reformation of Hindu orthodoxy have failed in the past and how it needs a complete transformation (Ch. 25). Our intellectuals are responsible for their lack of original thinking, inaction and failure to lead the masses in this respect (Ch. 26). The last Chapter (Ch. 27) recapitulates the central theme of the book with a plea to end our age-old tryst with tradition. Neither our sins nor our genes caused our defeats and our backwardness. They happened because our culture and our values were---and still are---at war with our need to compete in the modern world. The essential conflict today is not of theocracy or metaphysics but one of modernization; and we must make sure religion does not stand in the way. I advocate strong action, however unpleasant, to revolutionize our popular age-old values right from the roots to rationalize our thinking and transform our outdated value system.

Some very practical steps can be (Ch. 24): Build schools, not temples. Break bias, not skulls. Forget nostalgia. Speak out and act against blind faith. Encourage and depend on voluntarism, not government help in daily problems. Follow pragmatism, not God, in national affairs. Base actions (like cow slaughter) on social science, not on emotions. Stop romanticizing spirituality; we already had enough of it so far. Challenge myths. Spread rational ideas. Stop obsessing on trivialities like derivations of words, rituals, past glory, dreamy faith---wake up! Above all, all of us must revise our ideas of God and religion as proposed earlier (Ch.10) in order to enable us to do all the above without conflict.

A few clarifications will be in order before we proceed:

1. This book is not about politics, economics or history. It is about ideas, about something that goes beyond the routine perception of things---about their cause; and the cause of the cause. For example: India's poverty is a condition. Low productivity is one of its proximate causes. This arose from absence of innovation. Traditional beliefs are the ultimate cause of this absence or infirmity. I focus on them. Poverty is like the fruit on a tree, low productivity the stem, and wrong beliefs are the roots. I concentrate on the roots, not on the fruits, leaves or stem. Please do not expect economic quick fixes and easy cures for such chronic deep-rooted problems as wrong beliefs based on old culture and religion. But as Vivekananda said, "**Every improvement in India requires first of all an upheaval in religion.**" Nothing will change till culture and religion change. And THAT, is my topic.

2. The points made regarding general subjects like faith, rationalism, science and religion are almost universal in scope. These ideas may find a broader audience among many underdeveloped or developing countries. But the principal thread of my argument and the details concern India and Hindu religion as a specific example. 3. The subject being so vast, a separate book can be written for every idea or chapter that follows. But constraints of time and space, coupled with the need to focus the reasoning, dictate that we take small bites. This is to ensure that we do not miss the wood for the trees, however pretty one particular tree may look. 4. Please concentrate on real issues and the message, not on the messenger. If the idea is right on merits, it should not matter who said it or where it came from. 5. This is about social science, not natural science. So side arguments will always be there; but spotting trends and general directions is more important than exceptions and variations. 6. To preempt any controversy over semantics, I use common words in their commonly accepted dictionary meanings, except where noted otherwise.

7. This book is designed as a readable presentation for an intelligent reader receptive to fresh ideas. It is not an abstract research treatise for scholars, though they may find a new angle to look from. So I refrain from loading it with unnecessary detail. (Please See Bibliography at the end).

8. Unraveling the kind of complex network of inter-related ideas discussed here is really like playing three dimensional chess. A certain degree of cross-referencing, even repetition, is inevitable. So, please hold your breath; and your questions---chances are that your answer may be under a different context in another chapter. 9. I claim no originality except for the main theme of this book and the temerity of its presentation. The stories, the phrases, have been borrowed or adapted from a variety of sources, too numerous to be fully acknowledged, although I owe them a deep debt of gratitude. 10. Why do I tell jokes while dealing with a serious and sad subject? As Nietze put it, "I laugh so that I don't break down in tears."

SECTION ONE
THE SYMPTOMS

1. SCENES UNSIGHTLY
Glimpses of Life in India

What kind of India do we see in its heartland? The real India, not the glitz and glamour of its westernized cities but the everyday life of the vast majority of its teeming millions.

In the ever-shifting kaleidoscope of life, a few sights and sounds get permanently etched in memory. They develop a nasty habit of cropping up when least expected and flash upon what the poet Wordsworth called 'that inward eye'. Let us look at one such sight, a real life scene from India of the twentieth century.

Place: A big city in western India, a quiet little town square, in a middle class residential community.

Time: A cool breezy morning in the late 1940s.

The curtain lifts. A small boy is playing with mates, all below ten years, probably less.

A group of women appears on the scene. About a dozen of them. All clad in black saris. Heads covered with the end of the garment, pulled over the face.

The little boy is curious. Who are they? What are they upto?

The women are making some sounds, low, almost inaudible at first, not at all understandable, at least not to these innocent little kids.

But soon the tempo picks up. Are they crying? Are they singing?

Suddenly, the women start hopping on their feet! With both feet rising together at the same time! One woman would sing a few short phrases in a long drawl, throwing in somebody's name, and all the others would respond with a loud simultaneous cry of "Hi, Hi!" And all of them would be beating their breasts with both hands, all this while, palms stretched, feet hopping, in simultaneous, synchronized motion!

A senior playmate knows it all. "Somebody died," he explains gravely to all the kids. The kids understand only a little. Hardly anybody has known death before. None has ever seen this kind of a public display of grief.

And what a display it is! It continues for about half an hour. The women finally stop, remove their veils, someone pours water in their closed palms, they take a sip, start talking among themselves, one elderly woman even teasing another about her lack of skill in the performance. Everybody walks back home. Life will resume as usual. Everything will soon be forgotten.

However, not in the mind of the little boy. He will remember. He grows up, learns, travels, comes in touch with varied cultures of the world, reads history, philosophy, science. By now, he knows death, the lives it affects, the very natural grief it causes. But he will neither understand nor appreciate the curious custom of respectable women beating breasts and hopping in a public square in observance of death, a social tradition so bizarre that it would look funny if the occasion were not so distressing

Another scene, this time from a village in the same region of India. Again, in the late 1940s. On the outskirts of the small hamlet, on open ground. An old statue---a stone idol with barely recognizable features---stands on the side of a narrow dirt road. Two men are beating on leather drums hanging from their slim shoulders, with small wooden sticks. A crowd is watching the proceedings. A woman carrying a sick boy approaches the statue, puts the boy down, makes the boy bow down with folded hands, palms joined. The emaciated, half clad boy is trembling all the time. He has fever and smallpox, a god given malady for which no medical treatment is allowed to be sought by the devout.

An old bearded man applies wet red vermillion with his fingers, on the statue, and sticks some grains of rice on it. The man wears a length of fabric wrapped around his lower body and has no shirt on. He wears a long round of cotton thread coming down from his right shoulder and going around his left waist to complete the wrap around. He breaks a coconut, striking on a stone on the ground. The small crowd bursts into a collective chant of slogans: 'Sheetala Maatki Jay' (victory to Mother Goddess Sheetala), 'Jay

Baliya Baapa' (Victory to Father Balia)! Both words---Sheetala and Baliya---mean smallpox in the local language. The ceremony is designed to appease these gods.

How do we educated modern people in India look at such scenes? The most frequent reaction is a complacent comment that such customs are now dying. Yes, certainly they are. Breast-beating has ceased, at least among the urban educated. The terrible scourge of smallpox has been eradicated in the world as a result of mass vaccination, the god thereof consequently dying a natural death in India too. Am I then flogging a dead horse? No. The beast of tradition is not dead by any means. Orthodoxy in India is not a dead dog. It survives in myriad different forms. What is needed is not just flogging but dissecting the beast. Dissection can give valuable insights into the diseases that afflict this country, this great ancient land of a billion people armed with a few nuclear bombs and not a few Neolithic minds. The problem to analyze is not any particular custom as such, but the mind set it reveals: stagnation of thought, slavery to mindless traditions, sheepish one-track mentality.

A small story can clarify what I mean: A sweet young thing was in close embrace with her lover when the husband's footsteps were heard.

"Quick", she said, "jump out the window."

"I can't, we are on the thirteenth floor," said the young man.

"For heaven's sake, is this the time to be superstitious?" cried the woman in desperation.

Well, the young man's problem is not superstition; it is the risk of falling to death. In our case the problem is not just orthodoxy, it is the risk of a free fall to death of a great ancient civilization.

2. DARKNESS AT NOON
Problems in the Land of Enlightenment

Everyone knows that psychological aberrations in man can be every bit as serious as physiological diseases but they are much more difficult to recognize and treat. In many cases it is difficult even to get the patient himself to admit that a problem exists. King George VI of the UK used to personally take his own phone calls. A caller, trying to contact a mental asylum on phone, once got connected to the palace, through a mistake. The King answered: "King George speaking." "You, the King Emperor?" says the amused caller in disbelief. "Well, if you are a king, I must be Napoleon Bonaparte!"

Men often find it difficult to recognize not other people's, but their own true self, their own identities, afflictions and idiosyncrasies. It is no different with cultures, societies and nations. For example, an extreme form of nationalistic superego engulfed the great German people almost seventy years ago. They called it National Socialism, patriotism, Aryan superiority and everything else except what it really was---an aberration in the collective national psyche. It took a devastating world war to cure the very intelligent German people of Nazism.

It is truly shocking to see how much of India in this twenty-first century still lives in subhuman conditions. This nation that was the 'land of enlightenment' at the dawn of history is engulfed in darkness at the noon of civilization in the world today. It is amazing that it found itself difficult to survive in honor. It is still more amazing to see how even the educated people in India fail to grasp this simple fact or realize truly its full implications. Most urban Indians will not even acknowledge that we are backward.

After a long professional career in India, I migrated to the United States 18 years ago. Like all fresh immigrants of my generation, I went through the usual process of getting adjusted to what in reality was a different world altogether. We look at the skyscrapers, the flyovers, the tunnels under the rivers and wonder at the marvels of engineering in New York. We are amazed at the torrential traffic flowing so smoothly so fast. We are impressed, dazzled at the glitter. We are overawed at the tremendous economic, military, and technological power this country has acquired. We compare with conditions back home. And yet, we do not know the real difference between India and America. We do not know what we really should know and as Indians desperately need to know. Sounds a little strange but truth is sometimes stranger than fiction!

How do you explain to someone who can't understand that he does not understand? How do you explain something to someone who can understand but refuses to understand? Question: What did the man say when the elephant entered his home? Answer: Nothing. He did not notice. We do not notice. But it so happens that a democratic society that can't or won't notice is a grave danger to itself.

We claim that India is great, much superior to the other countries of the world in many respects. Need a proof? Let me share with you the following e-mail I received from an unknown but obviously well meaning Indian source. It reveals the mindset of our times, especially of the educated Indians.

"Subject: Fw: Proud To Be Indians.   **Date: Thu, 11 May 2000.**   **09:18:40**

Hi everyone. This is one of the best mails I have ever received. It makes me really proud to be an Indian. I request you to forward it to as many people as you can here in India and all over the world. Let the world know what we Indians stand for.

There are 3.22 million Indians in America. (wrong, actually1.7M). 38% of Doctors in America are Indians (actually, 5%). 12% of Scientists(?), 36% of NASA employees, 34% of MICROSOFT employees, 28% of IBM employees, 17% of INTEL employees, 13% of XEROX employees, are Indians. These facts were recently published in a German Magazine, which deals with world history. ------Facts about India:

a. India never invaded any country in her last 10,000 years of history.

b. India invented the Number System. Aryabhatta (astronomer) invented the zero.

c. The World's first university was established in Taxila in 700 B.C. More than 10,500 students from all over the world studied more than 60 subjects. The University of Nalanda built in the 4th century B.C.

was the greatest achievement of ancient India in the field of education---." (The long list goes on and on like this. Then come the quotes).

"(a) Einstein said: We owe a lot to the Indians, who taught us how to count, without which no worthwhile scientific discovery could have been made. (b) Mark Twain said: India is the cradle of the human race, the birthplace of human speech, the mother of history, the grandmother of legend, and the great grand mother of tradition. Our most valuable and most instructive materials in the history of man are treasured up in India only--- (Again a long list follows). All the above is just the tip of the iceberg; the list could be endless--I am proud to be an Indian. Are you? Please pass this on."

Great! Is it not? Grand history, big testimonials, lots of nostalgia and an overdose of wishful thinking coupled with self-approbation. Wonderful romantic words. I do not underestimate the importance of self esteem and feel-good factors; but the dividing line between self-esteem--complacence--bravado is quite thin, almost imperceptible. Self-esteem is a great feeling, especially so for children trying to grow up; but we adults need an occasional dose of reality and a look at the other side of the coin too, in order to gain a good perspective. Wish to have a little check?

Lots of good Indians in America? Great! Why did they leave India in the first place? What is it that motivates us to pay tons of money even to crooks to smuggle ourselves out of our 'great' country? India gets high praise from foreigners? It is common sense to note that (1) Almost all of it refers to the distant past. (2) There is no dearth of adverse comment on record regarding our miserable current situation. But the fact is that foreigners will naturally be too polite, diplomatic and sophisticated to criticize us especially when they don't have to. So we escape with indifference to our problems, faint praise for our efforts and eulogies for our past. Assimilated all invaders? Not the British, not the Muslims, the two most important. Not invaded anybody? Did anybody hear about a pigeon attacking an eagle? Is our non-aggressive stance a result of weakness or of our lofty moral principles? We need to investigate rather than assume a high pedestal. I do not wish to analyze the above list in more detail although it obviously contains many exaggerations and inaccuracies. In spite of the patriotic fires burning bright in the heart of a well-meaning Indian person, what is the real life situation in India at present? Let us look at a few facts. Facts have the power to shatter a lot of paranoia.

India is one of the poorest countries in the world today, ranking even below some African countries. We, the 16% of the world population, live only on 4.5 percent of the total landmass of the world. The highest numbers of people living below the poverty line--260 million--reside in India. So also the highest number of children--53% are undernourished (38% in Pakistan). The only countries comparable to India in this respect are the sub-Saharan African countries and Bangladesh, the poorest of the poor in the world. Almost a third of the population is condemned to live on less than a dollar a day when inflation has reached sky high. Our budget deficits are alarming---of the order of 10 percent. Inflation has reduced the value of our rupee to less than one-tenth of what it was in 1947 at the time of independence. In a particular year, we ranked 119th among 126 countries of the world in poverty. Average income spent on food alone (an indicator of poverty) is 48% in India, 24% in Mexico, 18% in France and 7% in the USA.

Our tiny neighbor, Thailand, has a per capita GNP of $ 1960. It would take India over 20 years to reach that number at a compounded annual growth rate of 9 % which is very optimistic. While China grew at the annual rate of 8% during the last ten years, we grew at 6. The foreign debt of India was the highest of all the countries in the world at the end of 1999. During the last decade, it has been hovering around 100 billion dollars, which is around 25 percent of gross national product. A huge 27% of the central budget income comes from debt. 26% of the amount spent goes into interest payment. The biggest percentage of the central budget goes into Defense, which (unlike creation of infrastructure) is naturally an investment with no economic returns, whatever its justification. Tax evasion is rampant. Government cannot enforce compliance. It periodically declares amnesty. In one such effort in 1975 during the emergency, cheats owned up over 14.5 billion rupees in undisclosed income, giving over 2.5 billion in taxes, wiping out more than half of the budgetary deficit.

Before we started modernizing our agriculture in the 1960s, India faced a major famine once in every four years on an average. About four million people died in Bengal in one famine alone in 1943. That is a number higher than the entire population of certain small countries in the world. The nightmares of flood and famine are hardly uncommon ones. United Nations Development Program prepares the Human Development Index based on health, literacy and other criteria. In this, India ranked 128th among 174 countries, below even Sri Lanka and Maldives. When the world is passing from the industrial age into the Internet age, agriculture is still the primary occupation of the people. 60 percent are still farmers. Vast numbers of people live a miserable existence not on farming, but on subsistence farming and as part time farm labor. The second largest employer is the oldest industry in the world—textiles--and that also is struggling to survive because it cannot compete with others.

Overpopulation? We know it all. Shortage of everything (water, fuel, housing, farm lands), congestion everywhere (schools, streets, trains), widespread destruction of good things (environment, morals, morale), increase in unwelcome things (corruption, pollution, slums), all these are too familiar to need description. Drinking water shortage is endemic in many parts of the country. Water is shipped in tankers as a relief measure in many places. Cuts in supply hours are routinely enforced in towns. We have alarming shortage of critical essentials like sources of energy---70 % of crude oil is imported. The big gap between demand and supply of energy results in frequent blackouts and shutdowns in spite of staggered supply hours. When a country lives on borrowed energy and borrowed money for so long, it lives on borrowed time. It is a sure prescription for impending disaster.

Unemployment is widespread. Accurate data is difficult to come by. Nobody even talks about partial unemployment, or unemployment among women, handicapped or disadvantaged persons. These are all taken for granted. It is not a popular practice to register oneself in employment exchanges and yet they are able to provide jobs to only one per 250 registered applicants.

Infant mortality rate is 43 per 1000 live births in China but 70 in India. India accounts for 30 % of the global tuberculosis cases and nearly half a million TB deaths per year. At least 40 percent of the confirmed polio cases worldwide have been detected in India according to the UNICEF. Here we are in company with Ethiopia, Nigeria, Pakistan, and Bangladesh. These are the last remaining countries where polio virus is easily spread. AIDS is spreading dangerously.

When "Literacy" is defined as broadly as to include anyone who is barely able to sign his own name, around 34 percent of the population is still illiterate. This means that the largest numbers of illiterate persons in the world are Indians, a number bigger than the population of the entire country at the time of independence. Female illiteracy is 57% in India and 25% in China. Educationists are unanimous that educational standards are falling fast and the effects will be felt after a few decades.

In the latest Olympic games India managed to win a solitary bronze medal. Many small little known or poor countries like Moldova, Bahamas, Thailand, Estonia, Lithuania, did much better. Ethiopia won 8 medals, Brazil 12, Cuba 29, China 59. Our poor show is nothing unusual. This year was only the second time in the history of the games that an Indian won an individual medal, never a silver, never a gold except in a group game—hockey—in which we finished in the seventh place this year. We are ranked 105th in football in the world, 108th in tennis, 12th or the last in Hockey in 1997. We were placed seventh in rank out of ten countries by the International cricket council in June, 2001----and this in a game that has become a national frenzy.

A quick look at the Nobel prize: Indians residing in India (not NRIs) have so far won this prize three times only so far, ever since it has been awarded. U.S.A. wins three or more as a matter of routine, almost every year. Our administrative and managerial incompetence is incredible. Compare the way we manage our airports, customs, courts, consulates, with that in the western countries. The problems are not due to inadequate resources alone. They are also due to lack of imagination and ideas. We don't have much to boast about in the intellectual field too (See Page 76--Innovation).

Exploitation of child labor and forced labor is prevalent. Authentic figures are not available, but a recent UNESCO report places the number of child laborers at 13.9 million--6% of all children between the ages of 5 and 14 years. Informal categories like domestic labor are additional.

We are destroying ecology and economy with egalitarian equanimity. Pollution of air and water is not news any more. The holy river Ganges needs a clean up. The Taj Mahal needs a restoration because of air pollution. Today's reality in pollution is much worse than the worst case scenario of just fifty years ago.

Law and order is breaking down. Earlier this was confined to backward states like Bihar. Now it is spreading in comparatively progressive states like Gujarat. Gang wars and caste wars are common. Kidnapping of the rich and the famous has ceased to shock anybody; it has almost become industrialized. Assassins can be hired with ease. Bomb blasts are frequent. Government is unable to control insurgency. Saboteurs have struck frequently in army, police and defense sensitive areas; two prime ministers, one ex-chief of the army staff, several government officers have been killed. Terrorists attacked a state legislature, the parliament, the Red fort, several army weapons warehouses; and exploded several bombs in the country simultaneously. Government resorts to bravado but is really helpless. We have become a 'soft' state. We cannot defend ourselves internally. Our internal weaknesses make us doubt whether we can win against a much smaller neighbor one-third our size in spite of our huge army. You see how awful it gets awfully fast.

People have already lost faith in the judiciary mainly because of inordinate delays in obtaining justice. A few numbers: Lawsuits accumulated in high courts are: Half a million pending since more than 10 years, 1.88 million since more than two years, and 3.2 million in all. These numbers do not include cases pending in lower courts (20 million) and in the federal Supreme Court (21,567 on Nov.1, 2000). Courts take twenty years to resolve contract disputes. Yet the prime minister and the chief justice of India recently blamed each other in public for this sorry state of affairs!

Slums worse than hell do not shock us. Suicide deaths are reported almost everyday in local news media and are rising. Most of them are due to unbearable living conditions, mainly, poverty. People are tired and turned off. Dowry deaths (bride burning), female infanticide, domestic beating of women, all these blight the landscape throughout the country. Millions live like animals and thousands even worse. Millions are neglected and thousands are being kicked around.

India today lives in an epidemic and endemic culture of corruption to the core, a cauldron of pathologies nurtured by culture. It is engulfed in a web of criminality, mafia and a striking absence of law. Unprincipled politics, frustration and disillusionment among the younger generation, social tension, growing secessionist movements and political horse-trading---all these have eroded people's faith in parliamentary democracy. In our dysfunctional democracy, for complex and unintended reasons too deadly to detail, people have simply lost the trust. The rot of morale, the social chaos, are undeniably terrible.

Our lack of punctuality and lack of cleanliness are proverbial, unfortunately real, subject of many jokes and need no elaboration. Any recent visitor to India will be able to testify to the negativity and cynicism pervading widely among the population and the distrust rooted in people's minds. Rampant corruption, favoritism for the privileged, exploitation and abuse of power---all these have created a well-merited distrust of politicians, bureaucrats, governments and institutions of all kinds. So many rumors and unauthenticated reports are circulating among the people and the press that it is next to impossible to determine what our national motto---Truth alone wins---represents.

We cannot cope with insurgency, overpopulation, pollution, corruption, you name it. We may not be broken but we have a hundred holes and a thousand cracks in the system. So we do what we always do----Nothing. Because it is no easy task to rehumanize a degraded society. We have a wholesome dignified society turned into a freak cynical nation; decent, God fearing people into immoral selfish freaks.

Well, the less we talk, the better. Let us call this second list B for convenience of reference. The list could go on and on. Like that story of an unhappy businessman who was describing to a friend the disappointing state of his business in boring detail. He said, "May was bad for business, June too was very bad, July was even worse and---and----", but the friend interrupted him. He said, "Don't bore me with your petty complaints. See what happened to me? My wife died yesterday. My son fell and broke his leg today and my dog is missing since morning. What can be worse than that?" "I can tell you what," replied the businessman. "August."

Want to say, "Cry the beloved country?" It is amazing that we still need to whip out statistics like above to convince people that we are in a mess. Poverty no longer pains us. Corruption no longer burns. Tragedies no longer shock us. It is all a part of routine everyday life. We are economically backward, strategically weak and intellectually stagnant. We are like a dead man walking in a town of the dead---dead emotions, dead sensibilities, dead hopes and dead ambitions. We do not realize what it is about this nation that makes it incapable of admitting the obvious: We are in a MESS. Period.

Clocks in India run ten and a half hours ahead of those in the East coast USA, but India is ten decades behind the USA in most intellectual, social and ideological fields. In manufacturing field, barring recent software, confused thinking and contradictory culture are the best products we keep making.

If these facts do not wake us up, what will? The first list A looks impressive; this second one B is even bigger and most depressing. So, which is the Real India? Is it advancing? Or is it declining, degenerating? Is it going forward or backward? Or is it going in circles? Like catch 22s---overpopulation causing poverty, poverty in turn causing population increase; corruption causing frustration, frustration promoting more corruption; lack of sanitation causing disease; and abundance of infectious disease resulting in more insanitation. If India is in bad shape today, how did we arrive at such a sad pass? And Why? Do we need to go back to our roots in the past? Or do we need to modernize?

It all depends on whom you ask. One section of Indians wish for a Utopia, which they call a Rama Rajya without really knowing what it means. They pine to return to the glory that was India. Nostalgia for a largely unknown past in an under populated country in an assumed era called Satya Yuga (Age of Truth) can easily distract us. Another section of Indians wishes to promote modernization; but after 150 years of English education we are still arguing what it is or whether it is good or bad for the country. Many pious souls advocate a compromise of the east and the west, not aware of what it means in specific terms. They advocate a synthesis of sorts, a mushy middle way that avoids the agony of an argument we dread and the mental gymnastics we are too lazy to go through.

The fuzzy logic, the lack of direction, even among the educated classes, is truly astounding. Life in India is often replete with sound bites, slogans and stereotyping. These produce sweeping summations and snap judgments. Generalizations abound and platitudes pervade all talk. Isolated images are proffered as an assessment of the entire landscape. We hear an endless torrent of stories and personal experiences, some of them so convoluted and confused that you need to ask the narrator: 'Are you criticizing or complimenting?' Most of the time this is called confused thinking but sometimes one does feel that something is really missing. That something may well be rationality.

The problems are complex. They are further complicated by our pride and inertia. Yet almost every bad story we read in the morning newspapers alerts us to the critical importance of our alarming problems. Surely, there must be an objective, reasonable way to look at these things and view them in the correct perspective, in order to analyze the facts and draw realistic conclusions. No magic bullet may exist for whatever it is that ails us but the right direction and path can surely be explored.

Human nature being what it is, all of us are apt to generalize from our limited personal exposures to men and matters. The educated rich person forgets that he is a representative of a growing but as yet a very small fraction—less than five percent---of the Indian population that is westernized, educated and happens to be quite rich by Indian standards. He thinks, "I don't know how India can be poor. I don't know anybody that is poor." This group is the most visible, vocal and dominant in India today. It exercises its influence over public life far in excess of its relative numbers. This in itself may not be a disaster if it were not for the fact that most people consider this group as a representative of India as a whole. Nothing could be more misleading. We like to concentrate on the parts of India that glitter. We ignore the unpleasant aspects—the poverty, the dirt, the corruption, the crime, the insanitation, the hypocrisy, all of which have become facts of daily life today for the common man. We are today a classic case of what some people in jest call SNAFU---Situation normal, all fouled up. In actual fact, dear reader, the situation in India is not as bad as you think----it is worse.

In a country becoming more and more desensitized, no longer shocked or angered by destructive behavior, it is time to take stock of where we have come from and where we are headed. Our generation will carry a heavy burden of responsibility if it does not do this. We cannot say ours is a case of frequent hiccups. It is more like a cancer eating away at our body politic. We are trapped in a weird cycle of a cancer crying for a cure; and possible cures producing still more cancers.

The most important fact, an amazing fact about our problems is this: It is not that we don't see the solution. It is that we don't see the problem. Like a fly on a wall, we witness everything but perceive nothing. Reality so far has been unable to pull the rug out from under our fantasy because we rest deep in the cocoon of our self-approbation. To feel better is not the same as to think better. And thinking, not feeling, is everything when it comes to seeing the world in the proper way. We must first admit that we have problems and then summon the will to make changes. That is often the hardest part. List B above compels us to ask the disturbing questions that we need to ask. How did the country that gave the Upanishadas become so ignorant? Why do we see so much unethical behavior in a nation that boasts a tradition of myriads of saints, preaching morality by the tons? How does a country that chews on the Karma Yoga of the Gita everyday harbor so much laziness and inaction? In a country where 'Truth alone Wins' is the motto, why can nobody dig out the truth from so much untruth floating around?

We must realize that if we keep doing what we are doing, we are going to keep getting what we are getting. Surely, patting on one's own back never helped anybody except kids and psychopaths constantly in need of reassurance and reinforcements. It is certainly not what mature adults do everyday in normal life. There should be no need to massage our fragile egos. I am second to none on manners and civility. But a debate on the past and future of a billion people is not a dinner party. If the opposite sides in a debate are poles apart in beliefs and approach, it is the duty of the intelligentsia to make those differences clear, not to play them down for fear that someone will be offended.

What we desperately need today is courage to face our faults. Not to denigrate ourselves but to see how one of the greatest early civilizations that prospered in the world can arrest and reverse its steep decline downhill into a state of such abject poverty, decay and degradation. It is a daunting task. But it can also be the highest form of adventure for those who might enjoy a challenging, vigorous critique of ideas. There is no way any reasonable person can deny India's problems; but intelligent persons can always make a detour and side-step their problems by concentrating on more favorable events or times. They can also wrap myths around unpleasant facts. We have such a myth---the myth of our past. Let us look at it now.

3. THE VINTAGE MIRAGE
Vanity for a Vanished Age

Can a look at history help us define our problems more clearly? Yes. Are we obsessed with our past? Do we harbor illusions about it? Certainly. Let us see how.

An interesting fact about Indian history is that the current (2002) BJP led government is the first Hindu nationalist government in India after 800 years of rule by foreign invaders. Eight hundred years of slavery? Yes, very true, but how many people realize this fact or appreciate its full implications? Actually, this fact can explain a lot of aggressive, assertive stance that the ruling majority community is adopting---like hypersensitivity about any comment on Hindus and attempts to sanitize unpleasant historical evidence.

Many myths about Indian history in the minds of the common man need to be clarified and corrected. We have displayed a pretty good talent for not making history ourselves and a still better talent for not writing it too. The dates of our best ancient personalities and events are often correct to an accuracy of a few hundred years here or there, sometimes even more. So our truly authentic history starts only with the Buddha, the Ashoka (Maurya king) Edicts and the Greek invasion.

India responded valiantly to the Greek challenge (after Alexander's invasion) in the form of the Mauryan empire (321 to 184 B.C.). Then came other aggressors from central Asia, like Shaka, Kushan and Hun. We faced up to that challenge with the most glorious period in Indian history, the Gupta period. That ended in 590 A.D. After that, Harsha / Pulkeshi were the only great Hindu kings. When Harsha's reign ended in 646 A.D it was almost the end of significant Hindu political power, except for brief, scattered periods, mostly in southern India.

After the first Muslim entry into India in 712 A.D. Mahmud Gizni invaded India in the first half of the eleventh century. He exposed our weaknesses convincingly and completely like none other before or after. He invaded seventeen times, went upto Kanpur, robbed the country almost at will and looted the Somnath temple (1024 A.D.), which was one of the holiest Hindu places of worship. He destroyed the idol of Lord Siva, the Destroyer of the world in Hindu religious tradition. He used three broken pieces of the stone idol as stepping-stones in his palace. Learned Hindu priests were sold as slaves in the streets of Gizni.

Did the Indians wake up? Did they analyze, organize, unite? Did they realize what was happening? No. Our only answer was shock, denial, fear and more of the same old stuff. Look what happened next. Another Mahmud (Ghori) destroyed Nalanda university, defeated Prithviraj Chauhan in 1198 A.D., and appointed his slave named Kutbuddin Aibak to start in Delhi the first foreign dynasty. It bore a rather significant name—the Slave dynasty. And that was the end. Never again would Hindu India be free from foreign rule until 1947. Allauddin Khilji (1311) conquered almost the whole country, stretching deep down the South, up to Madura and Rameshwaram. Looted treasures of the Hindu temples---always renewed by Hindu devotees---fed the armies of the Muslim conquerors. Queens of defeated rulers were consigned to the harems of the conquering hordes and their Sultans. Millions were converted or massacred.

The Muslim period was remarkable for stability only under the four great Mughals from 1556 to 1707. Barring this period, India was vanquished and plundered with remarkable ease by Central Asian invaders like Timur (1398), Changiz (1221), Nadir (1739) and Ahmedshah Abdali (1761). Then came the western nations who defeated us comfortably in the eighteenth century and ruled over us, until 1947.

After independence, we lost miserably against China in 1962. We fought three wars against a weaker, smaller neighbor in 1948, 1965 and 1971 but could not win decisively any time except once in 1971 when Pakistan, geographically at a tremendous disadvantage, lost its eastern part. In the latest conflict in Kargil we found it tough to tackle the camouflaged invaders in spite of an all out effort by our army and air force for three months. When at last they chose to withdraw as a result of international pressure, we celebrated our military 'victory' with a big fan fare!

Our history is not just a story of innocence lost. It is a story of being kicked, beaten and shot through the heart for a thousand years by scores of invaders. How many times has Delhi been burned and temples looted in India? We lose count. Such stubborn realities should have induced a painful reckoning of our past performance. But they have not. Even after a millennium of slavery and defeats, the grim reality of our situation has not sunk in our people. We still keep telling ourselves that it did not happen. We refuse to confront the demons in our past and refuse to acknowledge past disgrace. Not wanting to face reality, we retreated into denial. We pushed the thoughts of our weakness so far away that we ignored the miseries, insults and oppressions we routinely endured, like Rajput women committing suicide (Johar). Post traumatic stress disorder is a common psychiatric diagnosis in individual lives. I wonder if it applies to entire societies as well.

A kind of weird attitude—seeking solace in one's miserable current situation by dwelling upon other people's perceived misery in the past—is very common in India. Two commonly assumed and expressed statements by all Indians are: 1. India was civilized when the world was barbarian and 2. We survived while other civilizations perished. Now, what is exactly meant when we say that Greeks and Romans perished? They do exist today, just as we do, perhaps a little better. Jewism still exists. Aristotle and Plato still inspire. It is probably meant to convey that Hindu religion still exists. But how? In what form? Those who are proud of the survival of our society and culture (as contrasted with other cultures) do not appreciate the fact that survival in slavery is not the best form of self-respect, merit or wisdom. Dying is one thing; living hugely unhappy is another. Which one is preferable, honorable, boast-able? We have a pulse but we are dead. That is worse than real dead. A hollow bamboo burnt to the core from inside can appear to stand erect. The surviving or non-surviving is not the right question here; the right question is how. What we had to become to survive is the real question---poor, powerless, destitute, deserted, devastated, shackled, famished, insulted through a thousand years, dying a slow death. Is that a survival to be proud of? Decadence of a civilization is defined not by its past, poetry or art, but by its willingness and capacity to defend itself.

We internalized the insults and philosophized over the pain. Now at least, we need to analyze not only the political and military conditions but also the social situation prevailing in those periods, because no society but ours ever was magnanimous enough to make victory so comfortable for its enemies.

We suffered from history's tragic consequences. We are helpless victims of our history, captives of our past. We lost wars, we lost territory and we lost self-esteem. We were left truncated and cynical. Recoil syndrome grips us today. Ambivalence haunts us. We sublimate our egos and go into deep denial mode. We display xenophobia. All this is natural. But mature adults put such things behind them. Small groups of determined people can knock history out of its set grooves. We need not fear history, only its distortions by traitors to truth. We need not forget history, only our paranoid perception of it. Battles can be won or lost. Losing is not always a disgrace. But our defeats were endemic, our failures systemic and our diseases chronic. There is nothing sporadic or casual about them. "These failures are not, as some of us think, a chapter in a history book, but an all encompassing reality that is still with us today." When we form a habit of losing, when we are consistently defeated and subjugated by foreigners for centuries, it is surely a time to wake up and ask ourselves a few inconvenient questions. I hope to be able to do that in the following pages.

Our deep denial mode assumes various forms. To mention just one of them: "India was never a single nation in history till the Britishers ruled; so how could it unite against foreigners?" This is partly true in the sense that modern national states are a recent phenomenon. But that is true about the other nations as well. Why did they succeed and we did not? On the other hand: 1. Muslim invaders themselves---Turks, Afghans, Iranians, Mongols---were disunited, fighting among themselves, sometimes even more than we did. European nations were fighting among themselves when they conquered us. 2. Many Indian kings ruled over larger territories and were richer than the areas from which the invading hordes arrived.

Some of our states were and still are bigger than many European and Middle Eastern countries. 3. Many kings united India in the past---The Mauryans, the Guptas, Harsha and Pulkeshi and so on. 4.How many Indians are prepared to give credit to the Britishers for uniting us? Actually, they ruled over India, Pakistan, Nepal, Bhutan, Burma (Myanmar) and Shri Lanka too. We always argue that India is one, if not politically, then at least culturally and psychologically ("Unity in diversity", we call it). 5. If England and Scotland could unite 400 years ago in spite of deep historical and religious differences, why could we not? We need to analyze, not just assume. (More in Chapter 9---Why were we defeated?).

Earnest Hemingway once told his son: "Do you know what makes a good loser? Practice." Well, we have been practicing for centuries past. It is only our false pride that prevents us from acknowledging the fact. Unfortunately a man's vanity is often inversely proportional to the degree with which it can be justified. Soon after a trauma, we have a deep emotional need to alleviate pain and helplessness. But the time has come when the pain must be borne, we must look reality in the face and concentrate on clear headed unsentimental analysis so that we can effectively use the lessons for the future. Our deep denial mode and our swollen self-regard are not going to help us.

Vibrant nations absorb their fair share of hits and misses and move forward. Stagnant societies, once down, find it difficult to rise again because they rationalize their downfall through defeatist pessimist philosophies and resign themselves to their assumed fate. Arnold Toynbee, the historian, says that the kind of response a society mounts to meet its problems determines its survival and growth. (More later.) England recouped from the loss (1783A.D.) of her American colonies and rose to defeat (1815A.D.) the best military genius the world had ever produced in the person of Napoleon. Spain was subdued by Muslims just as we were, around the same time period as ours but she rose again to drive them out (1452 A.D.) and became the biggest colonial power on earth in the sixteenth century, conquering the continents of south and central America. When we were defeated, what was our response? We never gained independence again until 1947.

Glorious past? Yes, indeed, if a thousand years under alien rule can be called so. Glorious indeed if we can go back two thousand years and forget the most recent thousand years. We have a taste for vintage wine. Our strange myopia can clearly see the distant utopia but the ground under our own feet looks fuzzy, fickle and futile. We have a remarkably strange amnesia for recent events matched by an equally strong fascination for the distant past. Is it a kind of a strange Alzheimer disease affecting our collective psyche? We strain our memories through the mesh of what we can bear to believe. We cover them with the golden glow of what we wish to see. And then we call it history. Our self-delusion remains as boundless as it has been for centuries. We seek to deny how dismal we are now by asserting how great we have been. We look for easy solutions from the past rather than challenging ourselves to move into the future. What is better---inheriting a grandiose world or creating your own great future?

Most politicians and some intellectuals in India cannot speak anything about India without invariably using the words "glorious past, great civilization," etcetera. It is somewhat similar to the story of a loving proud mother being unable to name her son without drawing attention to his brilliant career. She runs to a lifeguard on a beach, shouting in panic, "Run, run; help. My son, the brilliant nuclear physicist, the eminent scientist, who won great prizes in the past, is drowning!"

We Indians possess a deep-rooted unwillingness to confront our limitations and we are blessed with a selective memory to support that lack of will. We have a great talent for glorifying our greatness and forgetting our failures. But naivete and arrogance is a deadly combination. Our pathological pattern of disregarding inconvenient reality can prove to be fatal. Gibbon, the great historian, in his masterpiece 'The decline and fall of the Great Roman Empire' enumerated more than a hundred factors that contributed to the fall of the most famous ancient empire in history. The golden age of India, the Gupta dynasty, deserved that kind of analytical introspection after it ended. All that it has got from us Indians is a bloated description and bravado of its undoubtedly remarkable achievements.

Winston Churchill said, "If the present sits in judgment over the past, the future will be lost." True. But what Santayana said is equally true: "Those who forget history are condemned to repeat it." Even as we wish to refrain from sitting in judgment, let us not forget the history of our weaknesses, so that we may not be condemned to repeat it. A false and mythical self perception of history can be suicidal to any society for its own future. "The greatest of faults is to be conscious of none," as Carlyle put it. If a sick man will not know or acknowledge that he is sick, he will not try to find a cure. To be really cured, "We must work on two fronts: A rhythmic alternation between attacking the causes and healing the effects."

Our politicians brag about our great past. Intellectuals glorify it. Laymen believe in it literally, not knowing if it is a part of history, myth or mythology. And everybody is happy and proud, content in his smug satisfaction, getting high in his own self-esteem. However, the dividing line between legitimate pride and unwarranted vanity is a very thin one. It is not always visible. Simple folks like me therefore deserve to be pardoned if they are saddled with doubts like the following: If my great grandfather was rich and great and I turned into a pauper in the street, does it prove my greatness? Or does it demonstrate my worthlessness? Is it a reason for me to brag about or to be humble about? And what do I need to do? Do I need to ruminate, dream about and harp merrily on how my forefathers used to live their grandiose lives? Or, do I need to analyze my failures and find ways to a better life?

We usually and instinctively make two kinds of assumptions in the study of history: 1.That our ancestors were just like us in their attitudes, beliefs and motivations. 2. That the course of history was inevitable. Both assumptions are wrong but they mislead most people. Example: We cannot and do not know if Rama Rajya in reality was what we think it was. Use of poorly documented history as propaganda props is nothing unusual for a people raised on folklore and mythical tales.

We are all memoirists and nourish a strong nostalgia for our distant past. The past remembered as idyllic has saturated our minds with nostalgia, vanity and worse. Our rearview mirror is much clearer than our windshield. Our rear defroster works better than our front defroster. Our past keeps mugging our present. It vitiates our present, befuddles our future and stops us from thinking clearly about our problems. Our minds are so mired in past glory that they almost seem antagonistic towards the future. We fondly hope to enter the gates to a bright future but are not prepared to close the door to the hazy past. Our creative energies are caught and immobilized in the dead weight of the past. When we are in a marathon race in competition with other societies of the world, we try to run forward, with shackles of the past tied to our legs, our eyes straining to look behind and our hearts fixated on a vanished world that mankind has left behind in its evolution.

We need not forget our past glory but we must not be controlled by it either. A society that forgets its roots will not be stable; but a society that is preoccupied with its roots will never grow to maturity. A society that is always debating who owns which root will miss the sunshine. There has to be a balance. We should not see the past as the future. We must learn to define ourselves by what we are and not by what we were. We must aim to thrive rather than merely to survive on past glory. We may remember our past, but we certainly do not need the hubris, the overweening pride that comes from vanity before a fall, as our own scriptures have told us again and again. Being at the bottom after being at the top is a terrible thing. It can leave us insecure, cynical, resentful, masquerading as morally superior, even insufferably petulant. But we need an ability to honor our past by moving beyond it.

There is no doubt in the mind of anyone that we had a glorious distant past. The Upanishadas and the six schools of philosophy (Darshanas) have been some of the best achievements of the human mind, handed down orally from generation to generation. Our Vedic literature is of higher antiquity than that of Greece. Our progress in Grammar, Mathematics, Astronomy, Logic and Medicine was remarkable. But three major pitfalls we must guard against are: (A) Forgetting that a large part of our history is unknown, unknowable or white-washed. Examples: Some neo-con Hindus claim that: 1. Aryans did not come from outside. 2. Ramayana date is 5200 B.C.; Mahabharat date 3600 B.C. But most Hindu and ALL non-Hindu world historians emphatically disagree with both these surmises based on the Puranas. (B) Fantasizing that we were somehow the **only** great people singled out by God, as the Jews used to believe for themselves till Hitler's shock. (C). Assuming that everybody else was barbarian when we were civilized.

The following short list of comparable periods in world history will put the matter in proper perspective:

1. 2500 to 1500 B.C.—Indus civilization / 1500B.C. Aryans arrive in India.
    1400 to 1000B.C. ---Epic   period (Ref: Bhandarkar Institute, Pune).
    Compare the above with:
    1500 –1027 B.C.-Beginning of Chinese civilization—similar time span
    4300--3100 B.C.-Sumerian civilization, art of writing, earlier than ours
    2396—2331 B.C.-Sumerian city states (like our Vaishali--300 B.C)
    2613—2494 B C. -Egyptian fourth dynasty, pyramids were built.
    1792—1750 B.C.—Hammurabi of Babylon
    900---800 B.C -----Poet Homer, the epics.

2. 550 –480 B.C. Period of Buddha (Buddhism) and Mahavir (Jainism).
    Compare this with: 628 to 521 B.C. Zarathushtra in Iran (Parsi religion);
    551—479B.C.—Confucius; and 570---517 B.C. Lao Tzu in China;
    399 B.C. Socrates; 427---347 B.C. Plato; 384---322 B.C. Aristotle

3. 323—185B.C. Mauryan empire
    Compare with: 744—609B.C. ---Assyrian empire---earlier
    700—800B.C.—Local city states in Greece
    570—322B.C.—Period of Pythagoras, Socrates, Plato, Aristotle

4. 320--590 A.D.—Gupta empire, our greatest period---Arya Bhat and others.
    Compare with: 31B.C.—14.A.D.—Emperor Caesar Augustus in Rome
    202B.C—9A.D.—Great Han empire flourishing, much earlier, in China.

It is quite clear that we were not unique. Many other peoples either were contemporaries or even preceded us in achievements of civilized societies. If we invented the zero as we often boast, the Sumerians (modern Iraq) invented the language-script as scientists have already proved.

During the ancient ages, mankind made comparable advances in civilization during comparable periods wherever civilization arose. Thus city states arose in India and Greece at roughly comparable periods in world history although there is little evidence of contacts between these two civilizations prior to Alexander the great. The intense intellectual ferment in India created by Buddha and Mahavir is comparable to the intellectual activity by other well-known philosophers---Confucious in China; and Socrates, Plato, Aristotle in the west. All of these lived during comparable periods in world history.

Greeks, Hindus and Egyptians all had polytheistic beliefs (many gods) during comparable periods in world history. Their mythologies have surprisingly similar stories with a few variations. Ex: Compare our Indra to the Roman god Jupiter and the Greek god Zeus, all three, kings of gods. Cupid, the Roman god of love wielded a bow and arrow like our god of love, Kamadeva. Their Vulcan is our Agni (Fire god). Their brave hero Hercules kills a nine headed Hydra as our Rama kills a ten headed Ravana. Compare our Valmiki to St. Moses the Black both of whom were robbers till converted to religion. What the westerners call the heathens had 20 or 30 thousand gods and we had 330 million! The Celtics in Ireland before the advent of Christianity venerated a host of deities, particularly goddesses like our Durga and Parvati--they named them Brigit, Morrigan, Macha, Epona etc. Our Kali and their Satan have similarities as also stories of their Noah's ark and of our Manu. A virgin mother, Kunti, getting a son (Karna) fom the sun god and abandoning him into a river, is nothing unique by way of a story. Exactly the same story is found in many cultures of old: Virgin mother Rhea Silvia got two sons from god Mars and left them in a river; they were saved and brought up by shepherds. These---Remus and Remulus---established Rome as early as 753 B. C. Our five Pandava heroes were sons of our gods through Kunti, as also most heroes in heathen mythology.

We had great achievements in language and literature. Sanskrit is a beautiful language and Kalidasa and others wrote powerful, impressive verse and dramas. But we don't remember that the Greeks had their Sophocles, Euripedes, Aeschylus, and many others. We had our Bhaskara (mathematician), they had

Euclid and Pythagoras. We had our doctors Charak and Sushruta, they had their Hippocrates. They had Pliny and Herodotus, the historians; and Archimedes the scientist; we had none to compare.

Inflicting pain on the body for the good of the soul (penance, Jainism) is not unique by any means. The same was preached by those who were known as the Stoics and they belonged to more or less the same period. Making allowances for differences in widely scattered societies of ancient times, it is clear that good moral values preached by our Rishis and pious men were similar to the values preached by all good men in all ages including Confucious, Jesus, the Quakers and Greek philosophers. It is also not necessary to assume that we were more advanced than the Muslims who conquered us in the beginning of the second millennium A.D. Just one fact of interest in this connection is not so widely known----writing paper was introduced into India by these Muslims who borrowed the art from China. The common man in India is naturally not familiar with such details of world history and thus is easily led into believing wishful myths about our superiority or uniqueness.

Talking about vanity? Under the British rule, we had around 400 local Indian rulers, most with only a fictitious authority over a few hamlets. To the merriment of the people and subjects of many good humored jokes, almost every such ruler claimed that his dynasty was a descendant of either the Sun or the Moon god!

Indians are fond of claiming antiquity. The more ancient the better, be it a book or a personality. If the Vedas and the first Jain god Rishabh Deva existed more than six thousand years ago, as widely assumed, logically they become either foreigner or non-Aryan Indian in origin. Because most historians agree that the Aryans came into India around 1500 B.C. Apparently, facts of this nature never stop us from claiming antiquities or being proud of them. Our scholars take great pains to stretch a minute detail, a myth, a semantic variation, and go out of their way to prove a minor favorable point about our ancient past. Scholarship is impressive and should be welcome; but it is necessary to remember that it is not correct to press the evidence too hard, especially when there is so little of it anyway. Given the certainty of this uncertainty, it is absurd to claim antiquity in the face of estimates, guesswork, margins of error, uncounted evidence, unaccounted for evidence and all that.

A museum guide informed a visitor that the dinosaur he was looking at was seventy million and six years old. The visitor, highly impressed, asked him how science could determine the age with so much precision. The guide said, "When I took this job, they told me it is seventy million years old. That was six years ago."

Our claim of antiquity, superior civilization or unique world status is just that---a claim. All nations make such claims for themselves. Defeated nations make them more aggressively. All nations find them useful, hardly a few are deserved. "The powerless lie about themselves and lie to themselves, since it is their only resource." As a matter of fact, we are not what we think we are; we are what we do. The world judges us by our actions, not by our pet peeves or vanities. President Kennedy said, "The enemy of truth is often not the lies—deliberate, contrived, and dishonest, but the myth---persistent, pervasive and unrealistic."

Most Indians find the possibility of less than perfect ancestors a lot worse than the prospect of perennial poverty. Our vanity is beating out our fears of poverty and backwardness. Vanity also trumps morality. Our scholars do not mind a little bit of intellectual dishonesty in devising tailor made proofs so long as they reinforce our ancestral superiority. Our love of exaggeration and neglect of history is well known. But while exaggeration may look attractive to the general public, constant hyperbole is taxing to a cultivated scientific mind.

In search of vindication, we tend to boast about things we should be ashamed of---like boasting about our non-aggressive nature to hide the shame of our submission into slavery. What price perversity? Let me call it a perversion of a misrepresentation of a twisted truth, doubly distorted by a slanted caricature.

"All the perfumes of Arabia will not sweeten this little hand," so bemoaned a grief stricken Lady Macbeth in Shakespeare. Well, all the honor and glory of our ancestry cannot blot out the shame of our current cussedness. A writer has put it so well, "A thousand years of starvation, defeat and deprivation are reasons to lament our failures. They are not reasons for celebrating the illusions of past perfection or dreams of future felicity. It is no consolation to celebrate our antiquity when it means nothing to people dying like dogs in the street. In fact, it is a cruel joke. Actually we should be apologizing to all these people because we are unable to see past the wreck of our own ancestors' failings. Otherwise, a toxic swamp of public cynicism and corrosive partisan bitterness could eat away----our nascent democracy."

Is there a relationship between historical achievement and future performance? Not by a long shot. All mutual funds in America warn us that past performance is not a guarantee for the future. In the corporate world of commerce, look at American giants of the past like Xerox, Pan Am, Polaroid, US Steel, and similar Indian names too that were the dominant reputed names in the past. They are but a shadow of their former selves, on the verge of death today. Look at what happened to once great cities like Babylon, Damascus, Pataliputra (Magadh empire capital) or Constantinople. In every case, the past does not guarantee the future.

To sum up this story of history, we have a huge problem: The basic problem of defending independence and living in dignity. It is the problem of a "soft" society unable to face its enemies for almost a thousand years and yet being proud of its supposedly perfect past. We refuse to face it squarely. Like Lincoln's little boy who hurt his toes in the dark. He said he was too old to cry but it hurt too much to laugh! In the previous chapter, we defined another big problem: Poverty and backwardness. Most of the current ills of India are secondary derivatives, only the outward symptoms of these two principal problems, for which we need to find causes and cures. It is unfair to hold the present generation hostage to the vanity of today's crop of charlatans who recall only those aspects of history that serve to glorify ourselves. A dreamy belief in the myths of our past glories can lead us to a disappointing disaster at home. It is imperative for us to detail our national hypocrisies and debunk our myths of superiority if we want to graduate from infantile pride to adult maturity. It is necessary to puncture our hot air balloon in short order. A man with head held high cannot get used to bifocals. A closed mind can be the worst prison. Analyzing our national minds will be beneficial for our progress, if such an analysis will foster links between ideas of thinkers and practices of public performers in our society.

We had a head start in history, we had good ideas and we had great leaders. But we, as a people, faltered. Why? Why do our institutions fail more often than they succeed even today? If the race is to the swift, why is it that we, the Indians, seldom crossed the Olympian finish line? Let the (Blame) games begin.

4. THE BLAME GAME
Perceptions : Popular and Perennial

The problem with India is not that people cannot know the answer; it is that every Indian thinks he does. That is exactly why he does not. Because he thinks in slogans and stereotypes. It will be hard to venture out without hearing an opinion---fervid in tone, purple in color and often as irrational as hell itself. We can summarize the variety of views of factors responsible for India's downfall as something like the following: 1.Politicians 2. Corruption 3. Illiteracy/Ignorance 4. Poor leadership 5. Overpopulation 6. Wrong government policies 7. Democracy 8. Exploitation by foreigners 9. Moral degradation 10. Fate, God's will 11. Cycles of time, like Kali Yuga. You can add a few more, depending upon your mood. Many pious Hindus believe in number 9, 10 and 11 above. Patriotic souls emphasize number 7 or 8. Economists blame number 5 or 6. Almost everyone blames the first three. So on and on it goes.

The usual problem with simple answers is that they are too simple, partial or casual. All these people may be justified in their own way, but only in a fragmentary and symptomatic sense. A deep-rooted chronic disease cannot be identified with a casual spur of the moment reaction. Nor can it be diagnosed by assumptions and halfhearted tests. If a disease has no medicine, it has a thousand medicines. Usually there is a multitude of causes as to why a particular thing happens. We have to delve deep and patiently trace out the root of the root of the root. We shall attempt to do just that in this book, but popular perceptions do have a grain of truth in them and they need to be addressed first.

Hardly anybody in popular parlance mentions things like climate or deforestation. Environmentalists and anthropologists emphasize them and they are certainly worth looking into. Geographical factors had a decisive influence on human development everywhere, especially in prehistoric times. But after the development of language, tools and agriculture, man developed culture that influences him much more than geography or physical environment, as we shall see later in this book. Culture also accumulates and is transmitted. Today with science, man has learnt to neutralize many adverse effects of geography. Besides, although India has a warm climate, she did not lack natural resources. She has abundant supplies of minerals like iron ore, coal, titanium and mica; a huge land mass; a long indented coast-line; fertile soil with perennial rivers; and vast human resources. In any case, since humans can do nothing much about factors like geography, accidental happenings or the supposed will of God, we shall not concern ourselves with them in this book.

Dadabhai Navaroji, Minoo Masani and others drew pointed attention to India's poverty. But why did we sink into such abysmal poverty? Representing symptom as cause is not an unusual practice. Many Indians honestly, but wrongly, believe that foreigners exploited and robbed India. But countries like South Korea, Hong Kong, Canada and Taiwan were colonized and yet have prospered. According to one estimate, the total wealth collected by the British prior to 1914 totaled four billion rupees, which, even allowing for inflation, is an insignificant amount compared to the gross national product of a big nation---11,354 billion rupees in 1996-97. These writers are all right as far as they go. But they don't go far enough. They elaborate on symptoms but do not diagnose the underlying disease. It is usually easier and far more satisfying to blame others for one's misfortunes. But think: How much can robbers take away from a vast country with such tremendous resources? Can anybody take away for ever our capacity to regenerate our resources? And, finally, why is it that Europeans discovered India and India did not discover Europe?

On the last question, we in India are accustomed to think that we had gold, we were happy; we were good; so we did not need to go out. This is only partially true. Every society needs to go out if it craves for progress. NASA did not develop the space program to obtain gold but rather to spend it. Alexander was not looking for gold. Constantinople, Baghdad and Damascus had quite prosperous Khalifa Muslim kingdoms. Iran was rich. Britain, France and Spain were not poor. The invaders looked for adventure, achievement, challenge; but we were contented and complacent. If they needed silk and spices, we needed many things they had which we did not even try to find out---like the paper, the compass, the gun powder, the technology, better weapons, better animal breeds and so on. In truth, foreign rule was the consequence and not the cause of the inner weaknesses of our society.

Conquerors are not always models of civility. Civilization is a comparatively young plant on the earth, hardly a hundred years old in a human history extending over several millennia. As recently as 1992 A.D. Japan admitted and regretted the fact that during world war second, her soldiers had forced tens of thousands of Korean women to serve as sex slaves. These are realities of life, bad as they are. The plain fact of life is that the winner takes all and nothing succeeds like success. It is pointless to point out that your conqueror robbed you or terrorized you. Why did you allow him to do so in the first place? Why did we always end up at the receiving end at the hands of so many foreigners? Why did we not rob the robbers? Why were we out-weaponed, out-numbered, out-classed? What were the ultimate causes? It does not help to blame the victor. But it certainly helps if we analyze our weaknesses and become strong ourselves. If you let anybody exploit you, it is your fault, not his.

During the war with China, the constant refrain I heard in India was that we have been cheated. But it is the business of the enemy to cheat. The days of Rama and Krishna are past long long ago. (Even they occasionally misled their enemies in battle.) If we are intelligent enough, enemies cannot cheat us. But like children, we always complain about being caught with our pants down---a la Kargil in 1999, a la China in 1962, a la ---.

We **hate to accept** responsibility for our actions and wrong judgments. Like us, South Korea, China and Singapore had low per capita income fifty years ago but they are highly developed today. Why did they outpace us? We have ready excuses in reply: "We fought wars, we have a big population problem." Well, South Korea fought a big war. China has a big population. But GNP in China is growing 10% per year, while we find it difficult to grow by even 5%. "But China is autocratic," we say. Well, autocracies are not necessarily advanced and all democracies are not always inefficient. Rather than fostering honest debate, our intellectuals prefer to make excuses. Instead of confronting the crises and taking responsibility for our infirmities, we faced our historical crises with hands folded, blaming everything and everybody except ourselves. Foreigners did it, Fate did it, Kali Yuga did it, it just happened. "I did not do it", as my grandchild always says.

Many Indians say absence of good leadership explains our backwardness. Nothing can be farther from the truth. Comparisons are odious but we certainly had better leaders and role models than what many other nations have had. The best leaders that America produced have been George Washington, Lincoln and Thomas Jefferson. The last was really a great man and the writer of the inspiring words of the famous Declaration of Independence. But "his ideals, vision and words were loftier, bolder, than his real life." He owned slaves. He had an illegitimate daughter from a black slave woman he owned. He could say one thing and do another. This is not to denigrate him in any way---these are facts recorded by American historians. Now look at some of our leaders---Subhash, Nehru, Tilak and many others. They can hold a candle to any great leader in any country, whether you always agree with them politically or not. Gandhi galvanized into action a huge mass of humanity, with his unconventional leadership that heralded the beginning of the end of colonialism all over the world. Clinton was a great success as an American president but he was not one of the greatest of men and certainly not a Rama or a Gandhi in his personal life. Indira Gandhi was a very efficient, decisive and competent ruler, not unlike Clinton, in effectiveness. Man for man, our leaders have been no worse than those of other nations. But when we talk of great leaders, we must be realistic enough to understand that they are not a dime a dozen and we cannot expect them to be born in every decade. Besides, leaders are thrown up from among the masses; they do not drop down from the sky.

The truth is that we are failing, not for want of good leaders, but in spite of them. But others are succeeding even with not so outstanding leaders. We need to find out why. There is a fairy tale where a fairy kisses a frog and turns him into a prince. We are acting out the story in reverse. Our society kisses a prince of talent and turns him into a frigid frog. In our democracy today, we have quite capable people capable of doing nothing. Many good people don't even wish to enter politics.

Most Indians hate politicians. We don't let a screen door slam on a cat's tail without rushing to blame the politician for the errant screen door problem. I have no desire to defend politicians. But consider this: Who put them in power in an open democracy like ours? Do we ourselves not bear any kind of responsibility for electing selfish, scheming, power hungry, incompetent, corrupt politicians? (I claim no originality for the adjectives. They are what the people always call them.). Can we not remove corrupt politicians as many other countries have done when found necessary? Can we not define procedures for their recall, impeachment, or arraignment before law? Just look how Americans handled Presidents Nixon and Clinton. We can repair the election system, we can redesign it, realign it, standardize it, make it a lot more foolproof. Can we not establish healthy moral conventions in this our land of 'great' morality, as the British have done in their 'sinful' country? Yes, we can. But we don't. We revel in an endless blame game of finger pointing, cursing the other guy, the other party. And when our own party gets a chance to do it, we shamelessly do exactly what we blamed the other party for doing. Each party thoroughly hates the other party; but within a single party, they hate each other too, with more enthusiastic bitterness. We have neither the sense to recognize this kind of inconsistency, nor the intellectual honesty to admit it.

We have made it a practice to prosecute politicians in a few cases but only after they fall from grace and power. But when politicians are in power, political cronyism rules the roost. The British worshipped Winston Churchill. He saved them, was a hero to them. But as soon as the war ended, they threw him out of power. Why? They decided that a different kind of leadership was needed in a post war reconstruction phase. And very rightly so. Note that president Regan was very popular with the American public; but when his grandson was found guilty for a minor crime, he was duly sentenced to six months in jail and the media did not so much as notice it. Contrast this with how relatives of Indian politicians are routinely lionized. It certainly does not have to be this way. We could change the way we do things. But we don't. And then we blame the politicians.

The plain fact is: It is not the politicians; it is we, the people, who have failed the country. We just do not have the kind of conscious, vigilant, discriminating public opinion so vital to the success of any democracy. A hero-worshipping, credulous, short sighted and sheepish population is least likely to check or discipline its politicians as other advanced countries routinely do. The culture of family and caste loyalties wins over that of loyalty to the nation and denigrates our democracy.

Nehru (Prime Minister), Jyoti Basu (Chief Minister) and Gandhi too were politicians. They were highly respected, even by their opponents. A large number of politicians even today are honest, selfless persons inspired by high ideals. Heroes don't come wholesale; but even today many politicians work long and hard, sacrifice their private lives, and barring a corrupt few, do not make enough money. We, the people, have become too cynical, too frustrated, to recognize them. Bajpai, the PM, one of the most respected leaders, was so much frustrated earlier that he wanted to quit parliament. On the other hand, we elect people like Laloo, Rabadi, Mayavati and Jayalalita, all becoming CMs of big states with majority support of rubber stamping legislators; and these legislators are elected with people's support. A criminal outlaw, a bandit queen, is elected to top legislative positions. An uneducated person is deputed to represent India at international conferences! People elected one eunuch as an MLA and another as a mayor in a town in central India just to show their cynicism and frustration with "impotent" politicians; not because they were admired for any talent or work. The absurdity of it all is obvious to everyone---anyone in India will be able to give any number of examples like these.

Our democracy is plagued by many politicians without principles. But what is more serious is that it is plagued by sheep without sense; sheep who have no sense to spot a wolf in sheep's clothing; sheep who elect and reelect and continue to support the wolf; sheep who deify the demon. We all know of criminals being elected with big majorities in spite of their bad records being well known. And this is not because voters are threatened or bribed. They are elected with enthusiastic support of the voters who are short sighted enough to believe them to be useful to local communities notwithstanding their well-known criminal activities. They have huge numbers of selfish sycophants supporting them. Common people condemn corrupt politicians in general but they think that their own corrupt representatives are doing a great job. People want a clean and efficient government doing everything, but one that accommodates their partial contradictory interests too. In short they are asking for the impossible. What happens when their partial short term interests are not compatible with the country's overall long term interests? We observe this almost everyday.

Compare the process of appointing cabinet ministers and judges in America with that in India. Merit is invariably the biggest loser in India. The only point of interest to the public and the press is how much representation the caste, the community and the state obtained in the loaves and fishes of office. The merit of the appointed person or his view on public policy is the last thing anyone cares about.

The almost eerie expectations we have from our politicians are exceeded only by our naiveté. Remember, we elect people, not saints. Even saints often cannot transcend self interest:--our ancient sages strongly advised kings to respect all sages; feeding Brahmins was incorporated in every Hindu ritual by Brahmins. Only the most starry-eyed among us would say that temptation does not lurk and self interest does not work. A politician cannot eschew self-interest just as you and I too cannot. A politician has to build effective coalitions to remain in politics. He has to recognize self-interests of members of his coalition and canalize them to the group's common goal. People who do not understand this will always criticize their leaders for selfishness. People who have an unreasonable fix in their psyche on renunciation and selflessness will always grumble cynically about the bad morals of their leadership.

You cannot blame a politician when he seeks votes or popularity in a democratic system. After all he cannot get anything done if he is not sure of support. Politicians cannot antagonize the people. So what do politicians do to retain popular support? When they honestly think that a popular course of action is improper and not in the interest of the country, they resort to ambiguous statements and double talk. Some examples are: our policy on cow slaughter, reservation for backward classes and women, petroleum pricing. Mamata Banerji, a respected politician in Bengal, is reported to have resigned from the central cabinet 13 times in one year. She resigned when electric power broke down, when a train accident took place, when petroleum and rice prices increased. She withdrew the resignation every time and continued to be a minister.

Walk outs from parliament on flimsy issues to placate the people and gain cheap popularity have become so common that a cartoonist recently joked: Several members of parliament walked out of the chamber to protest against traffic jams in the capital and collected in the cafeteria. Then they walked out of the cafeteria to protest against the poor quality of food served there and collected in the public square. When police tried to disperse them to smoothen the flow of traffic there, they protested against the high-handedness of the police and went back to the chamber to complain to the speaker!

A large number of small industrial units in Delhi operate illegally in areas marked for residential use only under the Delhi master plan. People complained about pollution generated in such populated neighborhoods. The Supreme Court ordered about 9000 of the worst polluting units to be shifted elsewhere or closed. This could not be done as there was a big agitation by the people against the order for several days, killing several people, torching public property and paralyzing life in the capital. People complain, people oppose. Vested interests bend public power for private advantage. Laymen second-guess experts' well considered decisions. Government and political leaders are helpless, unable to act. Then everybody blames everybody else for everything.

My educated friends blame illiterate persons for such things. That simply is not true. Education makes no difference in substance where self-interest, attitudes or deep beliefs are at stake. When educated people are involved, you have the same kind of shortsighted behavior, but with a little more sophistication. Many recent Hindi films illustrate the tie-up of politicians and criminals, but wisely refrain from telling the whole truth about the role of the public. A recent example may be interesting. In Bombay city, the business class has been worried about gang wars among criminals, kidnapping for ransom and killing innocent people for money. The press and the public shout from the housetops blaming the police and the politicians for inaction. Recently police arrested a rich diamond merchant for being involved in financing the activities of these criminal groups indirectly through films and could even obtain a proof and a confession from him. What do you think was the reaction of the public? Guess. The diamond merchants observed a strike for a day in support of their arrested colleague!

Public servants including politicians simply reflect the community they serve. It is impractical to hold them to standards much higher than those of the communities themselves. The times throw up the leaders they need. Politicians and even some of the intellectuals embody the crimped vision of our culture at large. Truly great leaders will lead, but great leaders are not born everyday. It is no use blaming the politicians. It is we who are to be blamed. I am to blame, you are to blame, and society is to blame. Simply because wrong practices could never exist in a society that cared enough about them. Let us either deserve to have good leaders or let us patiently suffer such as we deserve.

Healthy skepticism about politicians is good; the destructive assumption that they are an evil force is bad; we must not fail to differentiate between the two. To look at politicians to provide an exemplary model for us to grow up, like hapless children looking at Mom and Dad, is unrealistic. These kinds of assumptions and attitudes are insidious in a democratic set up where the government is:--Us.

Consider corruption, a popular subject. How is it that people with such deeply rooted spirituality since times immemorial are some of the most corrupt and dishonest in the world today? We simply do not realize that corruption cannot survive without people's cooperation. The giver of bribe should be as guilty as the receiver. But we create the environment that creates corruption and then we condemn the corruption, pretending to be shocked by it. This kind of double standard is common at all levels of society. Everybody displays indignation and assumes a high moral pedestal only when others are involved in corruption. And then merrily continues to practice it whenever expedient for himself. When I myself practice it, do I call it corruption? Bribe? Certainly not; I call it help from an obliging person, located at the right place, willing to assist, for a little consideration! Hypocrisy? Pretensions? Rhetoric? You name it. These have become passports to progress in our society. We have always been comfortable with hybrid identities. Daily life in India today makes inexorable demands on the people during the competitive striving for a decent existence. These demands have stripped large sections of the population of their natural innocence and made them maneuvering, scheming, manipulating mavericks.

Overpopulation is a fact of life in India. Malthus (economist) has been proved right many times over in India alone, with its history of periodic famines. Had it not been for the green revolution in the 1960s, the pattern would have certainly continued. Look at the problems of congestion, traffic, pollution, hutments, insanitation, shortages of water, power, and much more. Everybody agrees about the need to control population. With such universal agreement about the need to control it, we would certainly expect better results. Yet what is the record?

The problem is with the people themselves. The only strong and serious effort to make a dent in the population problem was made in the 1970s during the emergency. Incentives were offered for voluntary family planning. Small financial rewards were announced for motivators in order to create momentum for the movement among the illiterate masses. A few isolated incidents of reported coercion by some overzealous individuals were magnified out of all proportion by political opponents of Indira Gandhi, the then prime minister. An artificial scare was created that government was carrying out compulsory sterilization. A credulous, uncritical populace fell an easy prey to rumor mongering by interested parties and the momentum of family planning fizzled out in the sacred name of restoration of democracy. It was by no means a policy of compulsion but even if it were so, the country would have benefited immensely, as everybody admits in private talk in retrospect and as China has already proved. The country missed a crucial chance to break the vicious circle of overpopulation causing poverty, and poverty causing overpopulation. The result? Population hit a billion mark in the year 2000, more than twice what it was at the time of independence in 1947.

Why did this happen? Because we have vast masses of short-sighted incredibly credulous people easily led astray by propagandists having more than an axe to grind for themselves. And because people are not able to judge issues on merits. Indira Gandhi said, "Three things come in the way of India's progress: vested interests, vested interests, and vested interests." A people unable to see through the games of vested interests deserve the kind of politicians they elect, although they may cry hoarse denigrating them. Progress is the work of entire societies, not just governments. It is more than the calling of politicians; it is the calling of citizens. And our citizens have been found wanting.

A well-known ancient saying in India is: 'As is the king, so are the subjects.' That was in the good old days of monarchies. In a democracy, a more accurate statement is: As are the people, so are their rulers. A recent case: A thoroughly discredited politician punished by courts for corruption was elected soon after. Her party got a majority in the state and she took charge of Anti-corruption Department!

No politician will dare to make an unpopular decision even though he may be entirely convinced of its need and the whole body of objective evidence demands it. In Indian politics today, a gaffe (big blunder) is when a politician tells the truth. Simply because people will not let him. Atal Behari Vajpeyi recently made some hard unpopular decisions in the overall interest of the country. But he had to retract them because of popular opposition. Most rational people have by now grown increasingly dubious about any prime minister's ability to get effective action out of the boiling cauldron of public contradictions. Prime ministers are checkmated. They cannot muster the political will. Yet when public servants and officers become fearful of consequences for doing the right thing, we are indeed in real trouble.

Our people almost compel our politicians to hypocrisy. Not that I believe the politicians to be inherently good but leaders are under strong public pressure to act against their own best judgment on the merits of a public issue. Some lawmakers are committed in public to vote for a bill when they would secretly like to see it die. The support of some legislators to a bill is based in part on an assumption that it will not ultimately be going anywhere. We can see home ministers (in charge of the police department) supported by party workers who are but public facades for smugglers or gangsters. You can easily imagine what kind of pressure the minister must face from his best supporters if and when the police department arrests a criminal. It is easy to say that he must resist the pressure; but you have to be either superhuman or naïve or both to cut the branch of the tree on which you are sitting yourself. And so, pliant public officials kow-towing to the vagaries of sectional squabbles are forced to indulge in hypocrisy.

In almost every big city, illegal construction, violation of municipal building codes and obstruction of traffic are matters of everyday occurrence. But when public officials take steps to set the matters right, either politicians stop them under pressure from their constituents. Or the constituents, the public, themselves start agitations, take out processions in protest and resort to all kinds of direct and indirect pressure tactics. The public official is in most cases transferred for his indiscretion in trying to do the right thing in public interest. An officer quickly learns where his own personal interest lies. And the people? Some of them blame corruption, some blame vote hungry politicians, some bemoan the lack of morale or morals, some blame loopholes in the laws, and a frustrating cycle of finger pointing continues forever. The surprising part is that nobody sees anything wrong with the inconsistency of a fickle public, concentrating on selfish interests of small groups, unable to get the broader overall picture. When the law conflicts with what a section of the public perceives as injustice, the law is disregarded arbitrarily because of misplaced public sentiment. It is not appreciated that the law as the impersonal and unbiased instrument of democracy must prevail until it is changed.

We, the people, need to be brain washed of many irrational attitudes and thoughts. People do not care as much about roads as they do about what language the road signs are written in. We see everyday the results of narrow interest management. We have a huge appetite for self destructive behavior. People act and also vote against their own long term interests. And then merrily blame everybody else. We have growing greed and dumb deeds but does anyone care what the country needs?

Two examples will suffice to make this process a little more clear. 1. Some gas dealers in Mumbai used to adulterate costlier petrol gas with cheaper kerosene. This was dangerous and resulted in air pollution from partially burnt kerosene in vehicle engines. The gas companies responded to the public outcry with stricter and more frequent checks on the dealer storage tanks. But the dealers went on strike!

They obviously could not object to these right checks and defend their illegal activities in public. So they complained that they were being harassed! 2. People complained of corruption in the collection of Entry Tax on goods into the city of Mumbai. Some tax collectors were caught red handed and suspended. The result? Their union went on strike in their defense citing high handedness, harassment, and a host of other issues! And the original issue of corruption was effectively side tracked.

Democracy is the political system that puts faith in the power of the common people to do the right thing. Why do our democratic institutions not work? Some democracies are of, by, and for the people. Some others, like ours, are above, against, and beyond the people. The problem with India's democracy is not its power but the lack of it. It discusses and cannot decide. When it decides, it cannot act. If it acts, it cannot enforce or sustain. In most cases it cannot decide, so it leaves the decision to the judiciary, oblivious of the fact that the judiciary should not make political decisions. Forcing it to make such decisions costs it whatever little respect it has among the people. Combining judicial activism with intellectual sloth is a deadly prescription although it may save us temporarily from the effort of making a hard decision.

It is not necessary to elaborate. The ship of the state is sinking on the rocks of old habits, rampant irrationality and narrow interest management. People cannot see the wood for the trees. They fail to grasp the big picture. They cannot hold a vision. They cannot rise above petty local issues. They are their own worst enemies. And worst of all, they do not realize it. They always blame others for their own misery. St. Luke in the Bible (6:41) has answered them already: "Why do you see the speck in another's eye when you do not notice the log in your own eye?" Even the Koran says, "Verily, God will not change the condition of the people till they change what is in themselves." Patrick Moynihan said, "The truth is that it is culture--- not politics---that determines the success of a society."

It should be more or less clear by now that the popularly perceived causes of India's downfall are symptomatic and secondary in nature. The primary cause most responsible for our current plight is: WE--------and we alone. As a famous poet put it, "I am the dagger and the wound; I am the torturer and victim."

5. GOD JANUS INCARNATE
The Two Faces of India

A small puzzle for the reader: Can you find a group of people who is resourceful but poor; brave but defeated; intelligent but confused; scholarly with little common sense? You guessed it right---you can find lots of them everywhere you look in India at all times.

Am I concentrating too much on the negative side, turning a blind eye to India's current achievements? The achievements, of course, are not insignificant: 1.We have a large body of educated manpower---260,000 engineers every year, 3.1 million college graduates. 2. We raised life expectancy from around 40 at independence to about 60 years today. 3. We have escaped the curse of perennial famines. 4. We are one of the few nuclear armed nations. These are no mean achievements. So what's the problem?

To understand the above achievements in order: 1.Our traditional educational system before the introduction of English education (around 1840 A. D.) was based on a few local community schools like Pathshalas and Gurukuls for Hindus and Madresas for Muslims. They could never provide any worthwhile education of the kind we know today (Ch. 9). 2. Our Life expectancy has been raised mainly because infectious diseases could be controlled with the help of modern western medicines like antibiotics, not with traditional Ayurvedic herbal medicines that dominated the Indian scene for three millennia. 3. C. Subrahmanyan, the progressive-minded minister for agriculture in the Nehru cabinet had the good sense to invite a modern foreign scientist to reform the age old practices of traditional farming and thus initiate a revolution in agricultural production. This was done through disinfectants, artificial fertilizers and high yielding seeds---all of them products of modern western research. 4. Progress in nuclear and computer fields has been achieved as a result of western education and by our scientists trained in foreign countries, certainly not by the pundits and shastries that we turned out from the ashrams (schools) of Hardwar or Benares for centuries past.

Yet huge numbers of the population---English educated---are equivocal and critical of the benefits of English education. Unfortunately, such casual snap-shot judgments based on popular slogans have almost become a way of life in India. There is a strong under-current of resentment against what they brand as education designed by Macaulay "to produce clerks for the erstwhile English rulers." This is nonsense, pure and simple; but it is a very popular line in India, often among the so called 'intellectuals'. Just imagine where India would have been today without modern English education, not only in science and technology but also in the humanities and social sciences. Much more important than Macaulay's supposed intentions are the real consequences of English education. And these have been so great and good for us that English education is the best thing that ever happened to India. Even our great leaders who fought against the British had English education that brought the modern world to us.

One very important fact about India is that there are two Indias---one often pretending that the other does not exist. The first is a small, articulate, active, western educated, highly visible, urbanized minority, talking about reaching the moon. The second is a huge monolith comprising millions of backward looking, traditional masses, unable or unwilling to modernize their minds. And sandwiched between these two is a group of (ideologically) struggling individuals in a process of transition, too confused to decide for themselves which way to go; casting their lot with the first group today, with the second group tomorrow, making the landscape so fuzzy and fleeting. Just to clarify what I mean, I would say, in general, that Rajiv Gandhi typified the first (westernized) group; Charan Singh the second (traditional) group; and both were prime ministers of independent India. It is a well-established fact that most highly acclaimed recent achievements of India are the successes of the first group---a small minority of western educated modernized Indians who are most visible to the world. But the heart of the vast majority lies with the second group.

Our younger generation is certainly doing well in computers; but we must guard against complacency. Please consider these issues: 1. Our strength is only in software, not in hardware. Even in software, India's share in the world's software industry is rather insignificant (1.6% in 1999). 2. Our exports are nothing much to talk about---only $3.9 billion in the Information Technology sector in 1999, equal to the tiny countries of Israel and Ireland. 3. Only 2% of the companies used internet in 1999. 4. We have no basic research of our own in computer field. 5. Manufacturing employs just seven million in India out of 406 million workers, a tiny share. Fewer than two million account for computer related jobs.

Two hundred years ago, agricultural workers from India migrated to Canada, Africa and the West Indies. Around thirty years ago, many technicians like carpenters and plumbers went to work in Middle Eastern countries, remitted money, made states like Kerala rich and eased India's foreign exchange crunch. Today we are justifiably proud of the brilliance of our young technocrats in the internet era and India's future looks rosy. Hopefully, this is not a transient situation. But this very recent phenomenon is distorting our big perspective. As a very very minute but visible percentage of our one billion population, how do their numbers compare against those of other countries? Besides, we should not compare our best brains against other people's average ones and pat on our own backs.

All our modern advances have been made in the face of opposition by large groups of tradition bound orthodox ideologues. The current defense minister of India led strikes by public employees in the 1970s to oppose computerization. A former prime minister of India (M. Desai) was a strong lifelong advocate of urine therapy. These are no isolated incidents of idiosyncrasies of individuals. These kinds of ideas are but a reflection of the mindsets of these individuals and the masses they represent and lead--a mindset of traditional beliefs, distrust of modernism and rationalism, a strong belief in the supposed superiority of the indigenous Indian systems. Such persons are the natural leaders of the masses who constitute the huge majority in this our democracy of universal adult franchise. If you think we have been doing better in recent years, think again. Remember Rama Rao or Laloo Prasad Yadav. Remember Mayavati, Rabadi Devi (all CMs or Chief Ministers) and a host of current personalities in positions of power in every state and at the center.

No doubt there are a few politicians like Chandra Babu Naidu too, who are modern, progressive, forward looking. But how many Naidus do we have in this vast country? Our people are too reluctant to support even a moderately progressive politician like him. Also remember the opposition he faced, the difficulty he had, even in a progressive state, in his initial rise to public life. He needed support from a traditionalist nitwit like his father-in-law whom people gave huge election majorities. The best that can be said about the situation in post independence India in brief is that, on the whole, all things considered, it could perhaps have been worse.

India is a strange combination of orthodoxy and modernity, of a few success stories and many major tragedies. She can be pictured as a Burkha (veil)-clad woman riding a pony over a muddy village road, with a borrowed satellite phone, reciting Hanuman Chalisa hymns, not knowing where to go, except where the animal may lead her. It is not unusual to see leaders riding chariots, computers riding rickshaws, boilers riding bullock carts or saffron-robed saints in planes. India is like the mythical Roman God Janus with two heads looking at two opposite directions. Or it is that long limbless reptile with one head at each end, both heads pulling in opposite directions, unable to decide which way to go---forward or backward. We are schizo. We really don't know who we are. We are in a metamorphosis of sorts. We hardly notice the huge gulf between high culture and mass culture in the India of today.

The exotic modernized face of big cities that appears to the outside world is a pure fantasy contrasted with the huge block of real people of real India. This huge block today craves for modern physical amenities while at the same time holding fast to ancient mindsets. While we should not underestimate whatever little progress India has made so far, we must be clear in our minds: What there is of what could be called modernity in India is clearly western in origin. Overabundant pride in the current achievements of a small westernized minority can lead to false complacency. We shall see in chapter 9 how backward, poor, orthodox and narrow minded we were just before we came in contact with the western world.

Discussing the dark side of our past does not mean that the future will be necessarily dark; it only means that the dark side is what our crises have always been about. The hope is that analyzing our past failures will clarify the issues, warn against pitfalls and serve as a guide to the future, which we all hope will be bright. For, intelligent people need to be more often reminded rather than informed.

SECTION TWO
THE DISEASE

6. ROOTS OF REGRESSION
The Disease Defined

Prof. Jared Diamond of the University of California at LA wrote a bestseller 'The Third Chimpanzee'. Why did man overcome all other species? He proved that advances in Culture---like language, farming, sexual mores, etc. in prehistoric times were responsible for raising Homo sapiens above other animals, much more so than genetic or anatomical differences. In another good book ('Guns, Germs and Steel'---W. W. Norton) he asked: Why did Europe and Asia advance and the other continents fell behind? Development of technology of agriculture, transport and weapons was the direct or proximate cause of Eurasian societies advancing fast and subjugating others. To investigate ultimate causes, we need to find reasons for technological progress in one case and backwardness in another. His scholarly analysis concentrates on environmental and geographical realities that gave an edge to a <u>vast continent</u>---Eurasia <u>in prehistoric times</u>. For differences within <u>smaller regions</u> in Eurasia like China and India, and <u>in comparatively modern times</u> (after about 1450 A.D.), he rightly emphasizes the need to extend the investigation to "local cultural factors unrelated to the environment". He touched on this topic very briefly about China. I hope to add my bit in this book about India.

To pose the same question a little differently: Why was it that India could not develop technology----steel, weapons, steam engine, ships---that Europe did? Science has found no difference in neurobiology or genetics of different societies. Mere accidental events too cannot explain the difference. Ours was the most densely populated country with vast resources, brilliant minds and high ideals. Only an extraordinary genius could starve it of resources and motivation. That genius is our culture.

Chinese minorities in many Southeast Asian countries and the Japanese in Brazil have done much better than other ethnic groups in those countries, although all of them operate under the same economic and political systems of their respective countries of residence. Indians in America who have adopted western modes of ideas and work practices are doing much better than what they themselves were able to achieve before they had the opportunity to change their own cultural attitudes and habits while in India. David Landes ('The Wealth and Poverty of Nations') says: "Culture makes all the difference."

Values can kill, as nothing else can. Ours did. Values can drive a man to suicide bombing, to kamikaze, to Ku-Klux-Klan, to Sati. They can propel a society to its doom. Ours did. Cultural issues like innovation, originality and receptivity to new ideas are of critical importance for progress of any society. As Joseph Tainter points out in "The Collapse of Complex Societies", societies like ours can fail for various reasons like: Upholding tradition, they can maintain status-quo when changes are needed. Torn by clash of values, they can ignore harmful behavior. Concentrating on certain ideas, they can squander scarce resources. Individuals fixated on themselves can commit acts of incredibly damaging stupidity that injure themselves as well as society at large. We shall discuss such issues in this, the second section.

In Section one, we determined that:

(A) India has two basic and serious problems: A politically 'soft'/ weak state and Economic/intellectual backwardness. (B) While analyzing the causes of these, a complacent attitude of our supposed greatness in the past or our recent halting advances will not be right. The causes of India's past decline and current misery are to be found internally among its own people, not externally, as most Indians tend to imagine. We are weak because of what we are. The problem is US. The solution therefore is US and US alone. As Kabir, the medieval saint, put it, "I went out looking for an evil (person). I found none. When I looked inward, I found that there is none more evil than myself." Another poet said, "We don't have the courage to accept that we are bad, so we say that the times are bad." We now know the enemy. We have become the nation we have because we are what we are. Heraclitus said, "A man's character is his fate."

It is better to be direct and clear in matters like these, although it may not be popular or polite in public to say so. To put my thesis simply, bluntly and directly at the outset: We, the people of India, our own actions, thoughts, and beliefs are responsible for our downfall. These beliefs, thoughts and actions constitute our cultural ethos. Our culture is based on a history of long tradition and age old beliefs. It sanctifies orthodoxy, stifles creativity and discourages innovation. An overwhelming majority of our population has an irrational mindset because our culture encourages, promotes and preserves faith and irrational modes of thought. Finally, since our culture is based principally on our religion and is an indistinguishable part of our religious experience, our problems have their deepest roots in our religion, spirituality and our excessive obsession with both of these.

Shocking? No. As Thomas Paine put it, "Although a plain statement of the salient fact may seem preposterous, although the content may upset some people, unvarnished truth sometimes does help though it may shock. My boldness may alarm many but the times and the subject demand it." The time is long past when sophisticated speech, euphemisms and politically correct indirect statements would suffice. The above are serious statements with wide implications. The mere fact that anybody should have the audacity to make them concerning a proud people of so ancient, so sacred and such glorious heritage may be amazing. And yet, and yet, they are true, as true as truth can be, every letter and every word, in letter and in spirit in its entirety. But I don't expect you to accept them without thought. I am fully aware that I need to make a convincing case to establish them. The following chapters are designed to present the step-by-step evidence in support of these unpalatable unpopular facts.

A few definitions before we start:

What is Culture? According to Webster, culture is "socially transmitted behavior patterns, customs, beliefs, morals, expression and activity." It is the entire way of life of a society---its values, attitudes, orientations, traditions and underlying assumptions prevalent among people. It is this that we are going to discuss under the word 'culture'. Culture is much more than an evening of music, dance and drama or fine arts which we will not discuss here.

Any notion of a national psyche or culture is a volatile one in India. If you assume that there is a single national behavior, you are on a slippery slope. India is a complex conglomeration of various cultures---an ancient Hindu culture reacting with a central Asian Muslim culture, both in turn being wrapped over with a superimposed modern western culture. In a society dominated by ancient bonds of religion, the psyche is defined more in ethics and religion than in nationalism. Besides, Hindu community (I will include Jains here) constitutes the predominant majority and the most influential determinant of public policy. So the word 'Indian culture' in my current discussion will refer to Hindu culture. It does not mean that the other components are not important. It only means that they are not relevant subject matter under discussion at present. Unlike Indian culture, there are many easily identifiable characteristics that describe Hindu culture. There are also some clear tendencies that have contributed to making them what they are. We will be concerned with these.

It is necessary to explain the words "westernization" and "modernization". It is generally accepted that equality, dignity of the individual, rationalism, competition, discipline, secularism and such other ideals are valued more highly in the west than in the east. Eastern societies like ours have customarily placed more emphasis on inequality of status (as in caste, in feudalism, in paternalistic behavior), authoritarian structure, social conformity, faith, tradition, ethics, spirituality and so on. In this sense, whatever is being considered as modern today is to a large extent western in origin. Without entering into either the complexities of these value premises or the controversies of "east and west", we will use these words in their generally understood connotations. The word modern will be used more or less in the sense of western, although many eastern peoples who would like to call themselves "modern" have an aversion to the word "western". This is due partly to their patriotic fervor and partly to their sense of self esteem.

I shall use the words "advancement" or "progress" in this book in the sense of movement towards economic development and material well-being.

Modern education too does not necessarily impart a genuinely modern mindset, though it does generate a widespread hunger for modern gadgets and amenities. Even in most of the Indians settled in western countries, we see only a superficial cosmetic adoption of modern cultural ideas (see later).

With this basic nomenclature in mind, let us start our journey into the wonderland of our culture. To start with, we will document our downfall and then compare the outward manifestations of our culture with those of other cultures.

7. THE BEGINNING OF THE END
The Miracle We Missed

A good place to start in our diagnostic journey is in our history. If we were much better off in the past but are not doing well today, how and when did our downfall start? To better understand how to remove poverty, it is best to understand how we got into it. Well, our downfall started in the middle ages with our failure to graduate into the industrial age and it continues to this day.

Harsha (606-648 A.D.) and Prithviraj Chauhan were the last great Hindu kings. The latter's defeat by Muslim invaders in 1198 A.D. is the end of the period of early Hindu history. The way we fell an easy victim to Muslim invasions first and European invasions later, and our inability to recover from them until 1947, show clearly that our disease was deep-rooted and chronic. Our downfall started early and continued unchecked for centuries. Historical changes of such magnitude do not take place in a day. Nor are they confined within a single region. They encompass an entire culture, race or society. A single gust of wind or a decayed bunch of leaves is not enough to fell a mighty tree. It is only when the decay is deep enough to engulf the roots that the big tree is really endangered. The rot starts imperceptibly in one section but resonates over time in the rest of the body. What happens to some of us eventually affects all of us. This is the so-called Butterfly Effect. This has happened to the mighty tree of our ancient culture and civilization.

Up until the periods usually known as the Dark and the Middle Ages in the history of the world, India was on almost equal terms with the rest of the world, perhaps a little more advanced than most and certainly more wealthy. It is interesting to recall bits of information like the following regarding the times in Europe before the reformers arrived on the scene: 1. How many angels can dance on the head of a pin? This was a question being debated among Christian religious scholars for a long time. Some wise men said seven, some said five. 2. The Roman Catholic Church sold certificates reserving a place in heaven. 3. It was a fairly common practice to burn people whom the church disliked for any reason.

Religions in those times had this kind of orthodoxy and blind faith. But people like John Calvin (1509-1564AD) and Martin Luther (1483-1556) challenged this. Challenges to the establishment led to fresh ideas opening up original avenues of thought. Renaissance earlier and then Reformation transformed the western world completely, ended the dark ages and laid the intellectual foundations of the modern world, preparing the grounds for the subsequent industrial revolution.

The movement gained unexpected strength from king Henry 8 of England who had a penchant for divorcing his queens and even beheading them. The Pope would not allow a divorce and he excommunicated the king in 1533. So England itself was divorced from the Roman Catholic Church and thus was established the Anglican Church of England. The Pope in 1570 excommunicated the queen of England, Elizabeth first, from the Roman Catholic church. Many people somehow have not sufficiently realized the momentous significance of these events. For the first time in history, the primacy of a nation state over religion was established in England. This was the seed of what we call secularism today---the separation of religion from the state and the ascendance of the latter over the former. In Islam, more than 300 years were to pass before any nation (Turkey) did this---through Kamal Ata Turk. And he is almost unique even to this day, since Islam considers state and religion inseparable.

Early catholic priests had a monopoly on knowledge similar to that of our Brahmins. This was destroyed. Protestants challenged the monolithic religious hierarchy of the Roman Catholic Church. Its abandonment and publication of the English Bible (around 1610) served as catalysts for the creation of a great intellectual tradition in England. Tyndale, the man who translated the Bible into English was burnt at the stake by religious zealots. Scientists like Copernicus (1473-1543) and Galileo (1564-1642) questioned the deep-rooted beliefs of religious dogma. Newton laid the foundations of modern science. Invention of printing made books accessible to the public. Literacy rose. A king (Charles First) was beheaded, kingship was challenged and unconventional ideas in statehood took hold. It is difficult today to imagine how difficult it was to do all this. People like Michael Angelo (1475-1564), Leonardo Da Vinci (1452-1519) and Shakespeare (1564-1616) nurtured the intellectual ferment in Europe. An initial trickle of protest against religion and kingship triggered a torrent of ideas and turned into a mighty river of scientific achievement, democracy and the industrial revolution. The process still continues to enrich advanced societies.

The industrial revolution increased man's productivity in exponential proportions. Productivity is really the key to the elimination of poverty. When the gross national product of a nation increases at a rate faster than the rate of population growth, that nation accumulates wealth. When low productivity is combined with high birth rates, it becomes the surest one-way ticket to bankruptcy.

We in India own that ticket. We united low productivity in a holy wedlock with high reproductivity; and this eternal couple was blessed with a child. The name of that child is Poverty. Our birth rate till very recent times was 41 per 1000 population. Our GNP growth for decades was stagnant, hovering around three percent. Recent years have seen improvements but our death rate has also gone down. On the other hand our productivity is very low compared to that in advanced nations. Why? Mainly because for too long, we did not use mechanization and computerization that are the biggest aids to higher productivity. A random example of rise in productivity in America: In 1982 it took 289,000 workers to produce 75 million tons of steel. In 2002 it took only 74,000 workers to produce 102 million. We are not only less productive but also work lesser hours per man than Americans.

Industrial revolution in European countries opened the way to increased productivity through mechanization and technological innovations like the flying shuttle (1733), steam engine (1769) and electric power. It facilitated man's control over the forces of nature. Industrialization promoted population control, urbanization, transport and communications. All these taken together gave a tremendous boost in power and prosperity to the European nations that engineered the revolution. These were the nations that colonized the world and were destined to rule over it for the next few centuries---till today. The 20th century greatness of America too was founded on her great inventors (Edison) in the previous century.

Physicists know that static friction is higher than rolling friction and more difficult to overcome. When someone falls behind in a race, he will not catch up even if he runs as fast. Technology and progress feed on themselves. They advance and accelerate almost exponentially. The static nations of Asia controlled by orthodox theosophies and stagnant ideals could never catch up with Western Europe.

The industrial revolution transported society from an agricultural to an industrial culture. This kind of transformation took place in Europe only after the authority of the church was challenged. Protestant reformation melded Christianity with modernity and rationality. Though real modernization and industrialization began in England in the latter half of the eighteenth century, their cultural underpinnings were prepared by rationalism that preceded it by more than a century. Europe produced revolutionary writers like Voltaire, Rousseau, and many more thinkers like John Stuart Mill, Hegel, John Locke, Bacon, Descartes. They laid the foundations of what has come to be known as the age of enlightenment.

India was somehow left completely untouched by these momentous developments----isolated, detached, unconcerned, unaffected by what was going on. This kind of a giant leap forward, a far-reaching advance that was destined to transform human history forever, was unimaginable in the India of those days. We stood still for a thousand years. Why? That is a good question for us to ask ourselves.

No real change ever takes place until society is ready for it. Our society did not have the cultural underpinnings to give birth to a revolution, to encourage it or to sustain it. We did not have the creativity for fresh original ideas that gave birth to the subsequent industrial revolution. We lacked the spirit of innovation that was a prime condition for its birth. Foreigners did not defeat us so much as their systems of thinking defeated ours. We need to find out why.

A western educationist visiting a communist Russian primary school wanted to assess the arithmetical skills of the students. He asked a boy: "If I buy a chair for ten roubles and sell it for fourteen, how much do I earn?" The boy said, "Five years in prison for profiteering." THIS is revolution. A revolution implies novel and original modes of thought, new ways of thinking, a clean intellectual or cultural break from the past, a change in the value system. That boy grew up in a novel value system, whether we like it or not. When thought patterns are broken, new worlds can emerge. Creativity comes from a conflict of ideas, not from confirmity. A character in a movie (The Third Man) says: "Thirty years of noisy, violent churning in Italy produced Michael Angelo, Leonardo da Vinci and the Renaissance; while 500 years of peace and quiet in Switzerland produced the cuckoo clock!" Well, in India, we were hard pressed to find a better cow or plough in 2000 years!

When the intellectual ferment was going on in Europe, what was the situation in India? We had many writers like Tulsidas (1533), Mira (1499), Surdas, Chaitanya, Rahim, Narasinha, Eknath, Tukaram, Gyandeva, Ramdas and many more---ALL saints. We had no original thinkers or real innovators; no challengers to tradition but only those who illustrated and explained ancient theosophy. Religion by its very nature is anti-modern, traditionalistic, anti-change. A couple of saints like Kabir were a little less traditional but they had only a limited local influence and that too in religion, certainly not in science or other fields of endeavor. Compare these writers of ours (like the great Tulsidas) with contemporary Europeans like Shakespeare (1564-1616) and others and the contrast is obvious and striking. If literature mirrors life, consider, as a random example, the hauntingly beautiful soliloquy of a dying Macbeth in Shakespeare. The ideas expressed are so refreshingly contrary to the rehash of the devotional poetry that our contemporary poets routinely offered. The former formed the backdrop of a world winning English society of the future; the latter became a precursor to a decaying vanquished society.

We completely missed the boat almost 500 years ago. And THAT was and still is our problem. We have never been able to catch up with them to this day. We are always a few steps behind them in technology and research, as well as in humanities and ideas. Select any important new development in any particular industry at random. Compare the date it was introduced in western countries with the date it arrived in India and you will find the gap in time. We find little significant original research in India, and we also lag behind in borrowing and importing established technology. This is hardly surprising since we do not have adequate industrial infrastructure or capital resources. We missed the start of the industrial revolution and all the subsequent steps it led to including the steam engine, the railroads, the internal combustion engine and the electric motor. Industrial revolution proved to be the start of a chain reaction generating an ever-increasing torrent of technological innovation, increasing productivity, spreading wealth, bestowing power on the nations that started it all. All this while we have been playing a game of catch-up, narrowing the time gap at times but never really succeeding.

But what we missed was not confined to material progress alone. We missed what was even more important---the culture of progress, the ideas, the progress in the humanities. Technology gave rise to urbanization, to a new industrial culture, to different mindsets. We missed it all. Today our backwardness is evident in other areas as well, like finance, marketing, social sciences and such. These constraints are a direct consequence of our 'original sin' of missing the industrial and rationalist revolutions in the first place. Lack of industrial culture can explain many of the ills that India is experiencing today. Three examples may suffice:

1. Indians are proverbially lax in keeping time. This is a carry-over from our pre-industrial past. Agricultural communities had no need to stick to the clock. The sun is a good enough guide to a village farmer for all practical purposes. It is the industrial worker in busy towns who has to be punctual for his work and transport needs. Societies with low levels of industrialization and low productivity will generally have a culture that does not attach high value to time-keeping or time-saving. (I observed this at first hand in Mexico too.) It is amazing how much time we Indians waste in nonproductive activities.

2. Agriculture promotes overpopulation, a root cause of many covert and overt ills today. Industrialization promotes urbanization. Ideas, norms, and priorities change. Ex: In cities nobody can practise untouchability in public transportation; people also have to learn and be more vigilant about infectious diseases, sanitation and personal hygiene. Our well-known laxness in these matters may be, in part, a carry-over from our agri-based village culture that we find it difficult to outgrow.

3. Organization, orderliness and discipline are of critical importance in industrial societies where division of work, assembly line operations and mass production are organized. Not so in agricultural communities. India having been principally an agricultural community for the major part of its history, these characteristics have not developed in our culture. With the progress of industrialization, they are now beginning to be more and more visible, especially in big cities and western educated circles. But the country as a whole is still very much behind advanced nations in all these respects.

The industrial revolution changed the world forever. We missed it completely. And with disastrous long-term consequences. So the right question for us to ask is not why we are poor or backward. The right question is: Why did we miss the industrial revolution in the first place? Why was it that our culture did not support the kind of innovative thinking that created the industrial revolution elsewhere? **What was it in our culture that blocked creativity?** Do some cultures have beliefs, attitudes, institutions and commonly accepted norms that produce a weaker strain of society? A society that may be less adapted to promote creativity and encourage originality? Specifically, why did others advance and we did not? Is there something like the cultural DNA of progressive or retrogressive societies? To peel the layers off our cultural onion may prove to be a worthwhile effort even if we have to shed a few tears in the process. We need to see how our culture differs from other cultures that succeeded while we failed. These will form the subjects of our inquiry in the next few chapters.

8. THEY AND WE
America and India, the Culture Gap

Everywhere in the world where Indians have gone to live, they have prospered—everywhere except in India itself. Individual Indians have succeeded; Indian society has not. Why? When an Indian arrives in America, does he get suddenly transformed into a brilliant brain? No, but the intellectual and cultural atmosphere changes so much for the better that he is able to perform at his peak level here. The 'ugly' looking duckling from India (as in Anderson's famous fairy tale) gets metamorphosed into a beautiful swan overnight as soon as it starts swimming in the lakes of the west. A distinguished Indian person once said, "The day I arrived in America was the day of my liberation." Lack of patriotism? No, it is realism, lack of sentimentalism, painful admission of a distressingly evident fact of life. A Non-Resident Indian in America has earlier lived in India and India has lived in him. But a day comes in his life when India dies in him.

It may be useful to study the differences between societies that remained healthy and societies that did not. It was through Epidemiology that doctors discovered a link between smoking and lung cancer, between cholesterol and heart disease. When a sports team loses to a superior outfit, it tries to find out in what respects it is weaker than its opponents. When a good corporation starts making losses, it analyzes not only its own strengths and weaknesses, but also those of its competition. Nations and societies should be no different. What is it that is so different in other advanced countries that gives them an edge over us?

Some global companies (like GE) have bigger budgets than those of some countries. Management of modern business corporations is comparable to that of governments of small nations in many respects. Can we learn something from them? Two well-known management Gurus in America wrote a famous best seller—Seven Habits of Highly Effective People in American corporations. What, if any, are the habits and traits of highly effective societies of advanced nations?

When an Indian family arrives to live in America, it finds the difference in cultural experience so vast that we refer to it as a 'cultural shock'. It experiences a squeeze between two cultures. Rather than dilate upon obvious material differences like food, dress, and the like, I shall concentrate here on differences in culture---the people's habits, beliefs, approach to life and the way they act and react and so on. It is precisely these invisible qualities that we may neglect to notice. We easily adopt America's pop culture like food and dress but instinctively resist its high culture---like openness and independence of thinking. This is exactly the reverse of what we should be doing.

If we are too proud to learn from the Americans, the loss will be entirely ours. We can also learn a lot from the experience of people who have lived in and observed both societies at close quarters, the NRIs. I mentioned some of these cultural traits earlier----punctuality, cleanliness, discipline and organization as an accompaniment of the industrial revolution---and I do not wish to repeat them although they are quite important. The topic of cultural differences being so vast, I shall confine myself only to enumerating most of the cultural traits without going into details, except in the first point below, by way of illustration.

1. In my experience, the most critically important and the most decisive aspect of the American ethos is the amazing capacity of the American people for **Innovation**. It goes with originality and creativity. New products are introduced daily. Current products are modified, improved, repackaged, replaced by better and cheaper ones. No company can survive for long if it fails to do this or is slow to innovate. Whether it is a satellite or soap, software service, phone service or any other service, innovation and improvement are expected, achieved and delivered periodically, for an ever improving quality of life. It is not only the commercial products and the corporations. It is also the ideas. It is not only in technology, it is everywhere. You see a variety of creative ideas, insights, information, sharp and original thinking. This may not be obvious to outsiders at first sight; but everybody who has worked in America at a professional

level, especially in something connected with research, development or management activity, will have a genuine appreciation of what all this implies.

Innovation and productivity go hand in hand. Technological innovation, method improvement and work-study give the biggest boost to productivity. I attended several learned discourses on productivity while in India. They were great-----scholarly, methodical, informative. But my very first month on the job in the USA taught me more about productivity and innovation in the workplace than everything I had learnt in India for several years. Why? Because in America, innovation is not an option you choose; it is a way of life. It is a condition for survival. Survival of your job, survival of your company, survival of the president of the company as well, sometimes survival of an entire industry.

Innovation is so fast and furious that it is quite common to find children teaching their parents---how to run a computer, how to program a video, how to do this and that. We get outdated faster than we grow up, so great is the rate of change. It is exponential. Web content doubles every 100 days. Performance of computer chips doubles every 18 months and has done so since the first commercial Unimac computer in 1950. Computer speed has increased one billion fold since that year. If you put one dollar in the first square of the chess-board and double to two dollars for the second, four for the third, and so on, till sixty-four, how many dollars will you need to fill the board? Guess. It is 18 million trillion dollars! That is an example of exponential growth. Innovation in America is exponential; in India it is arithmetical, if at all. In America, there are many whose sole profession is inventing. Thomas Alva Edison, inventor of electric lighting, gramophone and cinema was a practical innovator, not a scholarly theoretical scientist. A strong streak of inventive, adaptive, innovative attitude informs American culture. School children are encouraged to be creative at an early age. Bright students do amazing projects at school. Schools in the US have produced a continued flow of inventors, designers, entrepreneurs and innovative leaders. Diversion and dissidence are not frowned upon. Experimentation is welcomed in all fields. Any kind of originality is richly rewarded.

I could give you impressive data about how much American companies spend on research and development (CISCO 2.70 billion in 2000—14.3 % of sales), what critical importance they attach to these and how many patents they get (IBM 2886 in the year 2000 alone, 2657 in1998); but this is information easily available elsewhere and it is not necessary to labor the point. It is more important to enquire why Americans have an innovative mindset, a questing spirit (Edison had 1093 patents); and why we don't. The key is in the culture; and this lies at the root of our failure to usher in the industrial revolution, as we saw earlier. For the present, let us stick to the enumeration of the other traits of American character.

2. Americans are a **practical** down to earth people. We are ideologues, they are pragmatists. We are more likely to revel in theory.

3. After a bitter controversy or fight, they have a capacity to forge compromises that respect the adversary. They acknowledge the merit in the reasoning of both parties, without necessarily abandoning their own personal views. This is a prerequisite for a democracy and represents **respect** for the individual and the adversary.

4. Americans are **information crazy** but we tend to act on opinion, surmise, judgment. Look at their market research and opinion polls. On the other hand, there is a general tendency in India to offer fact free opinions and base decisions on opinions rather than on facts.

5. We in India may be diverse in material respects---language, food, dress. But we think alike. Americans are **diverse** in thinking patterns as well. New ideas and opinions present challenges and richness of experience, sometimes including idiosyncrasies and weird behavior too in some individuals. People desire and achieve many options in lifestyles and ideas. We in India are more of conformists.

6. **Individualism** is a vital trait in American culture. Americans desire and respect privacy and individuality. We are self-centered, but less particular about privacy. We are good to our close inner circle but apathetic to others; yet we are conditioned to conform to prevailing societal mores and customs.

7. **Equality** is a basic tenet in American political and social philosophy----equality of race, religion, status, opportunity, sexes, you name it. Practices always vary, but in general, we Indians do not respect equality except in some books and talks. Look at the status of women, lower castes, and so on. Look at the way people treat men of any kind of fame or status. We are a status conscious society, with feudal attitudes.

8. **Independence** in thinking and living is highly valued and practiced. Small kids sleep separately from their parent; children start living independently as soon as they reach high school graduation age; there are no joint families; old parents are not dependent on children in general. All these have their advantages and disadvantages that we need not discuss here; but they do promote independence in thought and action in addition to occasional craziness as well.

9. The values that Americans live by are often directly contrary to what we and others too live by. Ex: 1. In a survey, they rejected by a majority of 2 to 1 the notion that **success in life is determined by** forces outside our control. Hindus are strong believers in luck. 2. **Tolerance** is valued highly.

10. They believe in **Dignity of Labor**. We consider manual work as derogatory.

11. They are more **professional** in work; we tend to be person oriented.

12. **Accountability** is specified, valued, encouraged and practiced more in America. We hate to take responsibility for our errors, misjudgments and failures. Preserving the face of 'Honor' is important to us.

Everything in America is not good and great. Americans have their own problems, some of them quite serious. But they are problems of plenty, of unrestricted freedom, of variations in ideology, of fierce individualism; they are very different from our problems. Above all, they recognize and discuss their problems openly and rationally. And that, is the big difference.

Lots of Americans are conservative but their conservatism is very different from ours. It is forward looking, rational and mainly confined to issues like opposing big government and abortion. It is not orthodoxy or excessive love of the past. Even in the Jewish religion, which is almost as ancient as Hinduism, a strong reform movement exists and the Jewish community is among the most advanced in modern times. A vigorous issue based debate (gays, abortion, stem cell research, marriage in priesthood) is a familiar feature also among Christian communities of diverse denominations. As an example, note this recently announced fact that ex-president Jimmy Carter resigned from the church to which he had belonged all his life because he did not agree with some of its public policy issues. President Bush (Junior) was born in an Episcopal family and raised as a Presbyterian, but now he is a Methodist.

Most people in India assume and assert in private that Americans are materialistic and we, the Indians, care more for love and family values and the like. Nothing could be farther from the truth. The notion that all Americans read playboy magazine or worship the dollar is not correct. (Actually, we do literally worship the rupee coins on Diwali day!). That notion misses by miles the deep well of idealism that many Americans display so much in life. I wish people in India knew a little more about Americans' love for animals, for adoptions, for donations, for volunteering, for human rights, for family life and a host of other matters. I wish they knew more details about the respect they have for human life, for freedom, for openness and for individuality.

We have made it a habit of comparing apples to oranges. We compare the best that India has to offer with the mere average American mind and become comfortable in the smug satisfaction that we are better. We compare the inevitable diligence of first or second generation immigrants with the casualness of some Americans and conclude that we are more industrious.

Almost all Indians settled in America worry about losing their cultural heritage and wish to ensure that their children do not lose this invaluable commodity. Little do they realize what they are talking about. I asked a highly educated, bright Indian whether she preferred Indian culture as a whole or American. "Of course, Indian," she said. Then I asked whether she liked social equality, privacy, and punctuality in her life. Her answer was an emphatic 'yes' to each of these separate questions. She was almost shocked when

I mentioned that these are western values, not a distinctive part of traditional Indian culture. A little reflection was enough for her to realize and admit the discrepancy in her two answers.

When Indians speak of 'preserving their cultural heritage' in foreign countries, most of them have in the back of their minds the preservation of their traditional orthodoxy, moralistic mindset, family values, sexual taboos and religion. In the case of a small secularized or westernized aristocratic minority, this means little more than copying dance and music from popular Hindi films. Hardly anyone thinks about differing beliefs or attitudes, let alone examine them.

Consider the following three propositions in a nutshell: 1.That culture influences progress; 2.That our culture is so very different from that of America; and 3.That America is advanced, India is not. If one even broadly accepts these three premises, what logical conclusion do they lead to? Think.

Many in India have surpassed Americans in food, fashion and frivolity. When shall we surpass them in openness, originality and organization? For us, keeping time is still a trauma, hygiene an insurmountable Himalayas and productivity a Pacific of despair. Our feminism is confined to hitting roadside Romeos with handbags; it does not rise to hit the corporate glass ceiling. Most of us are not able to recognize, appreciate or accept what is fundamentally good in American culture---its broad-minded acceptance of diversity, its down to earth realism, its capacity for compromise, its creativity, its fierce individualism and independence, its rational attitudes to life. Instead we have created in our minds invidious caricatures and negative stereotypes of Americans as materialistic money driven humans with no humanity, while we cozily and compulsively imagine ourselves as the most broad-minded, non-materialistic people in the whole world. We have sort of mass internalized the superiority of our spiritualism. We are in love with our self-image. If presumptive vanities were horses, Indians would ride. They would be the best riders on earth.

In short, American society is certainly not all materialistic or immoral, as many in India tend to believe from a superficial acquaintance with America. We have a lot to learn from it. If only we knew the real America! If only we ceased using stereotypes!

9. A SOCIETY THAT STOOD STILL
Why were we Defeated?

We had a glimpse of what a successful dynamic society looks like today. Since our Indian society stands out in direct contrast, we need to examine distinctive features of our own society. We shall do this only in case of the following three glaring inequalities that relate directly to our backwardness and persistent defeats at the hands of foreign invaders. They are very clearly visible in the stagnant Indian society of only a century ago.

1. **Status of Women**: Social and educational backwardness of women for centuries past has been responsible for serious problems in our life—like wrong child bearing and rearing practices, prevalence of non-hygienic conditions in families, spread of malnutrition and infectious diseases.

We know very well that the place of a woman in our society has been either within the four walls of a home or on the burning pyre of her dead husband. Look at the traditional way women were represented in our media as hubby worshipping wives. Look at arranged marriages forcing too many women to marry somebody against their own will. Our society's respect for the rights of the fair sex was limited to a worship of several goddesses who symbolized power and pelf. When it came to getting burnt in domestic abuse, or getting drowned in a bowl of milk at birth, the females were entirely on their own. The tragic condition of widows in Hindu society is too recent and too distressing to deserve any comment. Actually, not long ago, womanhood was considered a proper kind of penitence in Hindu society.

Women acted as brakes on the progress of a vast majority of bright men in India, not consciously, not intentionally, but naturally and compulsively because of their illiteracy, non-employment and consequent preoccupation with pettiness in life. Talented men had to become engrossed in trivialities, diverting their most precious resources---their brain and time---from productive use to petty matters. In most western countries, it is said that behind every successful man is a woman inspiring him. In the India of old, it may not be far wrong to say that behind every successful man is a wife bitching behind him! Contrast this with western couples like Madam Curie and Pierre Curie, both Nobel prize winners and hugely supportive of each other in their scientific pursuits. Until recently, it was almost a universal situation in Hindu families to find an illiterate, superstitious woman behind a highly educated husband. A well-known author, K.M.Munshi, writes (around 1930): 'My wife used to enter my room tiptoe and refill my inkpot when I was busy writing. That was her only contact with literature of any kind during our lifetime.' The litany of failed dreams, suppressed longings and unexpressed compromises in such unequal couples can only be imagined. The dilution of mental faculty in the progeny when unequal pairing continues for many generations cannot even be imagined or assessed.

Today after 150 years of English education, things are changing, but only in cities. Even today, only 52 percent of women in India are literate against around 76 percent of men. We are now witnessing a coil spring syndrome from urbanized women who were long oppressed under the holy auspices of our ancient culture but felt themselves liberated after contact with western culture. This is the same kind of rebellion that is evident in educated lower castes today against upper castes.

It is remarkable what empowerment of women can do. In America, women's movement established kindergarten, child health services and a separate juvenile justice system---all before women even had a right to vote. They have successfully mobilized to promote temperance, curb drunken driving and push for tighter gun control. They contributed mightily to the war effort too. We in India need to think: How can any society prosper while neglecting, subjugating, denying opportunity to half its citizens? How could we have advanced when multiple generations of illiterate ignorant traditionalist mothers raised almost all of us?

2. **Educational Limitations**: Our indigenous educational system had been a disaster until around the middle of the nineteenth century, when Macaulay and others introduced modern education. Till then

we had Gurukuls and Pathshalas, which were too scattered, too poor, too reserved, too limited in scope. Forget about ancient big names like Nalanda and Taxila; we are talking here about a thousand years before English rule, not about ancient times. I recently read an interesting account of how a rich family took its six-year-old child in a procession on horseback on its first day at school around the year 1845, so rare and remarkable was the occasion supposed to be at the time. Contrast this with the estimated ninety percent literacy among the North American whites in 1820. As late as 1938, my brother had to go to a distant town because my village had no school beyond the fourth grade of primary. It has been reported that Lal Bahadur Shastri, a former prime minister of India, as a teenager, sometimes had to swim across the river to reach his secondary school. The famous IIT's are a recent phenomenon, only a few decades old.

More serious than the paucity of schools was the fact that our traditional schools taught only Sanskrit language, philosophy and Hindu scriptures. No science, only a little practical arithmetic and certainly no technical education as we know it today. Imagine the consequences of this state of affairs for several centuries when the world of science was advancing by leaps and bounds. According to our wise men, the only knowledge worth acquiring was moral and spiritual knowledge. This was imparted well, but people had to go to places as distant as Hardwar and Benares for higher learning. Worse still, whatever little education was available was restricted to men only and to certain upper castes, specially the Brahmins. Indifference to women's education, even hostility, was routine in our society.

The constitution of independent India in 1951 laid down universal compulsory primary education as a directive principle of state policy. This may yet prove to be the wisest step ever taken by our country so far. But we need to keep in mind that it was taken as late as after 1947, by western English educated leaders, not by our traditionalist cultural enthusiasts. It was also not fully implemented.

3. **Caste** is an integral part of our society and has done tremendous harm to India. Many writers have criticized the caste system. We shall focus here only on some aspects relevant to our issues.

A Hindu is defined and circumscribed by his caste affiliation. Caste for him is a club, community, creed and faith, all rolled into one. As a kid I learnt soon enough from my grandparents the hierarchical structure in Hindu society, so evident everywhere. Ex-communication from one's caste was one of the most feared punishments a Hindu was afraid of. Castes promoted inequality, disunity and status consciousness. We are a divided nation—divided by caste, sub-caste and sub-sub-caste in addition to language, region, religion, sub-religion and all. We have not only untouchable castes; even the untouchable castes have their own hierarchy of upper and lower castes. And all these social rungs of the ladder still persist though abolished by law in theory. We are a highly status conscious society. It has been historically rooted in caste consciousness. Even our gods have echelons and categories of status. Status awareness shows in India in all spheres---in professional and political circles and even today after fifty years of democracy and independence. Mark when an average Indian talks. You cannot miss how he is conscious of and eager to emphasize his superior status, money or college degree. Yet our culture of inequality is piously denied, brazenly practiced and universally accepted.

Our feudal attitudes and consequent low productivity have their origin in the inequalities bred by the caste system or Varnashram Dharma as it is called. Even among professions, occupations often go from father to son---a lawyer's son becomes a lawyer, a journalist's son becomes a journalist, a chief minister's relative becomes a chief minister. Caste emphasizes seed, not deed. Talent is assumed, not needed, nor even expected. Caste has facilitated, actually guaranteed, the creation of a permanently privileged priestly class, almost obscenely advantaged just by the accident of birth. We rewarded those who had the foresight to be born into wealth or upper caste. (These days they call it the lucky sperm club).

Still we hear many learned apologists for our culture denying its origins, defending it and minimizing its impact, all in one breath. Apart from the usual dichotomy between precept and practice in our society, our learned men conveniently forget how and why: 1. Rama killed a low caste Shambuk. 2. A talented Karna (in Mahabharat) was stigmatized all his life. 3. Drona asked and obtained a low-caste Ekalavya's thumb; and 4. Lord Krishna in the Gita stated that he himself created the four castes. The Purusha Sukta hymn of the Rig Veda describes the origin of the four castes from the four parts of the body of Brahman and the same account is supported in Manusmriti. The most respected Parashurama, a virulent Brahmin Guru, an incarnation of God, killed the entire fighting class, the Kshatriyas, 21 times, merely to avenge the killing of his father at the hand of a Kshatriya caste king.

In American democracy today, the ruling rich men's plutocracy is smart enough to know that it is easier to rule if it can persuade the middle class to lobby for its policies benefiting the rich. Similarly in India, the ruling minority priestly class was also smart enough to know that it was easier to dominate if it could persuade the lower classes to adopt the values benefiting the priestly class.

When the privileged decision makers in any society are somehow able to insulate themselves from the consequences of their own decisions, that is the start of irresponsibility, blame games and downfall of society as a whole. The powerful Brahmin class acquired a status much higher than that of the defenders of the country but was itself not responsible for defense. It monopolized not only knowledge, but also power and status. Practical life got divorced from principles. The dominance of this minority precluded participation of the majority of the population in the affairs of the state. The state suffered, society withered, religion prospered.

For too long we judged man by the circumstance of his birth and not by the content of his character. Cult of personality and power prevailed. Caste perpetuated the gap in education. We did never realize that monopoly of knowledge and ideas is even worse than the monopoly of power or wealth. Meritocracy demands exactly the opposite. A society aspiring to be a meritocracy needs to shed its status consciousness. Meritocracy and democracy serve as great motivators for people in all walks of life. These two in America produced greater opportunity for more people than in any other country in the history of the world. Indians working in America know the difference between India and the USA in this respect.

Institutions of democracy are not as successful in hierarchical societies as they are in egalitarian outfits. When people have to make a choice between a classless modern society based on equality of status and a hierarchical ancient culture based on inequality of status, it is never an easy choice. It is easy to see that one of the main reasons why democracy is so difficult to practise in India is the hold of caste and status on the populace. People habitually and instinctively are more loyal to their caste affiliations than to political party affiliations or to any kind of principles. This largely explains the unprincipled voting we see so often.

A major consequence of caste was that manufacturing activity and useful technical crafts like carpentry, smithy, etc. were left to the lowermost castes and were assigned a lower social status than poetry or philosophy. Young minds that had qualities required for success in both fields preferred the poetic/philosophic to the scientific/technical field. Importance of productive work did not grow in the minds of the Hindu population. Technical progress became stunted. Also, marrying within caste only prevented cross fertilization of people, ideas and beliefs; and ensured the continuation of inbreeding. That is bad for any society in the long run.

Now consider the combined effect of the above listed three factors: Caste, problems in Education and condition of Women. How can any society advance with such inherent serious handicaps acting in combination for centuries?

Wars and revolutions are great drivers of social change. We never had real big all pervading wars. All we had was defeat, surrender and fatalistic acceptance of our fate. In a few exceptional cases where war did happen, it changed society in a profound manner, as in Shivaji's Maharashtra, for example.

Causes of our Defeats

Historians tell us that the most prominent causes of our military defeats in the past were 1. Disunity and 2. Failure to mobilize resources---human, financial, political, organizational. These are the common threads running through our history. Both are closely related to our social situation described above. In my opinion, a third cause---Our irrational beliefs and attitudes---has been even more important than the above two. Actually it is the basic underlying reason for the other two and yet we have consistently failed to realize that fact or acknowledge it clearly.

1. **Disunity**: This has always been our weak point. It was fatally obvious at the time of the Muslim conquest. The Rajputs who were entrusted with the defense of the country for centuries were a brave and noble community but they were always fighting, fussing, feuding among themselves over petty issues and personal rivalries. Jaichand Rathod (of Kanpur) fought against his cousin Prithviraj Chauhan (Delhi), Mansingh against fellow Rajput Pratap, and Jaisinh against Shivaji, all helping Muslims Ghori, Akbar and Aurangzeb, respectively. The mainly Hindu armies of the five small southern Muslim kingdoms destroyed the great Hindu kingdom of Vijaynagar in 1565 A.D. In 1857 vast segments of our people and rulers kept aloof from the fight for independence. Shocking examples of Maratha disunity (below) are well-known. India was united as one political entity only after the British rule was firmly and universally established all over India after 1857.

We observe disunity so frequently and consistently in our social and public life that it stands out as a feature of our cultural ethos. The petty quarrels we see in India today are hardly any different in essence from what we had in those dark days of our defeats and downfall. Cabinet ministers with collective responsibility not only quarrel, they do so in public. A minister in a full cabinet meeting can abuse the very chief minister who appointed him. Members of Indian cultural organizations and temple committees (even in America) quarrel and split over trivial egoistic issues. Religious sects divide over personalities rather than over principles. My own cooperative housing society in Bombay could never hold a peaceful, orderly annual meeting. All of us have seen some ghastly family quarrel that feeds on itself and never ends. It goes on and on. The routine is quite familiar. Pettiness? Small minds? Short-sightedness? Egos? I don't know what you will call this. But we are well accustomed to this kind of disunity and blame games in Indian society. For whatever reason, we Indians have an ingrained inability to work together to better ourselves.

Do some cultures have a tendency to generate more disunity and conflict? Do they tend to produce more egoistic personality types? Is anything in our culture that tends to divide us much more often than unite us? I cannot say and I do not want to guess. Perhaps somebody more knowledgeable than myself in this area would like to conduct research and throw more light on this subject. One view is that too much liberty in religious precepts tends to encourage the kind of attitudes that promote factionalism in society. Another view is that we mistakenly assume we are victims of something---casteism, racism, sexism, classism, and so on. This forces us to identify ourselves separately from another group. We fashion and refine the tactic to fight it and then assign morality to it. This tactic encourages the supposed or real victim to magnify his weakness and makes it impossible to ask what is in the interest of society as a whole. We never achieve unity as a result.

2. **Resource mobilization**: This has always been our weakness. When transport and communications were primitive, we had a natural protection from the Himalayas and the seas. As soon as civilization acquired a capacity to move large armies, our northwestern frontiers were thrown wide open. Alexander started the history of invasions into India with a huge army. An endless array of invaders like the Kushan, Hun, Shak, Afghan, Mongol, Turk and all followed. It has been noted that the army of Mohamed of Gizni looked like a big ocean. The question is: Coming from sparsely populated countries, if they could transport such huge armies through a very difficult terrain and sustain it for so long in an unknown foreign country with all its attendant problems and difficulties, why we, a densely populated country rich in resources, why could we, not raise comparable resources in our own country, when we had all the advantages natural to fighting on the home turf?

We know very well how America and England were totally mobilized to the last man and woman when the Germans lost both the world wars. Were the Germans not brave? They certainly were, but they could not match the tremendous resources that America mobilized. Germany fought almost to the last man, drafting even teenagers in 1945, since few eligible adults were left available. That kind of sacrifice and resource mobilization is needed in wars---even that is often not enough.

Our defense had a narrow base. With a huge sea coast, we had no navy worth the name. Masses kept aloof from politics. Social inequality bred by the caste system was a major cause. In the middle ages, the

Brahmins taught, the Rajputs fought, others were generally indifferent, even irrelevant. The thinkers did not fight, the fighters did not think. Of course, there were some honorable exceptions. But the exceptions don't count; the vast majority is what really makes the difference. Only the Kshatriyas were supposed to fight. According to one estimate, only a very small percentage of the population was real Kshatriya. The vast majority of the population belonged to the other three castes and were mere spectators, armchair critics or breast beaters. When a society excludes half its population (women) and whole big segments (non-Kshatriyas) from defense effort, how can it mobilize enough manpower? We competed with only a small fraction of our population participating. The defense of a vast country was entirely left to the Rajput community who though brave, were heavily outnumbered, outweaponed and outwitted as well. The bravest of the brave, Rana Pratap, faced the might of the Moghal army numbering around 75,000 soldiers, with his 22,000 ill-equipped men, many of whom were the aboriginal Bhils fighting with nothing better than bows and arrows. The arrows barely touched the iron clad professional soldiers of the Moghal force. The Rajputs found it difficult to assemble even this kind of make shift armies for want of personnel, finances and weapons. Pratap got financial help from a merchant named Bhamasha---but it was only a one time shot.

And that was another reason of our defeats-- the severe finance and resource crunch. It was the age of mercenary soldiers; nationalism had not crystallized. Most of our rulers had no effective financial management, no organized system of public taxation, no reliable sources of permanent income. As a result a large section of their armies was comprised of hastily raised adhoc bodies of voluntary fighters with outdated weapons and no discipline, little training and no long term planning or effective motivation.

Are we Indians physically weaker than foreigners? Perhaps. But consider these: (A) The Nepalese Gurkhas in spite of their short stature have proved to be some of the most feared soldiers in the world. (B) The smaller Japanese defeated the taller Russians in 1905. (C) Our North Westerners faced most aggressors most of the time. They---the Punjabis and the Rajasthanis---are tall, strong and hefty, not physically weak.

3. **Brainpower, Beliefs, Attitudes**: To realize all the above listed problems and address them adequately takes a lot of brainpower---in planning, weapons development, organization, strategy, diplomacy, motivation and clarity of thought----that, sad to say, we could not muster. Clarity is the first requirement in war. Keep the enemy arguing, confuse him and kill him---that is an effective military strategy. We lacked the clarity, the will, as well as the skill to face our enemies. Keeping ourselves open to too many confusing philosophical options, vacillating indecisively, not having firm guidelines, we were an easy prey to our enemies.

We lacked organisation and discipline. We were soloists. Harmonizing with an orchestra demands skills vastly different from singing solo. Individual heroism must play second fiddle to discipline, organization and strategy in a war. Pyrrhic victories won by individual heroism, though impressive, do not last. Men, however brave, cannot win with outdated weapons. Why were we out-weaponed? Alexander used fast cavalry; Babar (first Mughal) brought guns; we were stuck too long with arrows and swords. Our small brains failed miserably to grasp these facts and the shifting trends in military technology. Until too late. Until small but disciplined European forces started defeating our unruly outfits that we called armies. Then our rulers---Tipu, Scindia, Ranjitsingh and others---woke up and started engaging European military advisors to train our forces. Alas, it was too little too late. The undoubted greatness of these generals could not stem the overpowering tide.

Many otherwise knowledgeable people do not realize that India was almost like a ripe fruit waiting to be grabbed by European nations during the eighteenth century. With what ease they did this, we can imagine when we notice examples like the battle of Plassey. This is a famous landmark in the history of India. It is well-known that British rule in India began with victory in this battle in 1757. With almost a hundred thousand soldiers in the field on the enemy side, how many casualties did the Englishmen suffer? A mere 150. The Indians were completely outmaneuvered, outfoxed, some say cheated, by the Britishers. A similar fate had befallen the big army of the brave Rana Sang against the small band of Babar earlier in 1528. The Peshwas too in the closing years of the Maratha Empire were similarly outwitted. British diplomacy succeeded eminently in sowing dissention among the five big Maratha centers of power. It was but a pathetic footnote to the tragedy that engulfed the glory of the Maratha power. An Englishman said in another context: "We won the empire in a fit of absentmindedness." Our ice kings just melted into puddles. Compare all this with the fact that European conquerors like Cortez and Pizarro with extremely small bands of Spaniards overthrew the vast Aztec and Inca empires in the Americas in the sixteenth century. Is it a flattering thought to compare ourselves with those Red Indian societies?

The hard fact is that we became a nation of wimps who got self-destructed from within. We did never realize that we needed to save us from ourselves. We crumbled from within before foreigners broke us from without. Quarrels over trivial matters and inter-religious wars---Buddhist, Jain, Shaivite, Vaishnavite---too played a big role. Non-violence promoted by Buddhism and Jainism weakened society.

From 1756 to 1815 A. D. the hard pressed Englishmen's limited resources were overextended all around the world. The American colonies were in rebellion. The French were led by Napoleon in Europe. On the other hand, in India, the Marathas had recovered from Panipat defeat; Tipu and Nizam were strong; and the French were only too willing to help them. The American fighters for independence (1776—1783 A.D.) profited from the assistance by the French. But we could not profit from all these factors. The English were vastly more diplomatic. Though hugely outnumbered, they outwitted our rulers at every stage. They did not prevail simply because of their military, they prevailed because of their superior strategy, diplomacy and brainpower. They fought in three continents--Canada, Europe and India--at the same time and won all of them.

To put it directly and bluntly in perspective, our enemies had better brains, ideas, tact and motivation. This fact alone should put at rest fantasies of our own wisdom. We are accustomed to assume we are very wise; the facts clearly reveal that the truth is otherwise. This cause of our defeats was more important than our much maligned disunity. Actually, our enemy invaders too were not united, after all. The Afghans, Turks and Mongols quarreled among themselves; so did the English, the French and the Dutch. We could not benefit from their disunity; they could from ours.

On an individual level, we only need to read biographies of people like Thomas Jefferson, Thomas Paine, Benjamin Franklin and William Pitt (British PM) in the west and Nana Fadanvis, Bajirao, and Gangadhar Shastri (all Maratha statesmen) in India. They were close contemporaries. Who among them had better brains? With all due respect to a few of our people, it is clear as daylight that we were intellectual dwarfs. Before the third battle of Panipat, the Maratha commander Sadashivrao Bhau upset his allied Jat chieftain so much that he left the critical battle in which the Maratha power was crushed. In the sunset days of the Maratha power, the fundamentalist religious orthodoxy of the Brahmins around the Peshwa alienated a powerful caste (CKP) on a trivial issue: Can a CKP be called a Brahmin? The result? The CKP controlled Holker later looted Pune, the seat of his own Maratha power. Our stupidities contributed far more to our defeats than our lack of physical resources. Our patriotism should not come in the way of our acknowledging such simple facts. History is replete with them. Why did we grow so naïve?

Our beliefs in celibacy, nonviolence, contentment, self-denial, renunciation and non attachment to the fruits of our actions helped our enemies. The last one forms the crux of the Gita and is a great principle in personal life. But consider this scenario: My enemy is highly motivated and fights with passion to win at all cost. I am detached, resigned to any result, consider victory or defeat the same, fighting without much passion. All other things being equal, who do you think has a better chance to win? The enemy, clearly. We merely endure; the enemy prevails. Our contentment puts a stop to ambition. The world is full of willing people, some willing to die, others willing to help them. What is the difference between satisfaction and success? Well, we had the satisfaction and they the success!

Arjuna loved his enemies---Bhishma, Drona and his cousins too; so he did not want to fight. Krishna asked Arjuna to fight. Why? Because you must do your duty and nobody can kill anybody anyway since the soul is immortal. The entire emphasis is on philosophical reasons to fight, not on realistic practical reasons like hating the enemy or defending oneself or jihad. Can you fight an enemy you love? Yes, you can, sometimes, but certainly not as fiercely, as decisively, as when you hate him deep within your bones. The motivation, the will to fight, becomes diluted, hazy, less clear. A Muslim fights his jihad, a Hindu fights his Dharma Yuddha; so, that factor is common to both when they are fighting each other. What is different is that while the former hates the 'infidel' to the bone, the latter sees an immortal soul everywhere---even in his enemy. Who will be able to fight better? The answer is obvious and our history is a clear witness to its truth. The Hindu wins the philosophical point; the other guy wins the war.

An observation often made by our sports commentators is that our sportsmen often play well but they lack "the killer instinct." Note what General Patton told his soldiers: "We are not here to die for our country. We are here to make the other bloody damn guy die for his country."

Bhishma and Drona were great men---in certain respects; but they were silent spectators to the horrible insult to Draupadi. No amount of white washing can defend their inaction. Both of them sided with evil throughout. They did not have to do this for any vaguely patriotic or any other reasons. (If they were right, then Vibhishana who left his evil brother for good was obviously wrong.) Arjuna had enough reasons to hate these two opponents in battle. But he loved his enemies even as he fought them and he is our classical ideal---a confused commander and a talented hero. We Hindus are taught not to hate our enemies. Because the soul that resides in the enemy is a part of the ultimate reality that "cannot be cut, burnt, wetted, dried----," as the Gita preaches. We do fight but we do it for the wrong reasons and for the wrong goals. They fight to win, we fight to do our duty. They expect success, we expect nothing. They will not tolerate failure, we will tolerate everything, even success at rare times! We refuse to hate our enemies and they refuse to spare us. We don't like this evil world, so they send us to the next. We cannot save our skin but we save our souls. At least we think we do. How can we win?

A couple of simplistic questions may be excused, since the Gita is no ordinary book---it has molded our attitudes and our lives for thousands of years. How is it that our hero Arjuna developed cold feet at the very last moment? The big war was planned and discussed threadbare much earlier and everyone knew who is going to fight whom. Did he have to see everybody in person to realize that he was going to fight against his relatives? Questions are desirable during preplanning in a war, but positively harmful once the die is cast. What would you say about a wavering commander in chief---one who had no firm commitment to or conviction about his cause until he is given a booster dose of spirituality in the nick of time? Equivocation and equanimity in war equate well with weakness and defeat. Just think about issues like discipline, decisiveness, determined leadership, army morale, strategic planning and scores of other factors absolutely necessary before and during a war. These are precisely the qualities the Hindu mind has been found lacking in, during the course of our long history of defeats. An indecisive hero may win a war but the end result is a tragedy, whether the hero is Hamlet or Arjuna.

Woodrow Wilson, an American president, said, "We are not put in this world to sit still and know; we are put into it to act." Our ironclad illogic of concentrating on unattainable knowledge stopped us from decisive action even while we outwardly appeared like preaching action. As a matter of fact, the way people frame the debate on war---motivation, goal, ideals----goes far in determining its outcome. We never realized this and suffered the consequences.

A military defeat may or may not be a real disaster in the long run. But rationalizing it through philosophical fantasies converts it into a real and permanent disaster. Fatalism, Maya (Illusion), Non-attachment---all such concepts have served our society as such philosophical fantasies, although in personal lives of individuals they do have some utility and value. Our beliefs like these, our customs like Sati and killings of new-born females, our superstitions like omens and astrology----all these helped our enemies in the long run. We lacked the right attitudes. We lacked the kind of motivation that democracy and Churchill provided to win the world war. Wars can never be won with such inherent handicaps. In war, the will to win is important, the will to prepare is vital. We had neither. All we had was a pious wish to be released from this evil world. And our enemies obliged. We prayed and they slayed.

Social Realities only a century ago

It is obvious that our social systems proved painfully inadequate to cope with the challenges posed to our country by foreigners. Repetitive failure is never an accident. Our problem was one of systemic failure, not merely of infirmities. If anyone still has an iota of doubt regarding our bad social situation, let him look into our social situation around 1850 to 1900A.D. This specific period for two reasons: 1. It being comparatively recent, we have enough authentic information available, sometimes first hand. We don't have to guess. 2. English education had just been started but had not become widespread, and travel to foreign countries was extremely limited, so we can see our society almost untouched by foreign influence, unlike the mix we see today. So we have undisputed and unstained facts about the native Indian society. And most of rural India still continues to be more or less the same even today.

What kind of India do we see around this period? More than eighty five percent of the population lived in villages, practiced age-old farming, was illiterate, very superstitious, in short, very backward. A typical village had wells for drinking water, one for the upper castes, one for the lower castes and a separate one for the untouchables. Every caste had its separate locality to live in. People plodded on foot in the mud to go anywhere in or out of the village. Collecting cattle dung from the streets and drying it in cakes was a useful economic activity since those cakes were the most widely used fuel for cooking. Fetching water from the wells, taking care of the cattle and cooking kept the women busy. Herbal medicines and grandma medicines were popular since only these were available with ease. The village school, when it existed, had primary classes, but few attended. Unwilling pupils were bodily lifted by some hefty boys and dumped into the classroom where a stern disciplinarian of a teacher with a cane in hand took proper care of them.

Industrialization was nonexistent. Untouchability was universally practiced. Life expectancy was very low. The terrible scourge of the Pindharis and the Thugs (robbers) had only recently been eliminated. Outlaws and robbers were common, so wise men buried money in pits dug in mud floors inside their houses. It took the English viceroy William Bentick to introduce social reforms like abolition of Sati (woman burning after husband's death). Some enlightened Indians helped but they made barely a minor dent in the solid rock of social inertia and orthodoxy. The two real-life scenes we saw in the beginning of this book are from the 1940s but are typical of the times. A lot of specific detail is available for this period which clearly demonstrates the pitiable conditions under which our people lived. The current generation of young Indians is sometimes surprised and shocked to hear about the terrible state of affairs prevailing in India at the time. In those ancient prehistoric times on our planet, it was almost unheard of to find a woman in college. For children, working in fields was assumed. Attending school was a goal but never inevitable. College was hardly attainable, something to be proud of, a big deal. Widows were not allowed to marry, not in upper castes at least. Child marriages were common. My mother married at the age of thirteen. Tilak, a progressive social reformer, separated from his friend Agarkar (1895 A.D.) because the former could not or did not want to support a law banning child marriages before twelve years of age, as the latter did. 12 years!!! And that is a firebrand progressive leader for you!

Why is it that we were and still are submerged in a social situation so depressing and self-defeating? The roots lie buried deep within our traditional belief system that is closely intertwined with our culture. And that culture has its deepest roots in our religion.

10. THE SPIRIT OF SPIRITUALITY
Nature of Belief, God and Soul

The most important contributor to our political defeats has been our ancient belief system. When a belief is tenaciously held with unquestioning trust, especially in theosophical matters, it is called Faith (Shraddhaa). The entire edifice of our culture stands on the foundations of our age-old beliefs and faith. Our attitudes, actions, customs, traditions---almost everything in Hindu society---are traceable to our overabundant faith in spiritual matters. Therefore, if we are to understand our problems properly, it is necessary to have a proper perspective on Belief, Faith and Religion in general.

Nature of deep rooted Beliefs

It is universally accepted that religious beliefs are a matter of faith, not of rational thought. We acquire our most deep rooted beliefs either through upbringing or by feeling. Then we rationalize them. We filter facts through the colored glasses of our deep beliefs to accept only the matching facts; then our minds find reasons to reject the rest. An earthquake does not stop people from saying, "O God, thou art merciful." When facts contradict our assumed faith, we wriggle out using word games, clever arguments or even dishonest stratagems. Idol worship, slavery, jihad, persecution, cruelty, mythology, all have been rationalized at one time or the other by very decent, sincere, intelligent men.

None can stop you from believing if you are bent upon believing---not even God Himself. Man uses God as a tool to warp his logic. When my friend met with a serious car accident on a pilgrimage, he was positive that only a merciful God saved his life. That is the fantastic power of belief converted into faith. But he was not sure to whom he would attribute the pain and the several permanent disabilities---either to a devil or to his own past sins or to bad roads, bad weather or a bad driver. Many deep beliefs happen to be an obsession in search of a justification. A man assumes something and goes out to look for proofs. He always finds them. Another assumes the opposite and then goes out to look for proofs. He too finds them. The prerogative of belief is the liberty to formulate its own rules. Right astrological predictions strengthen people's faith but wrong predictions hardly cure it. We Hindus went to battles with Guru's blessings and Poojas; our enemies did not. But our too frequent defeats did not cure us or cause us to reexamine our belief in "Wherever there is Dharma (Religion), there is victory." Rather than question our belief, we coin new convenient definitions to make the facts confirm to our belief. Then we write impressive scholarly treatises to prove it.

If facts confirm the belief, the belief is strengthened; if facts go against it, the belief is strengthened even more---that is the beauty of belief. That is how cults prosper. We all wonder about some crazy misguided cults. But to their adherents they fulfill some hunger---personal, psychological or social. It is difficult to convince a desperately hungry person that what he intends to eat may be harmful. Cults prosper feeding unfounded deep beliefs to such people. "Fear of responsibility becomes a flight from reality. To make sense out of chaos, to explain personal powerlessness, to seek security in an insecure existence, people divide the world into simplistic categories--good and evil, saved and damned, good guys and bad guys--just as a child does. Dependency, debilitation, dread, desensitization---all play their part in influencing such minds." The end result often is a fanatical belief in something. The Solar Temple cult took 74 lives in 1994. Jim Jones promoted a suicidal People's Temple. And all Americans know about Charles Manson, the god man murderer. If such things can happen in America, it is not at all difficult to explain why godmen proliferate in every corner of a country like India.

One man's belief is another's jinx. People with strong beliefs are uncomfortable with other people's beliefs. To them, belief becomes faith, faith becomes fanaticism. These are not misguided people, as is popularly assumed. Fanaticism is but the other side of a coin that is called strong faith. Too strong a faith in my own truth leads me on to believe that my faith alone is the literal truth, the whole truth and nothing but the truth; and so, all others are wrong. Religions have a hard time being tolerant because it is in the nature of religion to go too far. Religious zealots are passionate believers in their own brands of truth and they hate (usually secretly) all other brands. Intolerance is but a natural consequence of strong faith, which by definition is unverifiable and unjustifiable through reasoned argument. Wounds in the wars of belief are too deep to be forgiven or forgotten. In parliaments, people with such strong beliefs hurl microphones. In streets they crack windows. In jihad they cut heads. Where every belief is untrue, we seek to convince everybody that our untruth is the only truth. This kind of ossification of the brain in set grooves is a tragedy of mankind.

Rationality is like RAM (Random Access Memory) in computers. It is randomly accessible and changeable since it resides at and operates in the outermost levels of consciousness. But deep beliefs like ROM (Read Only Memory) are ingrained in deeper levels of the subconscious and unconscious mind. Actually, deep beliefs act more like the operating system (DOS or Windows) in computers. Education or reason is not able to make a dent in them. A shock, an upheaval, a deeply touching event like death, will often change a conviction in a flash in a way that a hundred arguments will not. Reason falls flat. Such beliefs deeply affect attitude and behavior. Spirituality is the most powerful agent for change in these. So nothing will change until religion will change.

Here we are up against a wall. If deep belief is beyond reason, why argue at all? The search for rational cures for irrational beliefs may itself be an irrational undertaking. So why waste words? I am well aware that anything I say in the following chapters will be met with counter arguments by people adept at rationalizing their own beliefs. I will say it still, because: 1. People need to be aware of the other side, the other perspective. The fanaticism prevalent in the world makes any such effort worthwhile, if not to change, at least to attempt to show the hold of one-sided faith. 2. I hope wise men can discriminate between true and false arguments. 3. A few people as well as many bright youths do really have broad minds---they may hold beliefs and yet appreciate different viewpoints. With a little bit of luck, a few of the more open-minded fence sitters may be induced to reconsider their positions. In the process, if I can make even a few persons think afresh, I am happy. So I have hope. Even in a seemingly hopeless world.

The most important part of any culture is the beliefs it builds, promotes and sustains. Beliefs are the motivations, the invisible springboards of all our actions. Words, styles, details, stories may vary. We may not acknowledge or spell out all our beliefs. But they determine what we are, what we do, sometimes how we do it. It is, therefore, very important to analyze how our personal beliefs have affected all of us in society in practical life, although we may or may not be able or willing to reshape them.

We need not shirk from discussing religious beliefs even if they may be etched in stone. Why? Because attempts to transform any cultural beliefs without engaging in its theosophical underpinnings will always fail, since theosophy is the context of that culture. Religion transforms individuals, who form society. Even individually practiced, it has profound social consequences---good or bad. Questions of religion can also be questions of the world; they are not mutually exclusive. Religion, like government, is a social institution as much as it is a theosophical one. We debate government everyday. Similarly, we should not hesitate to discuss the positive as well as the negative social consequences of religious beliefs.

Organizations in time become ends in themselves. They decay. Yet when it comes to commenting on ancient religion, we demur, we defer, we back off. 'The defining dysfunction of our era is an honest critique of mystique.' Priest craft has effectively prohibited every comment on religions by pain and penalties. But it is imperative in this age of enlightenment that everybody is able to discuss all aspects of a belief without being called upon to judge the truth or otherwise of the belief itself. Whether a religious belief is right or wrong, desirable or undesirable, it must be judged by what it actually does as opposed to what supportive rhetoric it spews or what rosy pictures it paints.

Faith is a great and powerful force. Look at huge religious congregations reciting hymns, clapping, singing, even crying. Faith pervades. It penetrates. It provides the strongest motivation there is to man. Faith and religion can do amazing things to people. People will work for money but they will give their lives for meaning, myth or faith.

But there is no unalloyed good or unmixed evil in the world. Even a great thing like Faith can have undesirable or unintended consequences. Core convictions can help a man; but their subjectivity has led us to the most deadly conflicts in history. It took no less a sage than the great Hitler to say, "I believe that my conduct is in accordance with the will of the Almighty Creator." Religion can bind as well as blind. Extremes can be wrong even in goodness and virtue. Although too little of a good thing can be dangerous, too much of it is often weird and can even be fatal. This is as true of things like food, sanitation and emotion, as of spirituality and religion. Food is vital but too much of it can cause indigestion or obesity. Sanitation reduces disease but extremes of sanitation encourage disease through reduced immunological response. A famous mathematician was so paranoid that he used to wash his hands with soap scores of times a day! He became a real psychopath.

If you are a man of faith, will you be ready to look at the other side of faith? With all due respect for you and your faith, I shall view the matter from a different perspective—not to denigrate anyone's faith but to show that other viewing angles are possible, probable, or may be, even desirable. We shall see below the need for Faith in God as a desirable Value; but first, let us see the other side here.

Limitations of Faith and Spirituality

1. The biggest problem with religious faith is not that it is wrong, bad or undesirable in itself; in fact, it can be quite useful. The biggest problem is that it usually tolerates, promotes and sustains, directly or indirectly, **Irrational modes of thought.** Faith does not harm; it is the habit we form to accept things on faith that does harm. Faith builds an imperceptible wall between our common sense and us. Holding faith is not as harmful as cultivating faith. The former imparts resolve, the latter eats up reason. It is difficult to see the thin line dividing the two. Overemphasis on spiritual faith distorts objectivity, undermines capacity to reason and robs us of our will to look at other viewpoints. When a person is constantly encouraged to assume abstract concepts without reference to intellect, logic or common sense, he naturally gets into a habit of presumptive thinking. Since men's brains or personalities cannot be kept divided into neat compartments, such theosophical habits of thinking creep into non-theosophical fields as well. A society cultivates faith for too long and lapses into non-reason without realizing it. A society composed of a majority of such non-rational persons becomes ill-equipped to compete well with others. This has happened with us Hindus in India.

2. Spirituality diverted our most precious <u>resources</u>---human and material---to metaphysical pursuits at the cost of our progress in this world. (See chapter 12)

3. Deep spirituality when extrapolated to cover group dynamics in societies creates problems. Emphasis on spirituality tends to obliterate the finer points of distinction between <u>personal morality and group ethics</u>; between householders and ascetics; between inspirational poetry and true philosophy. Since we do not want to be self-centered narcissists, we must consider what effects our individual spirituality will have on the society we live in. We shall see this in detail in the following pages.

4. Spirituality may be good; but it is <u>not the only good</u>. Tolerance for other people and other beliefs is good; reason is good; love is good. Where there is a conflict between any of these on one hand and spiritualism on the other, we need balance. When we lose balance, we promote extremes. Extreme emphasis on certain desirable virtues in personal life---contentment, non-violence, sacrifice---ultimately and unknowingly created a soft and servile society in Hindus.

5. There are degrees and levels of belief in religious faith, as in everything else. In most people, blind faith and superstition go hand in hand with spiritual faith. Devout Hindu scholars believe in Scriptural word, wrong Rituals, inane Mythology and absurd Astrology with varying degrees of conviction. For a huge majority of people, it is faith that is preponderant, not reason. This degenerates easily and naturally into blind faith, superstition and worse as time passes. All believers have to confront this nasty question: 'At what point should faith yield to common sense? Never?' Think again. A married woman sexually surrendering herself to a respected Guru (God to her) ---how does this sound to you, dear reader? Such

anachronisms happen in Hindu temples and to brush them off under whatever pretext is another great anachronism in Hindu society. Faith can and does go berserk too often. In fact it is its very nature.

Even some intelligent people cannot differentiate between good faith and blind faith. A few oppose, some tolerate, most are indifferent; but social deterioration continues and society suffers. What fraction of society is always intelligent and discriminating? I personally know quite a few highly intelligent people who sincerely believe in the silliest of myths of religion. Faith in God is advanced as a justification for faith in myths. Myths justify miracles. Miracles justify absurd stories. Each one stands on the shoulders of the other. The result? Loss of common sense and spreading of blind faith. Criticizing stupidity is construed as criticizing faith. It is construed as a mark of disrespect, arrogance or lack of culture---and all this in defense of faith in religion.

The beliefs we hold are not merely private religious beliefs; they have public consequences in driving Reason's downward spiral. People derive their identity, orient their lives and interpret the meaning of life from the patterns first charted by religious ideas and myths. The mythical stories are not causative in any direct sense. But they exemplify and legitimize certain values. Therefore they create an environment that makes it seem sacrilegious to oppose or even question these values. But without questioning traditional values and modifying them as needed in step with the changing world, there can be no progress.

Unfounded mindless beliefs are so attractive because people don't have to think much---or even think at all. A culture based on many such sacrosanct certainties gets buried under an avalanche of assumed truths. The beliefs may be right or wrong to varying degrees; but in the long run these promote thinking in set grooves. Over long periods of time people convert assumed beliefs into social traditions too difficult to break. As an example, caste system in India might have originated anyway but it was firmly rooted in the belief that the Varna Ashram Dharma was created by God (based on the Purusha Sukta in RigVeda, references in the Gita and the Manu Smruti). Somewhere along the line it morphed into the ironclad monstrosity that included the tradition of untouchability as well. This kind of progression evolved with many of our beliefs and traditions.

Many practical questions in life cannot be resolved satisfactorily without a reference to some kind of a belief system. Abortion, stem cell research, criminal law, death, violence, facing or resisting evils of all kinds, and ethical questions---these are a few examples. So religion and God are not matters of idle curiosity and unnecessary controversy, as some people tend to believe. It is essential for all thinking people to develop a good perspective on both, in order to have clarity of ideas in practical daily life.

To Be(lieve) or Not to Be(lieve): Is there a way to bridge the unbridgeable age-old gap between believers and non-believers? Yes. Believers like mysticism; non-believers prick holes in them. But to start with, assume these two axioms: 1. Man needs God. 2. There is no God. The first is a desirable value, the second an objective truth. If we accept these two, the conflict between belief and non-belief disappears for all practical purposes. God becomes somewhat like Santa Claus. He is useful and charming, however unreal the idea. Several other concepts in history were untrue but essential---like Ether in wave theory in physics or Phlogiston in combustion chemistry. These did not exist but were needed at the time. Let us examine in brief how far reasonable men can accept these two axioms.

1. God as a Desirable Value----Do we need God and Religion?

We DO need God, whether He exists or not. Why? In brief, for two groups of reasons:

(A) Psychological needs of individuals arising from: 1. Man's helplessness against forces of nature, of society and of random chance. 2. Fear of uncertainty. 3. Fear of death. 4. Quest for meaning and purpose of life. 5. A convenient peg on which to hang all unresolved, unexplained and unexplainable questions.

(B) Societal needs of groups arising from: 1. Need for Ethical rules in communities---most important for building civilization. 2. Group formation, closeness, unity. 3. Hatred for enemies. 4. Means to motivate, manipulate and use large groups for certain ends. 5. Avoidance of boredom and distaste for mental gymnastics. Because of the above needs, people defend and rationalize God in all kinds of ways.

2. God as an Objective Truth---Faith or Reason? Is there a God?

How do we decide? The concept of God varies a lot. If we don't know what we are looking for, how do we find it? He may be beyond reason; but reason is all that we have, however limited. Inadequacy of reason is no reason to throw away reason. Even theology depends on logic and reason. Mathematical proofs are impossible but should we reject logic and common sense as well? When we find a jet plane inadequate to reach the moon, do we go back to a piston engine? Or, do we go forward and try to develop a rocket engine? Should we go back to the helpless caveman's faith and guesswork? If intellect has limits, faith has even more; experience too can be blind and speculation sterile. Stating that something beyond reason exists is an assumption, not a proof. When you face a solid impenetrable wall, it is futile to guess what lies beyond---a man, a mosquito, a bacteria or just a vacuum. Your guess is as good as mine. Inability to know everything is not a license to presume something.

Faith is no substitute for reason. It is a conviction, an opinion. It is not an instrument of knowledge as reason is. When we put religion out of the purview of reason, we put a huge chunk of life out of the purview of reason. We may argue about putting the truths of religion beyond reason; but there can be no argument at all about putting the practices, the rituals, and the personalities also out of the purview of reason. And yet we know that without these, no religion can survive. Think of questions like the death penalty, idol worship and life of prophets. Should we put them beyond the purview of reason?

Should we trust the saints who seem to know? They themselves tell us that they can only show the way but we have to realize God ourselves. To understand Einstein, I have to study physics, that is clear enough; but do I need to become Einstein myself? Even if I need to, can I become one? Even if I can, what fraction of humans can?

And why do saints differ so much about the concept of God? Buddha and Mahavira deny God; Jesus's God is all love; Mohammed's God punishes non-Muslims. Hindus have categories and levels of gods (see Ch 15). So whom do I trust? Going by birth, as most people do, only shows childhood conditioning, not any universal truth. When faith will not help, why not use reason in all these? There is no escape from reason in any case. We need it to weigh and balance conflicts in values and in discriminating between good and bad values. After all, man has become the supreme species mainly because of his intellect, so why denigrate intellect and ask it to play second fiddle to assumptions of faith? We can't have material proof for God; but we must insist on conceptual proof. Modern science too is all about concepts. But science concepts are logically provable, not just presumptive---as in case of theology.

People have asked many questions throughout the ages about God: 1. Why does a merciful God send earthquakes? All who die there cannot be sinners. 2. Why do good men suffer and bad men prosper? Why do innocent babies die? What kind of sins did the most virtuous lady in history---Sita---commit (in the previous birth?) to deserve the most miserable life in this birth? 3. Is an omnipotent God unable to destroy evil, Satan and Hell? Or, Is a merciful God unwilling to do so? 4. If everything must have a creator, who created the creator? 5. What was God doing before He started creating? 6. Nothing in the universe is single or unique. Everything (like electrons) exists in pairs or as part of vast conglomerates. Why assume then that something unique must exist?

The Soul: If there is no soul, there is no God or religion. How far can a reasonable person believe in the existence of the soul? Look at the difficulties here: 1. Dividing line between life and non-life is thin as air. Viruses are incapable of reproduction (hallmark of life) by themselves. Do they have souls? Does a mutating virus change its soul? The point of death is imprecise. After the heart stops, man lives on for some time and can even be revived. Brain dead people also live. So, when does a soul leave a body? Where is it? Already left? Still lingering in the organs? Waiting to be assigned another birth? 2. At what stage does a soul enter a body? At the sperm/egg stage? At the instant of fertilization? Or when a fertilized egg attaches itself to the wall of the uterus? Nature routinely kills billions of all these (souls) during each of these stages. Nowadays life can be born in the lab after both parents are dead. So immortality can reside in a freezer with stored sperm cells. 3. Organ transplants, cloning, stem cell research, genome mapping and other recent advances in genetics make it extremely unlikely that a reasonably well-informed person can believe in the existence of the soul, except only through faith. 4. Man has 300 trillion living cells in his body, each with its own metabolism. Certain organisms reproduce by dividing themselves. A plant grows from a single seed. Does each cell or seed have a separate soul? If yes, how many souls does a tree have? If no, how is a new tree born from a single seed?

5. Concepts of Soul vary from one religion to another. Do animals have souls? 6. The soul as described---immortal, unaffected by anything, a mere point of light, energy or whatever---why does it need God's grace? If it feels no pleasure or pain, what is Liberation and why does the soul need it? It is like saying, "John is not in jail. But he wants to escape from jail." In case of rebirth, how can the soul carry its merits and demerits with itself to another birth? 7. If and when chemists succeed in creating self duplicating protein molecules, what shall we conclude regarding the soul? This is not as far fetched today as creating carbon bio-compounds looked before the synthesis of urea in 1848 A.D. The child in me wants to ask the learned soul specialists and creationists: How was the first infinite immortal soul originally born and when? To all the above questions, believers say: "We don't know." And they are quite right. But the "don't know" provides the believer with a decent polite cover from the irresistible gunfire of reason and common sense. All religions have tried to answer these kinds of questions about God, religion and soul but the answers themselves cancel each other out. We are finally left to recourse to faith. Everyone tries to rationalize those beliefs that suit him and either neglect, ridicule, hate or kill the others with differing beliefs.

Why We Believe

The short conclusion to all the above is that reason not only cannot prove the truths of religion, it cannot even make them seem consistent, plausible, probable or intelligible. You need a very big leap of faith. Still many intelligent people subscribe to the concept for some of the following four reasons, even if they have overcome the above listed two sets of needs (no easy task for any man): 1. To uphold ethics (Ch.11). 2. Influence of some powerful spiritual personality. 3. Childhood conditioning. People acquire religion almost by default. 4. It is impossible for even the most intelligent people to remain rational every time, any time, all the time. They too are human, they too are hungry, and the hungry cannot pass up food. Non-believers too must understand and respect such people, if not for the truth then for the utility of their beliefs. Intelligent believers are not unable to think rationally, they are unwilling to do so. Moreover, when people attach a very great deal of importance to some idea, they will go to unusual lengths to defend it.

Irrationality is natural in man. The brain region responsible for irrational decisions---called amygdala---was designed by nature to protect us when danger lurked. This can circumvent the rational region, the prefrontal cortex; and actually does so frequently, when fear rules. That may partly explain why God is more popular at times of trouble (like death) and in poor or defeated societies like ours in India.

The conflict between Religion and Science is real and cannot be wished away in spite of all the compromisers and do-gooders. We must take the bull by the horns and honestly confront it. It would be nice if we could divide life into neat little watertight compartments, but we can't. Overlapping of territory is inevitable. The above approach of treating God as a Value, not as a Truth, can solve this complex problem that keeps on creeping up all the time when intelligent people formulate their views on topics as diverse as evolution, ethics or animal rights, all of which embrace both, science and religion, to varying degrees. All the major theosophies were propounded centuries ago when mankind did not have the benefit of the information that we have today. Kepler and Copernicus established only 500 years ago that the earth is not the center of the universe. Darwin proved only 150 years ago that man is not unique. But the last of the major religions (Islam) originated 1400 years ago. Microscope, telescope, paper, printing, oxygen, all were discovered much later. Theosophists knew very little about birth or death, about proteins or photosynthesis. Recent advances are changing our perceptions on the fundamental questions of life. Artificial intelligence and cloning of animals (even of man) are not yet the creation of new life but close.

When prayers, blessings and curses were the only plausible explanations for what was happening, there was simply no alternative to blind belief. If a blind man does not have faith, what else can he have? But if we continue to go solely by faith even when better tools of judgment (science, logic, mathematics) are available, we are like a partially blind man who continues to go by hunch even when he can have better sight with glasses. Well-meaning souls have dreamed up much semantics, pseudo science and pseudo theology. Some teenagers can insist that there IS a Santa Claus whom they knew and loved so much when they were kids. Ignorance may or may not be bliss, but it is certainly wise to accept its inevitability and stop weaving futile webs of fancy around it. Fancy can too easily become frenzy.

God grew to be the most illusory and yet useful, innovative, imaginative concept ever invented in history. But an illusion is still an illusion, however romantic, like Hindi films; however beautiful, like a rainbow; however useful, like ether in wave-physics. Life can very well be understood and explained without resorting to illusions like souls, gods, ghosts, witches, Santa Claus and fairies along with others like benevolent salesmen, selfless stockbrokers and pedophilic priests. A man at peace with himself, who can live with his infirmity, uncertainty and inadequacy, will keep an open mind and appreciate the good things in life without striving to guess meaning everywhere. He can resist the so called 'prediction addiction' of the caveman—to compulsively seek patterns where unfortunately they rarely exist or persist. If structure defines function, he will not presume causes for a functioning phenomenon that is life. But when one seeks answers where none exist, it is understandable that one will stretch belief up to and beyond its limits of reasonable credibility.

God can give us purpose, meaning, a reason for living. But so also can war. So also can Art; or almost any other passionate pursuit. Faith can in some cases be redundant or even positively harmful. In such cases skepticism or even ignorance, rather than faith, is bliss. Ritual is one such case. Astrology is another. As the poet Yeats has expressed: "The best (men) lack all conviction; the worst are full of passionate intensity." Thomas Huxley said, "Irrationally held truths may be more harmful than reasoned errors." While we cannot consistently explain events in our lives, we need not resort to the supernatural, outrageous or bizarre reasons for why things do---or do not---occur. As the famous psychologist A.H. Maslow said, "We need not take refuge in supernatural gods to explain our saints and sages and heroes and statesmen, as if to express our disbelief that human beings could be that good or wise."

With all the progress in science, some questions will always remain, not because of the nature of these questions but also because of the way we ask them. Man's body and brain are results of accumulated evolutionary changes over millions of years, changes that cannot be repeated, reversed or predicted. A mere speck of dust in the universe, a tick on creation's eternal clock, has the audacity to speculate and cast God in his own image today. But with increasing rationality, he will grow up one day and put his dear Santa Claus in his proper place----in the smoke stack of the chimney of history where he rightly belongs.

The above is a brief statement of my personal belief. But I certainly do not want to challenge anyone's religious faith. If you differ from me, I respect your belief. But I do want to map out some of the concerns and consequences of our beliefs. Taking our beliefs at their face value and on faith, we simply examine what kind of consequences flow from the fact that we hold those beliefs. So we can keep aside for a moment our personal beliefs in suspended animation and proceed with the rest of the discussion without affecting the essential trend of my argument in the following pages.

11. THE ETHICAL ENIGMA
Symbiosis of Ethics and Religion

Most common people confuse religion with ethics. Although they do overlap, religion and morality are not exactly identical. Many intellectuals profess religion only because of a vague feeling that religion is inseparable from moral behavior. The fact is that while ethics is absolutely indispensable for society, religion may or may not be so.

Ethics is the foundation stone of civilization. Why should a man be good? "Only the saints among us have not been tempted to ask this question. Only the fools among us presume that it has been adequately answered". Islam and Christianity say: Because God wants us to be good. Hindus say: Because good begets good in a theological sense. But there are other possible reasons why a man should be moral: 1. For the greatest good of the greatest numbers. Ex: Telling the truth or refraining from adultery promotes the greater good, irrespective of whether God desired it or Moses preached it. 2. Morality based on enlightened self interest. Ex: You don't need God's commandment to stop at a red traffic light. It is in your own interest to do so. 3. "Do unto others as you would have others do unto you" is a simple, effective, sensible precept that we don't need religion to teach us. Without going into details of these and other theories like those of Plato, Bishop Butler, Free thinkers, Utilitarians, Kant and others, let me go into my critical question today: Is it possible to dissociate ethics from religion, morality from metaphysics and goodness from God's grace?

Even non believers would not deny that we need ethics of some sort in our lives. Nonbelievers too follow the rules and restrictions of civilized society. Bertrand Russel, a nonbeliever, was one of the most decent good men. On the other hand, we cannot say definitively that men will be moral or virtuous solely because they are believers. Hitler was a good Christian. Good atheism can coexist with good ethics. You don't need to be godly to be good. Did you ever hear of an atheist becoming a religious crusader or jihadi? No. Do we know about immoral priests? Yes, we do. Lots of them. Quite often.

Forgetting negatives like crusades, jihad or terrorism and looking into the possibility of separation of religion from ethics, let us see how religion originated. How God created man is nearly not as important as how man created God. Gods were born in the minds of men when civilization was in its infancy. All societies were polytheistic in prehistory. Primitive man in his ignorance and fear attributed each of the mysterious things he saw to an entity he called a god. It is no accident that the earliest gods were forces of nature like Fire and Sun; or war-lords like Indra and Zeus. In India these were the Rig Vedic gods. Similarities in primitive societies about gods are so very striking.

When men emerged from the cave and organized into groups of initially hunting, pastoral and finally agricultural communities, they needed group formation and co-operation to face the stronger animals and cruel Nature. Rules had to be developed so that communities could hunt, share and care, live and work together. That is how ethics originated. The best way, really the only way, to promote ethical rules in those times was to do it in the name of gods. God concept acquired strength through society's need for orderly good conduct. Look at the way children grow up. Selfishness is a natural consequence of the instinct of self, but sharing and caring have to be taught--they are learnt values. So also are ethics and God. They are values acquired by children from family and society. They are also the values acquired by civilization in its infancy.

As society developed, the God concept was universalized in different ways in different societies. After the Rig Vedic nature-gods, the earliest Hindu Purana, the Ramayana, emphasized the regulation of the two biological instincts: 1. Need to broaden self-preservation to include family and community and 2. Need to circumscribe self-propagation by regulating the sexual urge within the rules of good conduct. The very first epic in world literature---the Holy Ramayana---is clearly the story of the establishment of primary ethical standards in the name of religion. Tagore even called Rama a pioneer missionary of the oncoming age of agriculture. Rama was not a God, he was the best role model available. Ravana was not a demon; he was essentially what all men were before they became civilized. Of course it helps a lot if we deify the one and demonize the other because it makes things much simpler and believable. Heroes became gods.

And so, this is the biggest, the best, the most important function that religion performed---it made man civilized. Nothing but religion could have done this in those times. Man had to have God. The story of religion is in short the story of civilization. When there was little knowledge, religion included everything under its broad canopy: science, logic, ethics, literature, psychology. God filled human needs. He turned out to be an excellent surviving and coping mechanism against worldly fears, frailties, anxieties, uncertainties and vagaries of existence. Exposed to the grim ennui of life man embraces the great unknown and calls him God. Being unverifiable is a great advantage since anything and everything can be attributed to Him without fear of contradiction. Search for meaning and curiosity about birth and death become a lot simpler if we postulate a useful concept like God. He lives on in people's minds largely because none can prove that He does not exist; and absence of evidence is not an evidence of absence. The unknown usually fires up the imagination, as witness issues like Extra-Terrestrial life, elusive El Dorado (paradise), the sunken Atlantis (the lost continent) and of course, life after death.

Religions arose out of societal needs. The nonviolence Buddha preached was a response to the animal sacrifices of Hindus. The brotherhood and iconoclasm Mohammed preached were a response to the tribal wars and multi-idol worship prevalent among the Arabs of the day. Sikh religion in India arose out of the need to compromise between the two violently antagonistic religions of the time. It is clear that religions do not come to us from the heavens, like the mythical Ganges River. They arise from local soils. Ethics and religion arose from basic human need for rules we can live by. Religion is not the product of God's wish to save mankind---assuming that He can have an earthly wish, if we can ascertain that wish, if mankind needs to be saved, if it can be saved, if it deserves to be saved, and so on.

An illusion does not become truth even when useful; even when we need it badly; even when it persists for a long time. The concept of God is a value, a deep desire, a useful illusion; but a value is not a truth. Calling it a truth helps establish it as a value. Treating it as a truth helps promote it immensely. Illusions can be enchanting. The danger comes when we believe them to be real, sacrifice everything and get carried away by them---like mirages to thirsty deer in a desert; like myths to credulous minds; like God preached to starving peasants; like jihad preached to young, impressionable minds. Then illusions become positively harmful, often fatal. The deer die. The minds metamorphose into mummies. Societies cannot compete. Civilization may not survive.

Today it is not impossible to imagine a civilized society without a concomitant and inevitable belief in religion. Such a society does exist in the Soviet Union, China and in some European countries, not all of them communist. Influence of religion is wearing out in most of the advanced countries, at least in public at the national level. Neutrality of government among different religions that secularism represents had been impossible to achieve until very recent times. Still, rumors of God's death are premature. Quite the contrary, religion has been resisting the relentless onslaught of the rationalist movement since the 18th century Europe. Its assertions on facts have been thoroughly and conclusively disproved, its beliefs have been strongly challenged and its followers have been exposed and discredited in several cases. And yet it survives. Why? Let us look at the relevance of religion in modern times.

Religion---The Positive Aspects---Then and Now

1. Religions preach certain common moral values (truth, love) that are basic to all civilized societies. But morality is largely a matter of simple decency and common sense. It is our shame that we need mirages and myths to promote it. Excellent nonreligious grounds for ethics, known to intellectuals (above), have not gained widespread acceptance by the masses. Until these get universally accepted, we shall need religion simply because society cannot dispense with ethics. This is the most important reason why rational people will have to live with religion, even while they continue to fight its irrational

and unacceptable manifestations. 1. Religion (or God) makes sense if and only if it promotes Ethics (or virtue). 2. Ethics makes sense if and only if it promotes Progress (and Survival). In both cases, the reverse is not true. In other words, 1. Ethics cannot be justified simply because it promotes Religion (or God). 2. Progress cannot be justified simply because it promotes Ethics (or virtue).

2. Religion gives peace of mind, solace and comfort in the vicissitudes of life, especially at death or in troubled times, making life more bearable. It saves us from the debilitating emotions of insecurity and uncertainty in this uncertain world. All of us crave for such support to lean on. Life as a doubting Thomas or a perpetual skeptic is too difficult to go through with equanimity for most men. People use religion as a momentary mood enhancer that leaves them in a fantasyland of good intentions. This need will always remain for weaker minds and backward societies. But with science providing a better understanding of nature and with increasing law and order in the world, its relative importance is now nowhere near what it was in earlier uncertain times.

3. Religion satisfies the urge to seek patterns and to hang our surmises. It provides answers, albeit assumed, to basic questions like meaning, purpose and origin of life---questions that arise in every mind at one time or the other and are too difficult to be tackled by humans with their natural limitations. Capacity to suspend one's judgment when no clear answers are available is not given to most men. This benefit does not have the force today that it had in earlier times when we knew a lot less about birth and death. Science has not answered all questions but a lot of cobwebs have been cleared. To a good mind, a sense of wonder and grandeur of life can remain even after science has revealed truths that may not be to our liking. But as knowledge percolates to the masses, people gradually learn to accept objective reality. If the reality may seem pale or bloodless to you compared with what religious grandeur and myth have to offer, you are welcome to the myths. Blind faith is a kind of price you pay to buy admission to the romantic theater of religion with all its consolations.

4. Religion encourages social interaction through shared belief and myth. It can unite communities through hatred of opponents as well. This advantage was also very important in earlier times but now it cuts both ways. Religion can now divide as well as unite. We see intra as well as inter religious feuds everyday. As a matter of fact, it may be the strongest practical argument against religion today.

5. A few other benefits of religion especially useful to us in India are: It provides escape from boredom to a big population that cannot afford other means of diversion. If an idle mind is a devil's workshop elsewhere, here in India, idle minds attend overflowing workshops at free religious discourses.

Some say: 'We cannot prove or disprove whether God exists; we cannot know what happens after death; Heaven and Hell may or may not exist. But why take a chance? Believe in Him. Just in case. Play safe. You don't lose anything.' The right answer to this is: Yes, you do lose something important and critical. You lose reason. You lose life. You lose the most precious gift of rationality. And that is too big a premium to pay for insuring a mirage.

The rule of law codifies modern rules of ethics. Our education is an expression of the values we desire to inculcate in our children. Our tax code is an expression of the values we practice. Up until recent times all these were weak or nonexistent; so threats and promises of divine justice were indispensable. Not any more. When these rules of law are accepted by most people, religion will become superfluous to many. As the circle of security expands, it will become superfluous to weak minds. As science overcomes more and more citadels of ignorance, it will become superfluous to curious cats. Finally, as man outgrows his infantile state, religion can wither away. I am not saying that it will. I am only saying that it may. The former is a forecast, the latter is a possibility.

Many established human institutions are changing fundamentally in modern times: Marriage is losing power. Patriotism is giving way to global considerations. Sectional loyalties to employers, Gurus, community, are being trumped by bigger loyalties. Government went from monarchy to autocracy to democracy. Religions too have to change; those that don't will die a natural death. Christianity was the first to adapt and became stronger through reformation. Islam is facing a challenge to its intolerant ways. Hinduism is at the crossroads where it has to choose between slow death and quick transformation into modernity. Civilization had to kill many monsters in its march to maturity: It killed the monster of immorality in ancient times through religion. It killed irrationality in the middle ages through science. It killed ultra-nationalism in modern times through technology. The next step may well be the killing of the monster of religious intolerance through global secularism. Failing that, mankind can destroy itself.

Religion should be accepted in public only if 1. It can be shown to be a logical truth OR 2. If its social consequences are excellent. Neither is true today. And of course, man can do the right thing for the wrong reasons or the wrong thing for the right reasons as well. Ex: Asked how he got his motorcycle, a mechanic explained: 'A beautiful romantic young woman rode up on it, jumped off, threw it to the ground, tore off her clothes and invitingly said to me, "Take what you want." So I took the motorcycle.' His friend approved. "Good choice", he said. "The clothes probably wouldn't have fit." Well, Religion is romantic, beautiful. It invites us to take what we want. It asks us to choose between this world and the other world. Which one do we choose and why?

Some people worry that abandoning religion will create a vacuum in life. There are three answers to this: 1. The above five points answer this partly. 2. This may well be so for some people but it is not true in my personal experience. Like many modern persons, I raised two great sons without indoctrinating them in childhood. They have grown up into two fine young decent men with great families without any adverse consequences at all. 3. I do not advocate abandonment of religion. I advocate acceptance of God as a desirable value, not as a truth. This means rationalism, secularism, open mindedness and absence of fundamentalism. It does not mean atheism or vacuum.

Since we all need **Ethics**, we will do well to recognize **its limitations** as well:

1. More is not always better. An overdose of ethical fumigation can kill many immoral mosquitoes; but it can also kill beautiful butterflies of sound common sense. Constant harping on restraining natural instincts can cause diseases like sadism, masochism and duality. Natural instincts pulling an individual in one direction and culturally enforced artificial repressions pulling him in the opposite direction can cause repressed psyches and confused personalities. The key is in balance, not in overemphasis on restraint. Stifling God-given urges makes many people feel confused about sexuality or food. As Freud proved, repression of the sexual instinct produces neurosis, reveals itself in dreams and causes a subconscious desire to fail, as atonement for a guilt feeling. Our widespread inhibitions are a consequence of our persistent emphasis on restraint. Many of our brilliant youths have split personalities. Discrepancy between what one is taught and what one experiences in real life can leave one sometimes caustic, sometimes bewildered and often cynical. The brightest among our youth who take their education seriously, grow up inward looking, sometimes even devastated, and less fit for the competitive struggles of life. The dimwits who learn nothing escape the undesirable consequences and often prosper more than the brighter lot. Starving scholars and silly Sethias (millionaires) are a familiar sight in our society. The former console themselves by preaching plain living and high thinking to each other. The latter indulge in high living and plain thinking; they congratulate themselves on their good actions in their previous births. The layman grows ever more fatalistic. Nobody ever questions the prevalent concepts, unrealistic education or the inane social structure.

Ethical values in proper balance improve a man's personal life. Carried to extremes, he can develop multiple personality disorder because the exigencies of practical life and the demands of ethics conflict with each other. Like a pedestrian walking in the middle of a busy street, his personality gets caught in the cross currents of traffic, making him jump at every passing car in life. That is in personal life of individuals. On a larger scale in society, we see occasional outbursts of coil spring syndromes from quarters least expected or to degrees unimaginably intense, like ultra modern liberated women; or like backward classes hating everybody and everything. They swing the pendulum to the farthest extreme on the opposite side. We encounter a lack of balance in response to another kind of original imbalance.

2. Laying down moral guidelines that in the first place are impossible to observe does more damage to morality itself in the long run. This encourages indifference, hypocrisy and worse. Ex: 1. Biological sex instinct asserts itself periodically in priests through clandestine sex and shocks us. Did they not hear

about God? 2. Financially corrupt public officials surprise us. Did they not hear about the Gita or know what is right? Instead of preaching morality, we would do better to carefully codify and enforce realistic rules concerning priesthood, campaign contributions, audit responsibility, and other relevant matters.

3. If for any reason (like hypocrisy, fanaticism, ritual) religion comes to be widely neglected, moral standards of a society will needlessly suffer. Ex: Disbelief in mythical Hinduism weakened not only religion itself, but also the morals associated with it. The way out is not to prop up the impossible myths but to demarcate religion from ethics. The myths are unsustainable, the ethics is indispensable. The latter must not suffer because of its nonessential association with the former.

God and religion are not ends in themselves; they are precious means to achieve the ends of human survival and welfare. Why? For this very simple reason, that there can be no ideas, no theosophies, no concepts of God or Satan, if mankind itself does not exist. There are no philosophers on mars or moon. There is no soul without survival first. Survival is the first right, duty and need, a pre-existing first condition for all of them---even to try for the bliss of Nirvana. Ancient societies utilized the God concept to advance much needed values like love (Christ), non-violence (Buddha), family values (Rama) and brotherhood (Mohammed). They succeeded admirably. The God concept grew as a kind of a valuable Means to the ultimate End through co-operation and shared values. In our zeal to build foundations for these values, we mistakenly emphasized the Means (the God concept) more than the End itself (survival and welfare). In fact we reversed them.

Which should prevail when Ends and Means clash? When men are violently intolerant of other men's Gods, civilization can be destroyed in this global age. Tolerance for competing beliefs therefore is a supreme value in order to ensure the ultimate value---the survival of mankind. If the concept of God itself is used to promote intolerance under whatever pretext, then the God concept is working against man's survival---ends are subordinated to the means. This is the danger that religious fanaticism has posed to mankind today as a direct consequence of some societies over-emphasizing spirituality, faith and God to the detriment of humanity as a whole.

SECTION THREE
THE CAUSES

This section will present a few theosophical ideas. If you need to skip through the detail, here is a plan: Each chapter in this section will present a few statements in the first one or two paragraphs that will be illustrated in the subsequent chapter. If you, dear reader, do not seek corroborative detail for any kind of reason, you can read only the beginning, skip through the rest of that chapter and proceed to the next one to see the subsequent step in the argument. This will save you time. But if you are interested in grasping the full force of my argument, please give me the gift of your patience and read the chapter in full to appreciate my reasoning, whether you agree with me or not.

12. THE BELIEFS THAT BLOCKED
Surfeit of Spirituality

Different societies live by very different motives and goals dictated by their beliefs. A few distinctive beliefs in our culture have held us back since long. Preaching money as evil glorified poverty and encouraged hypocrisy. Unquestioning trust in Gurus discouraged independent thought and creativity. Hindu belief in rebirth promoted good ethics but harmful fatalism. It weakened society through lack of motivation, ambition and competition. We wrongly assumed that virtue always wins. We became pessimistic, defeatist and negative. Obsession with spirituality diverted precious human resources from this world to the fantasies of the next. It promoted reliance on faith, not reason. People with sights fixed to the stars are more likely to stumble on the road. People who prefer saving the soul to saving the body are less likely to be physically very healthy. A society that lacks clarity, focus or balance in its ideas and ideals is more likely to falter and fumble at every step. Culture can kill--ours did. Repeated exposure to bloated beliefs can be lethal—ours was. Our traditional Hindu beliefs and assumptions deserve an honest debate and critical reexamination. We will list below a few of our popular beliefs that had harmful consequences:

1. Our belief is that **Money is evil**; contentment is good; ambition is bad. A durable delusion in our society is that poor people are virtuous, rich people have all sorts of vices. We in India are all heirs to a certain kind of naiveté about money as a motive.

The great Sankara Acharya, a brilliant saint, in his famous poem Bhaja Govindam says (Verse 29): "Consider money <u>always</u> as an evil. Truly, there is not the <u>slightest</u> happiness from it. The rich are afraid of even their sons. <u>Everywhere</u> this is the established situation." This is obviously a wrong and quite extreme idea but it comes from somebody whom Hindus regard almost an incarnation of God. Money is certainly not bad, greed may be so. But nobody can accuse me of misinterpretation here, since it is the simplest and clearest possible statement in standard Sanskrit. There is no problem of context too, because every verse in this poem is self contained and independent. Mark the words "always", "slightest" and "everywhere". Also note several other verses critical of wealth in the same short poem. Well, I need money for me, my family, and for many good causes (including religious ones). And I am certainly not afraid of my sons!

Is it any wonder that people who hold such a belief are one of the poorest in the world? Poor people often injure themselves with wrong values and self-destructive behavior. Our attitudes and beliefs make it hard for us to escape poverty. These cannot be changed easily except with the help of faith-based programs; and these programs do not discourage poverty, they encourage it. We liked poverty; we asked for it; God gave it to us. And then, when we became impoverished, we started whining about our bad lot. Our attitude to money is the kind of wrongful stereotypes in our belief system that our religion has been promoting through centuries. An Indian even in America sometimes feels inwardly guilty about money. He wants money no doubt, but he needs to cloak his desire for money within a moralistic framework that has its roots deep down in his cultural upbringing, unknown to himself. An American has no such imperative.

2. We believe that **Guru (teacher) is God**. Who said so? Our Gurus themselves, who else? Our cultural codes prescribe unquestioning belief in the Guru. They stifle a common sense discussion of obviously wrong ideas and transparent contradictions in the Guru's sermons. A whiff of sanity is considered heresy. A devout Hindu, for example, will never contradict what the great Sankara said (above) about money. He will stretch the meaning, twist it, modify it, reinterpret it, will put words in Sankara's mouth; he will broaden the scope of his statement; he will divert from the subject; he will accuse you of wrong intention, misinterpretation and of talking out of context. In short, he will do everything but accept the obvious meaning of his plain words. This is the result of centuries of mind conditioning in the service of our guru-tradition.

Respect for a teacher is necessary and desirable--no question about it--but respect is not agreement, blind following or submission. The idea of respecting Guru as God has obliterated from our minds the finer distinctions among respect, obedience, trust, belief or faith in the Gurus. Trust in anybody is not the same as belief in his views. I can respectfully disagree. There are good teachers and bad, just as there are good and bad doctors, plumbers or lawyers. To generalize about any profession is wrong. Within a noble profession too, there are good and bad individuals. No person deserves blind trust simply because of his age, beard, personality, profession or status. Respect should be earned and commanded on the basis of the merit in the message, not just demanded by virtue of status. Gurus who feel threatened by the questioning attitude of their disciples have an insidious expectation that gurus deserve belief at all times. The rewards for spreading unquestioning acceptance of irrational ideas are enormous as most of these Gurus exemplify.

When there were no books, no papers, no schools, high importance given to belief in a teacher was natural and justified. In those days man had no knowledge, no means of knowledge, no accumulation of knowledge, no precedents. The three L's taught were: Lie low, Listen and Learn. After paper was invented, it was: Read, Remember and Regurgitate---no criticism, no creativity, no circumspection. Modern society needs a different outlook; because a culture based on a blind unquestioning belief in the older generation can produce one-track minds, lack of innovation, out-dated-ness and credulity. A child cannot learn without faith in and respect for a teacher. But nobody should be treated as a child all his life. An adult needs a discriminating challenging mind to excel the teacher even while maintaining respect for him. To worship a teacher as God forever is to ensure continuity of tradition and adherence to outmoded ideas. People who have been taught submission only---to Gurus, parents, authorities---in the name of respect are less than likely to display independence, self esteem or originality.

The precept that faith is good and 'A doubting soul gets destroyed' (Gita 4-40) is a highly debatable and dangerous proposition. How can we ever hope to find various aspects of truth if we are always asked to accept The One and only truth? This is an excellent formula for maintaining faith among the followers, based on unquestioning mediocrity and credulous hero worship. No other society in history has enacted prohibition on thinking in such noble terms as we Hindus have done. If somebody wished to map out an elaborate well-planned strategy to sabotage our thinking faculty, he could not have done any better. Why is skepticism a wrong thing? Progress, innovation and creativity are products of healthy skepticism. Doubt may not be good in very few specific situations like war. But doubt is good; doubt should be encouraged, even in a child, especially in a child. But the Gurus of course don't like it.

The word for theosophical debate in our culture is revealing in itself. It is 'Shaastraartha' in Sanskrit, meaning '**interpretation** of scriptures'. Neither challenge nor questioning nor debate nor doubt nor discussion---only *interpretation* is allowed; all else is discourtesy at best and blasphemy at worst. Belief is expected and assumed as a matter of course. Some argue that Krishna encouraged Arjuna to ask questions. That is right. At places in the Gita, he did; at places he did not. But the public does not meet Krishnas in everyday life; it meets lecturing Gurus, mystically silent saints and a host of interpreters, orators and preachers; and we know very well how they discourage intellect and emphasize faith at every stage. Somebody has rightly said: "Knowledge that does not lead to new questions quickly dies out. It fails to maintain the temperature required for sustaining life." Unmerited, unqualified certainty is the road to intellectual ruin, though it may win a few battles in the short run. Dogmatic faith can pose a lethal threat to society.

3. **Rebirth**: Belief in Rebirth distinguishes Hinduism from other religions. Rebirth in turn implies its concomitant belief in the theory of Karma. The great positive side of this belief is that it gives solace and hope when current life is miserable; it also furnishes a powerful motivation for good ethical behavior. Why should a man be good? Other religions reply: Because God says so. Hinduism says: Because good actions reap good rewards, bad actions give you bad consequences, if not in this birth, then in the next. But now, let us look at the other side too, that had serious negative consequences on society:

(a) **Victory and Virtue**: Hindus believe that Dharma (Religion or duty) gives better birth and "Where there is Dharma, there is victory." This belief promoted good ethics but weak action; motivation for virtue, but no motivation for competitive success in practical life. Ethics is fine; but ethics is not all. Ethics is about values. It is different from competition and success. Being good is not the same as being strong or successful. Constantly worrying about values and virtues, we forgot strength and survival. We even preached the futility of survival.

In the marathon competition of life, struggle for existence and survival of the fittest, good men do not always win. We believe they should and in the long run--next birth--they may, but here and now, they do not always win. Evolution rewards those who get ahead, not those with the best manners. The Duke of Wellington who defeated Napoleon was a famous popular hero in English history. In private life he was quite fond of drinking, gambling and women. Hitler was a vegetarian and a teetotaler. Winston Churchill who defeated him and who won the biggest, bloodiest war in the history of the world for the British people, was a heavy smoker and drinker. He was not quite the kind of person whom we Indians like to call particularly moral or virtuous. On the other hand, many of our defeated rulers were virtuous scholars who knew the scriptures and recited the Vedas. Dara Shikoh, a liberal tolerant scholar, was defeated and executed by his fanatic brother Aurangzeb. Geneticists have found evidence that Changeez Khan, the cruel conqueror of half the known world, fathered so many offspring that 16 million men or 0.5 percent of the world's current male population could be the descendents of that evil genius!

Unfortunate as it may seem, the relationship between the morally good and the earthly great is neither straight forward nor well established. As nations go, the 'evil' westerners--gambling, beef eating, immoral (to us)---are prosperous and happy. I don't know if they will all go to Hell; but I do know that very pious virtuous Indians today are not too far from the hells of pollution, disease, hunger and suffering. What am I driving at? Am I advocating an unethical approach? Certainly not. I am stating simply this--that it takes a lot more than moral virtue to win in real life. Our belief that Dharma alone wins only illustrates the triumph of hope over experience. As the Christian scripture itself declares: "The race is not always to the swift, nor the battle to the strong, neither yet bread to the wise, nor yet riches to men of understanding, nor yet favor to men of skill; but time and chance happeneth to them all." (Ecclesiastes 9:11).

Good intentions alone cannot scrub the naughtiness out of this fallen world. If we find a risk in being fine and kind, we must find ways to avoid such risk. We need not die for being pious or polite. At times it is even necessary to learn to be able not to be good. A great virtuous act in a time of dire political need may simply be a waste of time, harmful or even dangerous. This is not immorality, this is practicality. Lord Krishna himself during the Mahabharat war exemplified this. Even Rama, the most idealistic role model of all time, made compromises during conflicts. Men must suit their actions to the times if they wish to succeed. Inflexibility finds it difficult to survive--whether it is in men, morals, plans, plants, doctrines, species or societies.

High minded idealistic concepts like non-violence often do not work well against less civilized men, beliefs or nations. You cannot shame a cat for eating a bird; you need to beat it with a stick. You need law and police to curb a crime. You cannot do without force in international affairs until that distant day when all mankind, hopefully, will subscribe to high minded principles like non-aggression and tolerance. Though it would be nice if you could possibly win the heart and mind of your enemy in the long run, it is foolish to try to do so now while you are actually engaged in a life and death struggle against him. Pious peaceniks 'turning the other cheek' to evil may go to Heaven for being virtuous. Those killing these 'infidels' on behalf of Allah too may go there. The only difference is: Before they all depart, the latter will rule this world; the former will lose it; so which is better? Good men find it difficult to believe that some men can be evil. Clever people can manipulate and dominate those who are trusting and basically good. The good accept reality late and reluctantly, if at all. This is a natural disadvantage that all virtuous people suffer from; because realism dawns on them almost always too late. Goodness is a desirable value in life but realism should be a good value to be desired.

When moral righteousness is accompanied by worldly success, it is great and very welcome. But when both are dissociated from each other and if you decide to sacrifice your worldly success in favor of righteousness, whether it is a good choice or bad, it is your own choice and you have a right to make it. But then, having made the choice yourself, don't complain if the results are not to your liking. You made a heroic choice and you have no reason to complain about your lack of worldly success. You must learn to live with the consequences of the choice you make.

The Gita has put it well. It says: "1.Where there is Krishna, the god of Yoga, 2.Where there is Arjuna, with his bow; there is wealth, victory, happiness. That is my firm faith and intellect." When both are together, it is all nice and simple, no problem at all. But when either Krishna (God, goodness) or Arjuna (weapon, strength) alone is present, what happens? Look at it another way. Could Yudhisthira (goodness) win the Mahabharat war without Arjuna (strength)? No. Could Arjuna win the same war, if Yudhisthira was absent for some reason? Yes, certainly. Righteousness by itself does not win wars; it needs to be supported by strength. On the other hand, brute strength has won innumerable battles---remember dozens of cruel oppressors like Changhis Khan.

Whatever the Bible may say, the meek do not inherit the earth. They inhabit it--ten feet under. When Mohammed Gizni has the military power to destroy my God's temple, what happens? His power wins, my God loses. The symbol, the idol, of my Great God (Maha-Deva) becomes the three footsteps to his palace in Gizni. The meek and the weak get sold as slaves in the open markets of Gizni; or they get slaughtered by the tribes of Timurs and Nadirs. When cultures clash, the loser is obliterated and the winner writes the history books that glorify the winner's cause and disparage the conquered foe. If life eats up life, if a big fish devours small fish, if "nature is red in tooth and claw" (Tennyson), why romanticize and deny it? Accept reality---we cannot change it.

To promote righteousness, we said that it always wins. To propagate it, we kept on repeating it. In the process we ourselves got convinced that it always wins. Two gamblers were arguing over cards. The first said, "I win. I have three Aces." The second one said, "No, you don't. I win. I have two nines and a gun." A Greek historian, Thucydides, wrote 2400 years ago: "The standard of justice depends on the power to compel. The strong do what they have the power to do and the weak accept what they have to accept." At the end of the day, justice is empty without force. This is not about what it should be; this is about what is. Terrorism may be the same; but a strong America can punish terrorists; a weak India cannot.

Pre-emptive wars--deceiving an enemy--are not for individuals in civilized societies but may sometimes be necessary for nations. Self sacrifice may be an attractive ideal for an individual; but the first order of business for a state is survival, not sacrifice. To believe that personal and societal morals are identical is one of the biggest misconceptions that we Hindus have had (Ch. 23, later). Devout Christian societies do not offer the other cheek to their evil enemies in spite of the famous Sermon on the Mount in the Bible. Scriptures are good for an individual; following them verbatim may have potential for a collective death wish for a society. But we Hindus have behaved as if our scriptures were a suicide pact for us; and at times, we literally celebrate the suicide with huge fanfare--bands, processions and all.

International issues can be approached through a moral, immoral or amoral perspective. We in India instinctively prefer what we feel the moral approach, even when our own interest clearly lies in the other direction. Our statesmen are never shy about preaching others from a high moral pedestal, though nobody may care or listen. We cannot keep quiet; we have no use for the delicate nuances of diplomatic tight rope walking. All this is in direct contrast with the practical approach preferred by many other nations. Note what two American presidents said: "Trust your neighbor but build a good fence," (Regan). "Speak softly and carry a big stick," (T. Roosevelt).

Moral principles are good for individuals in personal life in a peaceful society with established law and order; but they are not always germane to nations. While it is desirable to expect nations to act in a morally justifiable fashion, governments have to act with likely consequences in mind. In a far from perfect world, pure means do not always lead to pure ends. An action deemed evil by strict ethical standards sometimes becomes desirable to prevent a greater evil in the future. When nations are stuck with a choice between relative good and lesser evil, or when good is not necessarily wise or right, it is best to apply ethics with circumspection. In life, God may be necessary, but is not sufficient. We need a lot else to survive, compete and advance. Absence of ethics is a valid critique but presence of ethics is not a sufficient solution. We have presumed throughout that it is a sufficient solution, even the only solution. Therein lie the roots of our oversimplified ideologies, practical failures and softness of our political state.

(b) **Surfeit of Spirituality:** The second problem with our belief in the soul and its rebirth is that (apart from whether the belief is right or wrong) we suffer from **Surfeit of Spirituality.** Our constant obsession with spirituality has created a society that is philosophically and philologically potent but materially and militarily impotent. How many resources did we spend throughout history on ever bigger venerated stone statues? Even today while schools, hospitals and roads are starved of money, temples are ever flush with funds. They even produce murderous strife for control of their estates.

When America allocated more resources to space, it reached the moon. When a corporation invests in research, it can develop new and better products. You get what you plan for. When a society concentrates most of its resources on attaining merit for the next birth, its population may perhaps think it has attained a high spiritual pedestal but it will certainly limit its endeavors in this world. If we desire to advance in this world, we must focus on this world, not on the world after death. Our will must marry our goal. Our money and minds must match our intentions. Just think where we as a society applied our resources for centuries, and it will be far easier to understand why we are so far behind the world. President Roosevelt said, "No country, however rich, can afford the waste of its human resources." But religion and mysticism snatched from us many brilliant people like Vivekanand and Aurobindo. Our country lost concrete benefits from their undoubted talents. Subhash Bose was fortunately saved in the nick of time from his Himalayan sojourn and what a great leader he turned out to be! In the wars of the world, we did not need enemies to mislead us to divert our resources to the other front; we had our Gurus.

Why are so many intelligent Indians intellectually unproductive? Poverty steals their youth and spirituality their old age. In youth, compelled to struggle against poverty, most have little opportunity left for purely intellectual pursuits. In old age, most keep busy attending religious discourses or going on pilgrimages because the universal expectation in our culture is that they should seek God in preparation for the next birth. At all ages, they have little taste, time, inclination or motivation to make any worthwhile intellectual contribution to society. We lose brilliance by way of the lost potential for meaningful action. Good minds should be enjoyed as well as employed. We do neither.

I happened to meet a brilliant Hindu engineer, age twenty-five, with a saffron dot on his forehead, a man with loyalty divided between the internet world and the other world. If he chooses to concentrate on the other world as well he might, he himself may or may not go to heaven but his country has already gone to hell. He fled India for the USA in despair. When half of our intellectual resources are diverted to spirituality and most of the rest remain engaged in trivia, how much is left for constructive worldly pursuits? We have become spendthrifts of our own genius when we have so little of it anyway. We don't have an accounting method to estimate this kind of opportunity cost for lost talent and missed promise; but if and when Hindu society will find such a method, it will not just be surprised. It will be shocked at its own wrong everlasting priorities.

When I wager my precious life on the promise of a future heaven, I get virtual reality--the heaven is virtual and the scorched earth is real. Our desire to ensure a pleasant afterlife almost certainly guarantees a miserable current life for us. When I make a mad run for a never never land that I cannot reach, I can get too exhausted to aspire for anything else. We sacrifice the security of common sense to the silliness of self-delusion. We give up an assumed illusion to embrace a real illusion. Our search for afterlife never ends; our search for solutions in current life never begins. The cost of a search that would not end is a search that never begins.

How much time, money and effort we expend in India on talk about the soul and the other world! We witness compulsive, unrelieved, year round sermonizing on an endless chase of the will of the wisp. Scholarly saints sermonize ceaselessly. Congregations of over a hundred thousand people attend discourses in temples, town halls, open grounds, in the Amazon jungles, and now even in air and over the seas in specially arranged cruises. Spirituality has become a high flying flourishing industry with its own seminars and study courses in groups and Ashrams. It is difficult to survive the spiritual onslaught. The noise is omnipresent. It is as deafening to the ear as it is destructive to common sense. "The world is full of misery, it is an illusion; liberation of the soul, Nirvana, is the only worthwhile aim and purpose of human life", so say the scriptures, so say all the saints, and so say even the old illiterate women all over the country. Saints dilate on the futility of earthly existence and describe in vivid detail the properties of the soul. The soul, they have found out, is not matter, but it is the only thing that matters; the only indestructible entity in the universe; the only knowledge worth acquiring, and it is present as a brilliant light in every being, beast or bacteria. And God is so great, that a part of Him resides in inanimate objects too.

It is next to impossible in India (and now in America too) to count the numbers of Swamis, Sants, Gurus, Mahatmas, Maharajas, Mahants, Bapus, Dadas and Bhais who are compassionate enough to teach and preach theosophy. It is also impossible to list all the splendid adjectives applied to them--Holy, Pujya, Atmagna, Guru, Sadguru, Sarvagna, Bhagwan, and a host of others with several permutations. Our supply of simplistic sermonizing saints is apparently as limitless as the supply of spectacularly supine people willing to spend time on spiritual subjects. Brigades of saints invade America every summer preaching their own infallibility and assuming that we are dopes, simply because we are too polite to question them. They travel to a peaceful place like America--not to Palestine, Iraq or Kashmir--to spread their wonderful message of world peace. No Hindu saint earlier qualified for a label of a 'self-realized' yogi before he resided in the high Himalayas. Today no Swami worth his orange robes earns respect in India unless he makes a proper pilgrimage to claim American disciples. As for disciples, an Indian barely gets settled in a foreign country when his spiritual streak has him holding Sacrifices or Poojas, importing Gurus from India and building temples. News: The biggest Ganesh temple in the world will be built not in India but in California. Poor India! Even her Gods are deserting her!

An "eternal transcendental energy great Yagnam (fire-sacrifice) for world peace" was conducted in the USA in September 2000. The speaker of India's parliament laid the foundation stone of "energy location and spiritual center of USA". An ad in Indian USA papers eulogized Shri X as a great Guru who has "incarnated now to promote spirituality and cleanse our sins." It further informed that: 1. A cobra played on him and Goddess Shakti quenched his thirst when he was seven years old. 2. The goddess enters his body to enable him to cure incurable diseases. 3. He is none other than the goddess herself. Incarnation of god? All Hindu saints are. Peaceful cobra? Perhaps. Goddess entering a human body? Well, well--that is faith, after all. Faith as big as the Grand Canyon. No other people in the wide world do this kind of thing as compulsively, as seriously and as serenely as we Indians do wherever we go in the world.

It is simply amazing. Our soul syndrome has many symptoms. We don't let a sick dog howl without rushing gravely to explain the howl in wise theosophical terms. We inject spirituality in poetry, dance, drama, art, architecture, anything we do. Countless people are immersed in abstract pursuits that have little connection to reality. The other world and the future birth are all that matter; this world and this day do not matter. Even if this world mattered, we think that we can neglect this world and have it too; we can burn the body and save the soul. We prefer to fish in waters of the mirage. We like to fight over unreal images. It is like a dog chasing his own shadow. The impact of all this on society is bound to be severe when the masses reflexively care more about the other world than this world. Karl Marx made a huge understatement when he called religion as the opium of the people. As another author (Tom Friedman) put it in another context: "We have a hearts and minds problem with religion: we have given it our hearts and we have lost our minds. It is possible to do a good thing really badly."

What was the result of our exclusive focus on the other world to the detriment of this world? We did not like this world, so we lost it. We abandoned it to others, so they won it. We refrained from the race, so we gave ourselves no chance even to compete. To the injury of losing this world is added the onerous effort, time, money and anguish it takes to gain the next one. Do we have a reason to rue our backwardness? We are caught in the grip of an obsession bordering on universal paranoia. Being obsessed with the other world is like committing suicide out of the fear of death. We would rather risk our world being destroyed than slow our race to build something to escape it. Reality is not allowed to intrude on our obsessions. For us a bird in the bush is worth two in hand. The world stands in awe before the grandeur of our obsession. We need to ask ourselves seriously: Is the need to attain salvation our most pressing problem? What percentage of the population needs it? How can the people who are supposed to know all about God not know anything about what God is all about?

The doctrine of supremacy of the soul and inferiority of the body had disastrous practical consequences like neglect of hygiene and sanitation, encouragement to fasting, and malnutrition in an already impoverished people. It takes a foreign Mother Teresa or a valiant Baba Amte to save leprosy patients abandoned to misery in the name of sins of earlier births. Our saints get eloquent preaching huge assemblies to wash out their sins. It would be far healthier instead if they asked people to wash their hands twice a day with soap. We need to reframe in a much more positive light our notions about our bodies.

It is almost a disease. Call it Spiritualitis. Millions of pious Hindus have perished as an indirect consequence of this disease. It is spread by preachers and priests. The symptoms are pieties and platitudes. It is chronic as well as infectious. Infectious disease infects and impresses the body; spiritual disease depresses and destroys the will. Fen-Fen and Vioxx were pills in America that promised weight loss and pain relief but delivered heart disease. Our spiritual pills promise salvation (in the next life) and deliver damnation (in this life). When we describe the shining light of the soul, we forget the depths of darkness in the daily lives of our people. Descriptions of immortality of the soul conceal the mortality of underfed children. Actually, fasting in empathy with the hungry is better than fasting for your own selfish soul. When people starve, it is the vilest of sins to focus on the liberation of my own soul, because no religion ever preached selfishness. Our self-destructive self-centered ethos is self-evident in our civics, politics and religion. Should it be allowed to overpower our social ethos? Think.

Piety has won to the point of enshrouding people in a soft, easy, cozy blanket of spirituality. Myths by the shovel are freely offered with religion by the teaspoon. Metaphysicians have a metabolic urge to maximize their mystic missions. This antiquated tool of exploiting the people in the name of spiritual salvation dulls and deprives the masses of the will to live, to fight, to think for themselves, all for the benefit of professional preachers. Ideas, real ideas, are dangerous; so we do not want people to think. If they think, they might realize what they are missing. The only real thing we want people to do is to choose which spiritual mirage to adopt for real. In an increasingly infantilized society whose intellectual faculty is reducible to listening to Guru delivered lectures, adults are distinguishable from children only by their choice of medium---Bhajan, Pooja, cassettes, CDs or videos. This is "intellectual" progress: More sophisticated delivery of the same old stuff.

All this has been going on for centuries past. For too long a time our culture has carried the burden of the S-word on its shoulders. Emancipation from excessive spiritualism is our crying need today. Not that spiritualism is bad or wrong per se. But we took our spiritualist pursuits to extremes that ceased to make sense long ago. In fact it began begetting an all-pervading nonsense. I may go to a special pleasant place when I die; but I want to make sure my life is special pleasant while I am here. Brahma may be the ultimate reality and life a mere dream; but if the dream is going to last a hundred years, I may as well wish for a pleasant dream.

A specter haunts us all Hindus---the specter of Spirituality. A ghost beckons us all---the ghost of our immortal soul. A magic wand has cast a spell on us---the stupefying spell of our sacred sermonizing. The great ancient Hindu civilization can implode of its own decadence, a natural emancipation from its own metaphysically accumulated debris of a wasteland. Our extraordinary failures in social economic and political fields owe their origin in our glorious success in the spiritual field. If the battle of Waterloo was won on the playgrounds of Eton; for us Hindus, the battles of Panipat were lost on the ghats (banks) of the Ganges. Our hopes lay wounded on the pathways to Heaven in the high Himalayas. Our will to fight was broken with severe blasts of spirituality from saintly scholars. The ultimate became the enemy of the proximate. The perfect became the enemy of the good. We simply forgot that the vitally important can be effectively impossible; that liberation **in** this world is much more necessary than liberation **from** this world.

We fight our theosophical and ideological battles everyday in our drawing rooms and halls. Those are the battles that need not be fought. We withdrew from life's real battles in order to fight imaginary battles---like the celebrated Don Quixote attacking windmills. If everyday is a battle to survive, to compete, to advance in the world, thinking solely about the soul everyday is certainly no help. For, what kind of fasting can help man fight malnutrition? When did a sermon save you enough money to tide over your old age? Which temple bell, however loud, can awaken my dying child? Assuming, asserting and passionately believing that our soul is a bright light is not going to remove the darkness that has engulfed us all our life, even if our belief is the truth, the whole truth and nothing but the truth.

(c) **Fatalism:** The third damaging consequence of the belief in rebirth is the concomitant belief in fatalism. Fatalism had literally a fatal effect on Hindu psyche. It robbed them of ambition. People assumed that the world is a slave to the inevitable. They missed the motivation to do anything worthwhile. A social system that teaches fatalism is unlikely to produce great effort and supreme endeavor. And these are precisely the things that society needs when threatened either by external aggression or internal problems. Facing the trauma of a powerful invader like Gizni, our pious people believed that God would destroy an evil like him. When exactly the reverse happened, they believed that it must be our fate. The real problem with such beliefs is not their truth or otherwise. The real problem is that they prevent us from concentrating on the question of whether we were outweaponed, outmanned, outwitted, (or all of it) and why we really lost. Contrast this with Christian free will and Islamic aggressiveness and you know why we lost to both.

I had a health problem in my younger days. My devout parents believed on the authority of a priest that it must be the consequence of a sin I had committed, like criticizing a priest. Since I was known to be a well behaved person, the conclusion was that the transgression must have been committed in the previous birth and the suffering was my preordained fate. The remedy? None. Every soul has to bear the burden of his past Karmas (actions). Just accept your bad luck---either no medical treatment; or delayed treatment; or wrong treatment dictated by superstition. I was asked to use the most sacred wash water obtained from a ceremonial bath given daily to the idols in the temple. The only condition was that it must be done with enough faith and trust in the remedy. This had the added fringe benefits of saving money and boosting religious faith. And if the treatment failed to cure you, it only proved your own lack of faith!

Fatalism is worse than laziness, since it provides us with philosophical foundations to justify our laziness and failures. I have no way to control my past births. If my birth, social status and everything else are beyond my purview, why bother being industrious or ambitious? Even if I bother, will it help? Fatalism imparts an aura of respectability to our inactivity and passivity. Do we have the power to shape our destiny? The regular answer from our populist culture of fatalism is a resounding No. How can this culture ever have a motivation to strive, struggle, win or advance?

Three interesting facts about fatalism are: 1. You can never disprove it-- whatever happens is exactly what was destined to happen! When you don't know where you are going, any road will lead you there. 2. Fatalism can become a self fulfilling prophesy---like the stock market. 3. Logically speaking too, the doctrine of predestination makes free will invalid, morality unnecessary and God's grace a superfluity.

Invoking fatalism or inevitability is the pet recourse of all ideologues reluctant to allow their destinations to seem like choices. Our philosophy resorted to fatalism and shut out hard work as a possible choice. It succeeded. This induced passivity concerning this world and active pursuit of the other world; and that was exactly what the ideologues wanted. An almost wacky detachment from real life coupled with chimerical notions of real reality took hold of the minds of the masses.

We humans have little power against nature. Chance and accident also play a big role in life. These can be improved with better attitude, industry, and positive outlook. There cannot be immunity from life's vulnerabilities; but that is not a reason for fatalism. Because I cannot control everything, does it automatically follow that I cannot control anything? We don't have total control, but we can do a lot to increase the likelihood of desirable outcomes. A proactive policy is the answer. And that begins with anticipation of events and ends with a decisive response. Our culture never appreciated this fact.

(d) Our philosophy is **born out of defeat.** In a cycle of catch-22, repeated disappointment moves from fatigue to cynicism to fatalism, which leads to more defeats. Our failures metastasized our view of the world. Our theosophy's dismal outlook on life gained deep widespread roots in our minds after repeated defeats. Earlier it was only a viewpoint; later it became the focal point in our outlook on life. Fear and despair have now come to define our culture---fear of the unknown and despair of the world, despair of this world and fear of the next. Psychologists have a theory: Facing threat or distress, the nervous system has a fight or flight response. Learning to accept distress in life is the best way to cope with continued stress/distress/disappointment. That is what the Gita also teaches best. And that is our culture's response to repeated defeats. Can anyone count how many times was our Indra (king of gods) defeated and ran weeping to Lord Vishnu to save himself? Did we not make a virtue out of necessity? Our moral pontifications resemble what William Blake, the poet, said, "The cut worm forgives the plough." The worms have neither sense nor strength to wriggle out of the paths of the ploughs. So they forgive the ploughs of their plunderers.

(e) This philosophy gives good support to distressed inward looking people to bear the misfortunes of this life with equanimity and hope for a better life in the next birth. But it is **pessimistic and unconstructive.** It is no encouragement for ambition or achievement. It neglects the sunshine in life and focuses on the shadows. A believer in this is like a man who always carries an umbrella, prepared to walk in eternal rainstorms. Countervailing optimism is never factored in.

(f) Belief in rebirth needs a tremendous amount of **reliance on faith as opposed to reason.** Hindi movies and Hindu beliefs both require a breath-taking suspension of disbelief and a fantastic leap into fantasy. There is no way you can check on myths or wild guesses regarding earlier or subsequent births. My cousin will be skeptical if I told him that we have skyscrapers in my countryside. But he readily believes in his Guru who has told him that there are seven kinds of heavens above and seven kinds of hells below. He can even name them all! The oddest thing about our obsession with rebirth is how much of what we think about it is right, down to personal names in past scores of births. A Guru will invariably paint the past birth or recommend a long term next world view with its golden vistas and dreamlike happy Nirvana. The short term view can be inconveniently verifiable and its proponents held accountable. So the Gurus invariably preach faith in the next world, leaving the laity to fight their own battles in this world with whatever little rationality they are left with, which is not much.

(g) We preach **contentment**. But progress is never a product of contented people.

The above, then, is a short though incomplete list of our harmful beliefs. A thousand stories, films, novels, popular passages are there for anybody to see, detailing such beliefs. Their stereotypes, slogans and platitudes have become staple food for the consumption of the masses in India. All such beliefs have meshed together to produce the fabric of our culture. We need to test this fabric for strength and quality.

13. THE WALLS WE BUILT
The Culture That Killed

The preponderant message in any culture, even if implied, gets through to people's minds. Man almost inherits his cultural chromosomes and cannot outgrow the compulsions of his birth, his nurture and culture. It is said that a Frenchman will burn down the station when the train does not come. A Spaniard will curse the authorities. The Englishman will look at his shoes; then he will look at the sky. I shall let the reader guess what a Hindu will do. Cultural ideologies can put pressure on individuals to behave in ways that are detrimental and even destructive. We are all bound in chains. But chains are what we love.

Certain distinctive features in our culture act as solid brakes on our progress and doom us to failure. Our misplaced values make our self-damaging behavior seem rational to us. Our popular culture discourages innovation, independent thinking and modernity; promotes uniformity, tradition and negative attitudes; has a narrow focus; and loves verbosity. Our society is paternalistic, status conscious and hero-worshipping. Many of our problems can justifiably be ascribed to elements in our culture and character. For examples: (A) A culture that would prize ascetics over men of action will produce more renunciation than action. Our culture preaches suffering as noble. We have become more suffering and perhaps more noble than others, but certainly not more strong, proactive or achieving. (B) Old agrarian societies in a sparsely populated world prized children. Today when overpopulation has become a big problem, Hindu society still clings to notions that consider a childless woman a bad omen. (C) We know about lack of cleanliness and prevalence of infectious diseases in India. It is rather difficult to convey the concept of dirt and germs to a population nourished for centuries on ideas like sacred cow urine and ash clad saints. A large number of wrong cultural attitudes have become hallowed traditions in our society. We will list a few of them here.

1. **Innovation:** Our culture <u>discourages Innovation</u> and independent thinking. This is in stark contrast to what advanced societies have done and are doing (Ch. 8). We have a deep drought of creativity and originality. But innovation is the warp and woof of progress---if you make a better mousetrap, the world will line up before your door. Biological species transform through mutation; human communities advance through innovation; individuals improve through experimentation. England led the world in innovative ideas after the dark ages---in science (Newton, Darwin), in political democracy (The Magna Carta), in philosophy (JS Mill), in literature (Shakespeare). England established an empire from which the sun never set. Was it just a coincidence or fate? Hardly. The Englishmen dominated the world in the 18th and 19th centuries because they created such an original innovative society in the two previous centuries.

In India we see stultifying intellectual conformism. We need to find out why we lag behind, not only technologically but also intellectually. I can understand why India did not produce gun powder or steam engine. I cannot understand why she did not produce a single priest like Galileo, when our long tradition of knowledgeable priesthood included thousands of brilliant minds. In modern times, why did we not produce a Walmart? An Ibsen? A Picasso? Why did we not discover Retail Franchising, Kindergarten, paper, ink, a better novel, a sonnet? We, a predominantly agricultural country, did not improve our traditional farming for two thousand years. But did we improve even our toilettes? Almost every new residence being built in India today prefers a western style toilette to the conventional Indian style; so the advantage is obvious. We are too decent, some say too inhibited, to ask such questions; but let me ask it anyway: Why did we need the 'evil' westerners to show us the natural art of defecating in better style?

Poverty explains our lack of innovation only in some cases. Simple improvements in daily life, a change in process or procedure, marketing innovations---all these do not take a lot of money; they take ideas. It is not money that limits growth, it is lack of human ingenuity that does. Angola is a country rich in resources; Japan is not that lucky; but look at the difference! Metallic ores may be scarce in a particular country but man has developed products like plastics, ceramics and fibers to replace conventional metals. Think of the originality and creativity so obvious and striking in American toy design, in children's literature, in film stories, in new financial products, to cite just a few instances at random. Compare these with our indigenous toys, our writings and our formula films. It is not just money; it is their freshness of approach and our stale stereotypes that are responsible for the wide disparity that is at once so obvious.

Why does our culture produce so many sheep in men's clothing? Consider how we bring up our children. Our motto is a plain and strict "Johnny, don't." We encourage our children to be dependent on us, to obey and follow us, to confirm to social mores. An American child sleeps in a separate room. He is on his own as soon as he finishes high school. But we decide what career our son follows and where he lives; and we choose a girl for him to marry. We depend upon him and he depends upon us all our lives. He is raised but never grows up. Enforced conformity wins over any individual choices he may have. Better or worse, American children grow up far more independent minded than Indian. They may or may not become as virtuous or as docile as ours but they do end up being more self reliant and creative. An Indian child grows up in an environment where he is stigmatized by society for being independent. An American child grows up in an environment where he is stigmatized by society for not being independent.

We invented cultural cloning long ago. Most persons belonging to a particular caste in a particular language group in India will not only dress and eat and talk alike, but also think alike. "We are a facsimile society. Every person mirrors every other. Originality never happens; replicates repeat daily." Our education tends to turn out stereotypes and persons whose education is conventionally complete rather than persons who think for themselves. Invisible shackles of peer pressure destroy the integrity of our personalities. If we divert, we are intimidated by social pressure. We forget that the best way to get people to think out of the box is not to create the box in the first place. Steam rolled uniformity also results in lack of interest and boredom. If boredom in daily life alone could kill, India would not be overpopulated.

Competence, creativity and intelligence have a relationship; creativity can build upon intelligence. More intelligent individuals have a greater chance of being more creative if they possess the requisite imagination. Receptivity of society to innovative ideas is at least as important as innovation itself. Inventions occur less often from brilliant ideas or rare geniuses than from tinkering with existing ideas, fooling around with gadgets, trial and error and finding new uses for available products. Culture influences all these. Considerations of social value and prestige, vested interests, hostility to change, self-approbatory vanity---all these can prevent acceptance of new ideas. A strong streak of individualism promotes innovation; our strong family ties work against it.

We need to consider whether rote memorizing of scriptures made Hinduism and Islam more hostile to innovation than Christianity. Rote memory overload is so intrusive that the subject becomes inherently less creative. Creativity flows directly from certain deep cultural foundations. Only a society with such deep cultural base can constantly renew itself and generate innovation. Tolerance for dissidence and freedom of thought are the necessary foundations for all creativity. In the suffocating world of one truth, one way, one leader, society moves only one way---backwards. Creativity and innovation can flourish in an environment where individuals are not afraid to be intelligent risk takers. When a society is bothered by diversity or divergence, when it encourages defensive mindsets, it will not be able to provide the proper environment essential for creativity or innovation. This has unfortunately happened in India for far too long. As a consequence, our culture cannot act, it can only react; and react defensively, passively and traditionally. As they say, "It's the process, stupid." We just can't abide the process.

2. **Modernity**: The second distinctive feature of our culture is that our outlook on life has a certain basic hostility to new ideas. Our theater and films mock at modernity. Most educated people stick to orthodox ideas. To us, old is gold, ancient is better than modern and old men/ideas are better than younger ones. These beliefs can be true or false in their own places; but they do encourage a mindset opposed to modern ideas. To the average Hindu mind, nothing is really true that is not assumed as sacred. And nothing is as sacred as ancient. But to any modern mind, nothing is as absurd as an outdated idea. Today's problems cannot be solved at the level of thinking we were three thousand years ago. We

75

need a change of base. But we simply do not get it. Anti-modernism is in our drinking water; iodination may help. While technology has evolved fast enough, our minds have been slow to keep pace. While knowledge accumulates at exponential pace, the debris of outmoded ideas has kept us buried deep in our own dumps. We are like actors on a stage who have not noticed that the audience has left the theater. No culture ever practiced the art of planned obsolescence the way we have. None was as proud of it the way we are. But success goes to those dynamic people who can adopt change and adapt. The fittest and the flexible survive, be it a species or a nation. "He does not stop at red lights," that is the title of a biography of an Israeli prime minister. An apt title for a historical biography of Hindu society may be: "It does not go even at green lights." Traveling on the historical highway to progress and modernity, this society never goes at green lights; it halts, hesitates, and never proceeds till prodded and pushed. Little wonder everyone overtakes it.

When finally after a thousand years we get a chance to catapult the country into modernity, we clamor to push it back into the distant past. Recent news: The IIT at Delhi will teach "ancient Sanskrit scriptures as an alternative source of science and technology and will present an 'alternative cosmology' written in ancient texts." Cosmology in ancient texts? Alternative? Perhaps it can teach us that eclipses are caused by the two demons, Rahu and Ketu. That whatever is known about geography and astronomy in the last 2000 years was already known to our Rishis. Forget about the telescope and Galileo, forget about calculus and Newton. Rama traveled in a plane and Hanuman reached the sun. Arjuna obtained his weapons from heaven and Bhima reached the netherworld. Well, all this is coming from a government that tested nuclear bombs and missiles too. And this kind of cosmology will be taught at an institute whose brilliant young graduates have made a name for themselves in modern technology around the world!

3. Our minds have a **Narrow focus**. Our civic sense, civility, morality, all are confined to our close circle of family and friends only, not to others. We merrily dump our garbage in the neighbor's courtyard. We fret and fume about petty issues all the while. As a writer put it in another context: "Tearing down a mosque and building a temple may be critical for the dignity of a Hindu mind. But how we resolve our conflicts, what kind of maturity we bring to bear on our problems---these are also critical to our dignity and standing in the modern world. We should be concerned with old questions but they are not the only questions. A people that can ask only one question can go only in one direction---downward. A people that can have only one vision, Tunnel vision, can only move in one direction—backward." Our culture's crimped vision has slid us downward with ever increasing momentum. We have no global outlook. While other countries are focused on developing world-class competitive industries, we are focused on protecting our uncompetitive ones. When other world leaders are building their legitimacy by pushing compromises among nations, ours are building their legitimacy by pushing regional, religious and caste conflicts. When others are making microchips, we are making only potato chips. When the world is talking post modernism and neo-modernism, we are debating whether modernism will be good for us. We live our life in a bubble. Although we can see out of this bubble, the view is hazy. We are perfectly happy with this kind of view because fog and haze is all we have seen.

Nationalism divided Europe for a long time but they were smart enough to know it and overcame it in spite of tremendous odds. Today the western European Common Market is a kind of the United States of Europe, already the second largest world economy. In Asia, religion divides us more than anything else. Hindu obsession with competing with a backward Muslim fundamentalism rendered it blind to the vast progress being made elsewhere in the world. If religion could be confined to private belief, Asian nations could see a resurgence surpassing anything else anywhere in the world. But alas! We have no global outlook, no long term perspective to realize such things.

Our straitjacket thinking in the Indian arena has put us in dire straits. Within the narrow confines of a cultural straitjacket, with rigid morals and manners, with prudish and puritanical predilections, Hindu society has lost all touch with real life. All our thinking is as if passed through a keyhole of our culture to streamline and conform to a narrow vision. Our experiences in a stagnant society have given us one-track minds. Culture is constructed for us for mass consumption and control. We are fed these ideas in cute little packages and we adopt them wholesale. We don't question mass culture's neatly packaged stereotypes, since we are unwilling to tiptoe around complex issues.

4. We love **Verbosity**. We waste words. We are mesmerized by words. In meetings, we find it difficult to remain focused on the relevant subject and tend to go off at a tangent. A person often has nothing new to say but he will say it still. He will insist on adding insignificant details or personal anecdotes. We love to hear the sound of our own voice. It is perhaps natural for most men of commonplace trivial existence to grab their chance of five minutes of fame (that last too long too often). Because we have so little to say, all we really care about is the chance to say something just about anything. Politicians keep talking till the audience drops dead. Our meetings are endless. Information overload renders us unable to discern the difference between the merely topical and the critical. Words can delay decisions. If brevity is the soul of wit, the sole wit we can summon is a torrent of words. There are strong indications that long windedness is one of the traits of most Indians. The river Ganges has 108 sacred names, God Vishnu has 1000. We have such extensive literature on every subject that no human can ever finish reading a small fraction of it, however brilliant or devoted he might be. Thus we have the four Vedas, Upanishadas, Bhashyas, Commentaries, commentaries upon commentaries to explain the earlier commentaries and so on. The Gita uses no less than seven verses (1-12/18) just to list which warrior blew conch shell of what name! Karma is of 12 kinds, heavens and hells are of seven kinds each, Gods are of----it goes on.

Indian immigrants face a communication problem in the USA. In addition to accent, certain ingrained habits like verbosity come in their way. They interrupt others; speak too loud; cannot stick to the point or do not know how much to elaborate and when. The roots of such problems lie in the culture that they have grown up with: Temple bells and drums do not promote soft speech. Slogan mongering mobs do not appreciate fine nuances of speech. It is futile to wait for your turn to speak in huge crowds.

Laconic speech? Look: 1. A close friend requested President Coolidge to give a speech, saying he had made a wager that he could persuade him to speak more than two words on a particular topic. The president, without a moment's hesitation, said, "You lose." 2. In a murder trial in America, an accused said to the judge, "I am innocent. I did not do it. God be the judge." The judge delivered what must be the shortest, pithiest judgment in history: "You are not. You did. He is not. I am. Twenty years."

I am told this is a real life story. Contrast this with our courts—orations, appeals to emotions, witnesses, postponements, piles of papers, summaries. No wonder they can never find enough space to store documents. There are places and times when details are not only desirable, they are of vital importance. But Verbosity can easily hide the real truth or at least make it more difficult to dig out. Committees and commissions appointed to look into these problems have only added more mountains of paper without touching even the fringe of the problem. It takes judgment to know exactly how much detail is relevant in any specific situation. We cannot focus. We are casual where real depth is needed.

5. We have a high tolerance for **Repetition**. Rote memorization was normal in a paperless civilization but we cannot change the habit even now. We repeat truisms and slogans ad nauseam, parrot-like. A devotee will write the word 'Rama' a million times. Huge assemblies will recite the same sacred Mantra nonstop for twenty-four hours. If a Mantra is so effective that its recitation only will save my soul, why do I need to repeat it ad infinitum? If our truths are so self evident, why do we need to go on repeating them? The fact is that we have perfected techniques like repetition to reinforce faith. Repetition is contagious in a crowd and breeds blind acceptance. Ideas become accepted clichés after enough repetition.

6. Too many children are imbued with **Negative attitudes**, unsuitable for success in this competitive world. Schools, parents and priests do not equip them with skills and habits for lifelong strife, struggle or competition. A lot of negativism passes off as virtue in our society. But in real life, attitude is all. It exerts a dynamic influence on individual behavior. Luck boosting involves taking advantages of the opportunities that come your way so they come more often. Wrong attitudes can act as luck blockers. Two footwear market researchers surveyed a remote poor region. One reported: "Situation hopeless; nobody wears shoes here." The second one reported: "Glorious marketing opportunity here; nobody has shoes."

7. Indians have an above average proportion of people having **Duality** or double standards about many things like money and skin color, for example. Preaching a lofty ideal totally divorced from practice is not considered anything abnormal in our culture. 8. We are **Indirect** in speech, writing, logic and relationships. 9. We as a people think we are **Know-alls**. We have acquired paranoia of dinosaurian proportions. The will to preach and teach others oozes out every time an Indian speaks even in foreign countries. 10. We are **Hero worshippers** to a fault. We deify great men. To us the personality of the messenger counts more than the quality of his message. 11. Our culture had **Economic constraints** that circumscribed expansion: We had joint families (good in agriculture), but no joint stock companies (good in industrial age); no patent laws; not even good partnership laws for long range business. Absence of institutional change delimited our businesses. Ex: Others profited from our spice trade, we did not.

The list of negative cultural traits can become longwinded and other people will modify the list. But it is not necessary to harp on the subject. Our culture, that once uplifted and inspired, now debilitates and destroys. It is extraordinarily traditionalistic, unusually contradictory, fantastically illogical, abnormally orthodox, amazingly irrational---and apparently, we are proud of all these things. Even a devil can quote scriptures and even a Nazi can sometimes stumble upon a small truth. Hitler's air chief Marshal Goring said: "When I hear the word 'culture', my hand goes to the revolver." Had he seen Indian culture, he would have perhaps wished for a machinegun. Some of our decayed cultural predilections that cannot be rejuvenated need to be shot down as Goring's planes were in the Battle of Britain. In China, they had a cultural revolution in the 1960s. They did not need it. We did. We need it now.

Do I find nothing that is good in Indian culture? Nothing could be farther from the truth. Like everything else in life, our culture too has its positive as well as its negative sides. Our arts---poetry, literature, music--are something we can and should be proud of. Why then do I concentrate on the negative side? Firstly, we are not talking fine arts here. We are talking about our actions and beliefs which have been lopsided and unbalanced. Secondly, our exercise here is to analyze the causes of our downfall over the past, which merits an in-depth discussion of the enfeeblement caused by our cultural traits. How did we acquire the debilitating cultural traits like those we mentioned above? It is essential to trace the roots of our culture to view the foundations of the vast and intricate edifice of our Hindu beliefs and practices.

14. A TRYST WITH TRADITION
The Triad of Tradition, Culture and Religion

Our culture has been tied up with tradition since centuries past. This is evident in all fields. Even the most intelligent people follow wrong tradition and rationalize it because religion deeply influences tradition. Our insistence on maintaining the 'purity' of our culture and isolation from the world are responsible for this. So no improvement in Indian society is possible without first an 'upheaval' in religion.

Indian arts have all along been dominated by religion. Our architecture was predominantly temple architecture. Dances start with a hymn in praise of the goddess of learning, or lighting of a sacred lamp. Our literary works began with incantations in praise of gods. A huge part of our literature is based on religious themes--Krishna and Radha, Ramayana and Mahabharat, were and still are favorites. Most leisure time activities of the general populace in India are predominantly of a social or religious kind. It is comparatively rare to spot anything connected with literature, music, health and an endless variety of such other subjects that we normally find everyday here in America. Even the names of persons and buildings refer to gods, saints, mythological characters. In western countries it is rare to find people named as Zeus or Jesus but in our UP state, almost every fourth person's name may either start or end in the word Rama. Why should we be healthy? A statement often quoted is from Kalidasa: "Because the body is the first instrument of attaining Dharma (religion)." Mark here that Good health is not an end in itself; it is subservient to the principal purpose of life, which is Dharma. Contrast this with other cultures and the relative priorities are clear.

There is anything wrong or undesirable in all these things. My purpose here is only to point out the outwardly spiritual bent of mind of the general public even in routine worldly matters. Can you recall such predominantly spiritualistic inclinations in matters of daily lives of ordinary people in any other country? Scratch a Hindu and you will find a philosopher. Gently tap two of them and you will find three theosophists. Two major religions—Hinduism and Buddhism—originated in India as also several smaller ones like Jainism and Sikhism. The convoluted strands of belief and culture, culture and tradition, tradition and religion, got so intimately intertwined and intermingled in India that they immensely influenced each other for centuries. It is therefore next to impossible to meaningfully discuss our culture separately from our traditions or from our religious beliefs. **As Vivekanand put it, "Here in this blessed land, the foundation, the backbone, the life center is religion and religion alone---Every improvement in India requires first of all an upheaval in religion."**

Even the worst of the crazy customs has its defenders. When it comes to tradition, we are all conformists. We see it as the way things have always been (which is not true), or the way things have to be (which also is not true); or we presume that society will collapse if we tried to tinker with it (which though desirable sometimes, is not true either). Therefore we place tradition wholly outside the purview of what we will consider to change. Reflexive defense of the status quo, fantastic ability to cling to tradition and complete dissociation of actions from any kind of common sense—all these come naturally to us. Many otherwise intelligent people rationalize wrong customs because they are traditional. Ex: We Hindus offer sweet food to crows (birds) every year in the belief that it will reach or it will do good to the souls of our long dead forefathers. We take a bath and offer alms to save the sun from being swallowed by two demons during an eclipse. (I am told Doctor C.V. Raman, the Nobel laureate in physics, used to take a bath after an eclipse). A community lunch, sweets included, is quite common on the 13th day after a death.

Why do even the most intelligent people in India follow even the most stupid traditions? The reasons are: 1. Sanctified by religious practices 2. Indifference 3. Habit through repetition 4. Fear of social isolation. Defenses of tradition assume various forms---pseudo-scientific, psychological or health based. But the basic truth common to all champions of wrong traditions is simple: they are sustained by a strongly orthodox religious mindset which they are unable or unwilling to recognize in and by themselves. Religion is basic to our problems. Everybody talks about it (like the weather), but nobody does anything about it. We utter oaths to ethics when our true allegiance is to religion and tradition. We confuse ethics and religion with familiarity and orthodoxy. We always find good reasons to rationalize everything in philosophical and practical terms for every one of our superstitions and evil customs. Tradition and blind faith are not matters of belief or disbelief; they are matters only of varying degrees of refinement and sophistication. Disowning other people's custom and myth, a few good people will still weave endless webs around their own assumed myths, rituals and practices.

It is difficult to flip over the flat rock of orthodox inertia in our society. We tied ourselves in ropes of orthodoxy that can be burnt but never unraveled. We seek to preserve, protect and defend the perversions of our past traditions even when we secretly disagree with them. It has been a hallmark of Hindu culture to indulge in the complete dissociation of common sense from its traditions; ascribe all kinds of symbolism, metaphor and interpretation to them; and to be mighty proud of it all. In other societies such silly traditions are considered strange and unfortunate when they happen; in India, they are considered strange and unfortunate when they do not continue to happen. Thus my own people considered me something of a freak, a strange person, when I did not participate in the community feast after my mother's painful death. Bad tradition is comparable to a nuclear arms race---it hurts everyone involved but is supposed to pose a risk to anyone who opts out. And so it continues. And it continues to become stronger and stronger in an isolated society like ours, with limited contact with the outside world.

Our Isolation: Hindu society represents an independent civilization that evolved entirely separated from the rest of the world for two reasons: 1. Protection by the Himalayas and the Oceans. 2. Our insistence on guarding our pristine culture from the influence of the evil outsiders. India was like a gigantic virtual island protected and segregated from the world. Separation can breed stagnation that in turn can promote decay. Fish or frogs that live in a deep well are different from those that live in a river. Borrowing, adaptation and emulation of ideas are at least as important for progress, as any original invention because they can act as springboards for fresh ideas. But we created lots of taboos against reacting with foreigners.

We shunned outsiders as if they were radioactive---except when they conquered us. We treasured insularity and became paranoid about our purity. Our culture had a 'Touch me and I die' attitude with an impudence to match. We prohibited foreign travel. In the 1890s Gandhi was expelled from his caste (a big punishment in those times) for going abroad for education. Compare this with other countries. Around the same time period, James Joyce wrote a novel set in Ireland while he was teaching English to Italians in Austria-Hungary. Niels Bohr of Denmark published his classic paper on the Hydrogen atom in English under the guidance of a New Zealander who lived in Canada. Al Barauni came to India around 1030 A.D. But our deep-rooted aversion to immigration or emigration inhibited our social vitality and creativity through blockage of fresh contacts. Arrogance of ideology won over experience of common sense. We succeeded admirably in keeping ourselves in a state of putrefied piety, fossilized frigidity and intellectual stagnation. If our ingrown culture had ever listened respectfully to ideas even mildly opposed to it, it might have avoided some of its most serious errors.

The evil effects of isolation are evident from the cultures of the Aztecs and the Mayans who, before the arrival of Europeans, had organized societies whose beliefs and traditions resembled ours. A comparative study of these gives extremely valuable insights into how ancient primitive cultures think in parallel. These societies, isolated from the world by two oceans, could not advance and were defeated by outsiders just as we were. To mention some exchanges at random, Europeans got the tomato from these people and gave the potato, the horse and smallpox to the Red Indians in the new world!

Nothing gives us a truer perspective on life than international exposure. Ignorance, ambiguity and doubt are cleared by men pooling their brains, discussing, debating, in a give and take of information and insights. If societies and cultures are cut off, they develop into stagnant societies, as the Red Indians did, as we the real Indians did. This is the kind of cultural interaction that we Indians opposed vehemently in the recent past. Inability to change ideas in step with the times is lethal for any society. The physical world not only keeps changing, the rate of change also keeps on accelerating. But our minds do not change that fast. Static concepts in a dynamic environment are sure predictors and predecessors of backwardness of any society. Flexibility and adaptation ensure survival and success for a species or a society. We refuse not only to adopt but also to look at other differing ideas on life. (The "we" here refers to the vast orthodox indigenous majority, not the westernized globe-trotter minority of recent years.) We liked petrified ponds and were scared of streams of fresh water. We would much rather have pre-chewed food churned out centuries ago than fresh fruit of recent growth. We see hostility to modernization, to winds of change, even among scholarly persons. Our isolationist culture must bear responsibility for our closed minds.

Can we transcend and break out of our tryst with tradition? Isolationism, Tradition, passivity are not just personal traits. They are also products of vast social forces and of the structure and organization of society itself. Can we defeat these without destroying their strong cultural underpinnings in religion? Do other religions also have the same problem? Let us see what we can learn from them.

15. RUMINATIONS OF A RATIONALIST
Religions, Good and Bad

When so much religious fundamentalism and fanaticism threaten modern civilization, it is useful to have some understanding of comparative religion. Hindu beliefs like soul, rebirth and liberation are not supported by other religions. It is not easy even to decide what can be called religion and what is a mere sect, cult or faith in powerful personalities. There are fundamental and deep differences among major religions of the world. There is simply no way to decide who is right. So let us make a cost-benefit analysis of religion here. Religion fulfils some deeply felt needs of individuals; but today the negative and harmful impact of religion on society far outweighs its positive side. Modern man finds it difficult to accept old precepts and dogmas of religion. Modern science has started delving deep into the study of the brain to explain theosophical matters like consciousness, self awareness and perception. Biological reasons for religious impulses are being studied and are quite interesting.

Christians and Muslims believe that only humans have souls. They permit humans to eat animals (other souls?). They do not believe in rebirth of souls. While this does not make soul or rebirth right or wrong per se, it certainly makes it worthwhile for us Hindus not to be so passionately definitive about its validity. But almost everyone in India has regarded rebirth as a self-evident truth for at least 2500 years. In the history of human ideas, there is perhaps no more remarkable fact than this---that a doctrine never logically demonstrated should have been so passionately and persistently believed by such great numbers of people for so long. And yet, in Hindu society, it is considered absurd to ask, impossible to know and heretical to show doubt about soul and rebirth. Many philosophers (like Hume) have proved that God could not possibly exist in the form handed down by organized religion.

It is strange but true that it is not easy to decide what is and what is not religion. We have five major religions in the world plus Jainism, Sikhism, Scientology, Bahai, Mormons and many others. We have too many cults, many claiming direct revelation from God. (Ex: Charles Manson in USA, Aum in Japan). Do all these count as religions? On what basis? Christianity and Islam were insignificant for long periods before they attained prominence. Some like Jainism attained a limited following. Some like Buddhism prospered and then declined. Many are born but few survive. Cults that gain a huge widespread following become religions in the end. Like bewitching brand name products of commercial corporations, religions are born, have a lifespan and then they die. Messiahs sprout up like flowers in spring and all of them have followers, staunch and fanatical, ready to die for their supposed saviors. These considerations should help us put a damper on our fanatical belief in any religion or any belief in fanatical religions.

The world has religions that command that no outsider will be shown mercy; that make sure that nobody will have the least bit of fun; that make sure that no good man will ever eat enough. To cite just one odd example of crazy sounding beliefs: About a hundred thousand Mormons, a branch of Christianity, live in North America. There are more Mormons than Presbyterians in America. Mormonism was established by one Joseph Smith who claimed a meeting with the angel Moroni. The Mormons believe in polygamy, superiority of the white race and the right to commit homicide in the name of Christ. They believe the end of the world is imminent. How much of all this can you believe in?

Hindus had six Schools of Thought---Sankhya, Yoga, Nyaya, Vaisheshika and the two Mimansas. Every one of these schools of philosophy has its own varying concept of God, the first even denying God. They split hair so fine that we need a super microscope to see the definition of the concept. Only one clearly supports Vedanta, which got popular acceptance over the other five. What leads one to believe that all the other five are wrong? The concepts of soul as a Karta (do-er) or a Bhokta (object, receiver) are contradictory in our principal scriptures. Confronted with such contradictions, the hair splitters downplay intelligence and advocate faith, self-experience, meditation or what have you. And all this is done while advocating intelligent inquiry. A highly respected modern Hindu scholar (L.S. Joshi) has explained in detail that if an intelligent man believes in the Karma theory---reward as per actions---he will find it quite difficult to explain issues like: 1. Repentance 2. Accidental or non-intentional acts 3. Shraaddha (after death) 4. Free will 5. Physical suffering even after Realization of God 6. Transfer of Merit or demerit from one soul to another. Also think about this: Karma is a fad concept if you believe in God, His mercy and His prayer. God Himself is a fad concept if you believe in fatalism or determinism. Fatalism is a fad concept if you believe in knowledge, devotion or action as a means. Elaboration on all these will need a separate book but no amount of verbal gymnastics can overcome these inherent inconsistencies.

How does all this relate to our argument against one sided fanatic religious beliefs?

Firstly, let us have the courage and the honesty to face it: There is no reasonable way to believe in ephemeral concepts like a Personal God, soul and rebirth except through faith as we saw earlier (Ch. 10).

Secondly, it is clear that passionate and intolerant belief in any theosophy is unwarranted in scope, unjustified in theory and harmful, even disastrous, in practice.

Finally, there are fundamental and genuine differences among religions of the world, not just the superficial differences of form. Practices will always vary, so let us use only the precepts for meaningful comparison. All religions have a moral code, a ritualistic cult and a metaphysical creed. But each one differs basically from another in all these three respects. In fact, theosophists disagree about almost everything except how much they consider each other wrong. The usual assumption--that all paths are good, take any one--simply will not wash. Only the platitudes and moral commands are common. Here too there are fundamental and irreconcilable differences as in the ideas on treatment of animals, questions of sex, usefulness of penance and many more issues. The highest common factor among all religions is nothing but a couple of precepts of virtuous behavior, a genial and general goodwill that everyone accepts anyway. (That is ethics, not religion.) But the differences are glaring and vital. Islam advocates breaking idols. Hinduism is just the reverse. The ideas on God, soul, rebirth, nonviolence and so on are fundamentally contradictory in most theosophies. Jesus' God is a loving God; Allah is revengeful to infidels; Brahma, the Hindu God, is a do-nothing non-attached manager of Karma (actions). Even Buddha and Mahavir---otherwise so close---differ fundamentally on penance.

The good souls that believe that all religions are the same make three assumptions: 1.That Religions do not differ significantly OR 2.That the differences do not matter. OR 3.That they are infinitely malleable. All three axioms are wrong. The best argument against any specific belief of any particular religion is another religion. If a Christian believes that Jesus is the Son of God, you need not argue with him, just refer him to a Jew. If a Jew believes that eating ham is bad, ask a Christian. If a Hindu says eating beef is sinful, ask the others. They all question each other and cancel themselves out.

When asked, most people will overwhelmingly support religion. But ask the inevitable next questions---which religion, which principles---and the surface consensus evaporates. A most virtuous man like Socrates did not qualify for salvation under Christian belief (not baptized), as well as under Islam (non-Muslim, hence infidel). But he preceded Mohammed and Jesus both! How can he be baptized? Can you believe in theories that teach that holy persons like Confucius, Socrates, Rama, Buddha, Zarathushtra and Nanak are unable to qualify for God's grace? Please be prepared for a lot of quibbling and semantic gymnastics from apologists of the biggest religions of the world in order to extricate themselves from such an impossibly messy position. After enlightenment's rationalist onslaught on religions, Christianity started making improvisations to take care of such obvious inconsistencies. Today some broad minded persons believe that religions other than their own are possible paths to God. But this still does not apply to vast populations, not even to a lot of intellectuals.

Since we saw the positive side of religions earlier (Ch. 11), let us now see the other side as well:

Religion---The Other side

1. Religions encourage, advocate and promote **irrational modes of thought.** Dogma, gullibility, blind faith, speculative and presumptive habits in society are a natural and direct consequence of theosophy

promoting non-reason. Assertions regarding prophets and scriptures have to be believed on faith alone, because there are no logical narratives and there are huge gaps and inconsistencies in the accounts.

2. Religion promotes **cults of personality** and ritual. In fact, it is its very nature. The least ritualistic of all religions, Islam, also promotes a tradition like stoning the devil to death at the time of Haj in Mina. The devil obviously does not die since the ritual is performed every year but scores of pious old Muslims are trampled to death in the million strong crowds. The inferior status accorded to women in all traditional religions---think of Hindu widows, Saudi women---is too obviously irrational to need elaboration. In Medieval times, the very personification of God on earth---one of the Popes---is reported to have had eight illegitimate children. Of course things have now improved a bit. Nowadays, priests only molest children, do not produce them. But bishops defend such priests or even promote them.

3. Religion, like money, can unite as well as divide. Historically, religion has served to **divide more often** than to unite. Good ideas like peace and brotherhood are reserved for followers of the same prophet; for others, they are quite the opposite. The fights are not only between different religions, but also within each particular religion. They are not only about theology but also about petty issues, personalities, power and property. You pick any religion, its sect or sub-sect and the above can be proved. Why does this happen? While rational questions can be argued, there is no way to settle faith-based issues except on faith. And your faith is as good as mine. And that is the catch.

4. Each religion passionately believes that it **alone holds the truth**, the whole truth and nothing but the truth. This naturally tends to promote intolerance, as the world is now experiencing. Even the famous scientist Michael Faraday was one of the members of a small sect of Christians called Sandemanians. They honestly believed that they alone had the key to truth and they alone would go to heaven.

5. One remarkable facet of all religions has not received as much attention as it deserves. No religion made much headway until some kind of military success or **state support** was available. Christianity was but an insignificant influence until the Roman emperor Constantine embraced it and proclaimed the Edith of Milan in 313 A.D. It was then that Christianity gained its biggest jump start. Islam could not even have started if the Kuresh tribes of Macca had not been defeated by Mohammed after he escaped from Mecca to Medina. The line of succession to the prophet was won with the sword. Islam bifurcated as well as spread with the sword of the powerful Khaliphas. All this is well documented Buddhism and Jainism in India have been claiming the Maurya King Bindusar (Shrenik), as the principal follower of their two contemporary founders. Sikhism became really strong after its militarization by Guru Govind Singh. As for Hinduism, Rama and Krishna were both kings, as also was Indra, the king of the victorious Aryans. No religion could stand tall without state support, at least in the beginning.

6. Religions often depart from God and prophet. What Christ taught and what the Church preaches is different (casting the first stone, offering the other cheek). The Vedas asked for favors from gods in return for Yagnas (sacrificial fires); the Gita asks that fruits of actions should not be expected.

We know quite a lot of cruel and awful things done in the name of religion and still being done today. Islam originated in strife and is the cruelest of all religions in practice and precept (Death by stoning, cutting off arms of thieves). Christianity preaches love; but you would not think of love if you read about the horrid assassinations of nations and the unrelenting vindictiveness, with which the Bible is filled. The bloody persecutions, the tortures unto death, the crusades, the burnings and killings of millions of the so-called infidels, pagans and heretics---all these have been well documented in history and were carried out in the name of this impious thing called revealed religion. They were not carried out by despots and cruel men only, but by holy Popes and priests. Gibbon (historian) has shown how uncouth and downright distasteful many of the martyrs and popes of legend really were. All this has been done, defended and justified in the name of this monstrous belief that a merciful God has spoken to man.

Many who choose to inform Allah five times a day that He is great must be people good at heart. So also those who choose to hear every Sunday that God loves man. Jihadis and crusaders are, in the very nature of things, minorities. But Hitlers are not born in millions. Talibans were a minority. Yet

Germany had to be destroyed and Kabul bombed. Counting numbers in such cases is not the real or relevant issue.

A very popular perception is that we Hindus are tolerant. This has been only partially and recently true. Hindu King Pushyamitra Shunga (187—157B.C.) who ended the Buddhist Maurya dynasty, rewarded with gold anyone who brought the skull of a Buddhist priest to him. There is good reason to believe that Hindus became more tolerant in history only after being defeated. I can be wrong but I have a strong suspicion that most people become ideologically more tolerant after they are militarily defeated. The strong usually tend to be intolerant; the weak sing the virtues of tolerance.

Spirituality is born out of a healthy hunt for knowledge, an inquiry for truth. By its success it produces religion that needs adherence to one truth, abandonment of healthy inquiry. Thus spirituality by its success subverts its own intellectual prerequisites.

I do not mean to demean spirituality. I only try to turn a searchlight on the shackles that tie people to irrational religion. I only try to expose hype and hypocrisy in matters of religion. If and when mankind will be able to strip religion of the above negative and irrational aspects and look at it strictly from a worldly utilitarian angle, religion will serve a useful purpose in life. For this to happen, the entire goal, emphasis and scope of religion have to be defined in practical rather than theosophical terms. Enter Humanism, Rationalism, Utilitarianism and so on.

A prominent author, Thomas Paine, who was a believer in God but an opponent of established religion, said this: "Of all human institutions that were ever invented, there is none more unedifying to man, more repugnant to reason, more contradictory in itself, than this thing they call religion. Too absurd for belief, too impossible to convince and too inconsistent to practice, it renders the heart torpid and mind numbed. As an engine of power, it serves the purpose of exploiters. As a means of wealth it serves the greed of priests." Doctor Johnson, the English writer, once said, "O God (if there is a God), save my soul (if there is a soul)!" We may add: O God (if you are there), save yourself (if you can) from your followers (if they will let you)! Truly, God (whoever He or She may be) needs to save Him(Her)self these days!

All religions depend upon revelation of truth to someone by God. Granting that this is possible and probable, the problem still remains that God's revelation is revelation only to the first person; it is hearsay to all the others. As soon as any person repeats the Word, it becomes second hand, however greatly we respect that person. In most cases it is hearsay heaped upon hearsay, after decades or centuries. Men of religion believe that the Bible, the Koran and the Vedas are the word of God. A simple question is: Who said so? The answer is that nobody can tell; only we tell each other. So who told whom? It was communicated to the world by mortal men, through several persons and several generations. The Vedas are called the Shruti or Overheard. Heard by people whom we call by the general name of Rishis (Sages). All we know about them is their names. But the names are also generic, not specific. At other times we also call the Vedas Impersonal, meaning they are eternal and originated before man originated. But what came first, man or language? Naturally, there can be no language earlier than man himself. In that case how can we call the Vedas as impersonal or non-personal?

There is more than enough evidence in the Vedas themselves and elsewhere to prove that the Vedas are man made. They show distinct signs of development over a period of time. The poets of parts of the RigVeda themselves mention predecessors in whose praise they sing, whose songs they desire to renew and speak of ancestral hymns produced in days of yore. The ten chapters were composed by different Rishi families and Rishi Kanva is the most frequently mentioned name. Internal evidence from language, grammar, meter, and organization of material strongly supports this tradition. So there is no evidence to believe that the Vedas are the direct and original word of God. This applies to all holy books. Revelation can be a philosophy, morals, or commands from God. Revelation cannot be applied to something done on earth of which man himself is the actor or witness. But this is the major part of religious books. The fact of the matter is that these books are the works of poets and itinerant preachers who mixed poetry, anecdote and devotion. The word prophet in ancient days actually meant a poet.

Did I choose Hinduism because it is good or reasonable or logical? No. I just inherited it. We outgrow our childhood things like our dress, innocence or fairy tales, even if we love them. We grow up, make decisions and change a lot. Why then stick blindly to the beliefs we acquired simply by virtue of our bringing up? We should encourage people to choose the religion they want after they are grown up, instead of assigning to them a particular religion by birth as we do now. The inherited religion should not enjoy any unfair advantage or head start over other competing theosophies. Make it a matter of free and personal choice. Let religions compete for the minds of men on the basis of reason, not prejudice, just as other beliefs (capitalism, democracy) do.

For an intelligent modern person, the problem is the same that Shakespeare's Hamlet had to face: To be(lieve) or not to be(lieve). That is the question. But let us assume that I sincerely want to believe. The matter does not end there. I need to decide whom to believe in. The saints are so impressive that I want to believe them all. But you simply cannot, without contradicting one or the other on theosophical and practical issues (above). Assume that I keep aside all the above differences (although I can't); brush aside my reason; and decide to believe in some religion. Even then the problem is far from solved. Next I come face to face with the inherent contradictions within my own chosen religion. Every religion has them. I have to decide what parts to believe in and what not to believe in. Taking Hinduism as an example, I will have to make decisions like God or no God, Karma or Knowledge, Ritual or no, etc. in theory and in practice. What do I do in all honesty, if I don't agree with and can't accept some five verses of the Gita, for example? Some say, "Don't accept." Firm believers say, 'You can't disagree." So the problem becomes not of faith, but of degrees of faith. But if religion is all about universal truths and eternal values, how can you have it in varying degrees?

Rajaneesh called all religions 'anti-life'. Religion should be God-loving, positive; rather than God-fearing negative. A prominent writer (Clark) has opined: "Religion is a disease of infancy. It prevents the search for God if there is one." Another writer said, "Considering the millions of sinners worldwide and given war and despair and suffering of billions, can I honestly believe that God (or Karma) has time or cause or capacity to tailgate my every act and thought?" To any truly reasonable mind, revealed religion is an unrevealed hallucination that evolved into a dangerous heresy and sometimes into an impious fraud.

There are biological reasons for religious impulses of men or prophets. When the brain's circuitry goes awry, many aberrations can take place. Modern brain imaging techniques like MRI and PET scans are being used today to explain theological matters like consciousness, realization of self, hallucination and meditation. A branch of science called Neurotheology is in the process of development (Newsweek May 7, 2001 OR Readers' Digest Dec.2001). Any ophthalmologist can tell us how changes in the retina can cause visual flashes, blind spots and such other phenomena. Researchers in psychology have long held that "Religious hallucinations are quite common in schizophrenic people. They are signs of illness, not religious insight. It is no easy thing to distinguish between mental illness and religious insight." (Prof. George Graham). (For a short list of recent books on the subject, please see Bibliography at the end)

"The (psychotropic) herb Salvia Divinorum is a type of sage plant that can cause intense hallucinations, out of body experiences, and when taken in high doses, unconsciousness and short term memory loss. Users have also reported sensations of traveling through time and space, assuming the identities of other people and even the feeling of merging with inanimate objects (NY Times 7-9-01)." This is only one of many and varied herbs with psycho effects.

Child psychologists know that a child starts distinguishing between thought and desire, between desire and objective reality, around the age of four. When the brain does not make a clear distinction, a kid finds it natural to assume that he owns the toy he covets. A similar thing happened to civilization in its developmental infancy---men honestly believed that the thought was the truth. Many intellectuals too have difficulty in distinguishing between the state of their mind and the state of the world. Huge numbers of honest good men fall a prey to wishful thinking. Passionate believers believe God exists simply because they earnestly desire that He did.

Millions of modern men today are starting to lose faith in miracles of faith. They realize that reason can never be rooted in rudimentary religion. And yet what makes many good intelligent people blind to obvious facts and common sense? Faith does. Their need for God does. Need for religion is confused with the need for guidance. Not because people don't see but because they refuse to see. After they master the art of a willing suspension of disbelief, it gradually metamorphoses into a willing acceptance of any belief. To start with, people with deep faith do not like rationality; after a while they do not want to like rationality. To start with, faith is characterized by a refusal to think, not an inability to think. Through constant practice and teaching it can end up as an inability to think. Religion is more pre-rational rather than irrational. If it were more non-rational rather than anti-rational, it would not be as harmful.

Doubt, ethics, social needs, innate curiosity, fear of uncertainty, childhood indoctrination and absence of a viable alternative keep many from disavowing religion. Most common people do not have courage, originality, maturity or mental preparedness that would challenge the prevailing culture. In some cases people do have all of the above, they can also be honest and intelligent and yet they can hold a wrong belief. Such rare examples are: Thomas Jefferson on slavery, some environmentalists on global warming and some scientists (like Faraday) about God. Besides, nobody can remain rational consistently and permanently under all circumstances. An unusual personal experience, a touching circumstance, or contact with an extraordinarily powerful personality---all these can have profound impact on people's minds. An honest difference of opinion in all such cases must be allowed and accepted.

Still, it will never fail to amaze me how otherwise intelligent and even brilliant people sometimes seem to disconnect their brains each time they hear some off the wall piece of theosophical bigotry---bigotry that cowers them into believing that what they hear is the Truth. When an intelligent person allows his intelligence to become subservient to other aspects of his personality, he can behave in an irrational manner. None can guarantee to be reasonable all the time without a break. As Hamlet describes his own wavering mind: "I am but mad north northwest. When the wind is southerly, I know a hawk from a handsaw."

16. POETRY OR PHILOSOPHY?
The Fine Art of Interpretation of Scriptures

In Hindu thought, more than in others, many debates boil down to language as much as to logic. Interpretation of Hindu religious texts is a matter of huge confusion, controversy and recrimination. Mutual accusations of misunderstanding, misinterpretation and neglect of context are frequent but meaningless and nonproductive; because ancient scriptures are vast, unclear and inconsistent. The difficulties are compounded with our huge penchant for Redefinition of common words. Language can be used to confuse, obfuscate or evade issues. When we interpret ideas using words as vehicles of thought, we face tautology, truisms, etymology, connotation, denotation and a host of pitfalls to negotiate at every turn. I shall list them very briefly along with errors that creep into texts. As for Hindu literature, it is extensive, impressive, ambiguous, unauthenticated and impossible to interpret properly even with the best of intention and effort. Metaphor, hyperbole, ambivalence, myth and jargon are preponderant. Beautiful poetry is mistaken for philosophical truths in Hindu thought.

(A) **Word Pitfalls**: 1. Meaning of words is subject to progressive change or complete reversal (Ex: liberal). 2. The same word often means different things to different persons. Ex: (a) A policeman saw a woman knitting while driving. "Pull over!" he ordered. The woman said softly, "No, officer, socks."(b) A child asked me, "Do you have holes in your socks?" I said "No." He said, "Then how do you get your feet in it?" 3. Etymology of words is uncertain and speculative. Ex: "Brahmin" can be a caste; a seeker of Brahma; a twice born; a cultured person; and so on. We Hindus have most of the world's leading experts on the former meaning of fossilized words. 4. Words have shades, degrees or nuances of meaning. Ex: In ascending order, the following are applied to describe from the least to the most intelligent persons: idiotic, stupid, silly, average, clever, intelligent, bright, brilliant, genius. To fib, overstate, distort, misquote, fabricate, falsify or invent---all these are varying degrees of a plain truth called "lying".

5. Words have a value judgment wrapped in them. If I like you, I call you frugal or thrifty; if not, miserly or cheap. Look at this: "I am firm; you are stubborn; he is an obstinate mule." 6. Words can mirror as well as mar the truth. If I need to defend a thief, I can say that he did not steal but simply borrowed without asking. 7. Tautology is saying the same thing indirectly, employing the very definition of the word to describe its properties. People **define** God as one who is omnipotent. Then they **describe** God as all-powerful. We forget that we ourselves assigned omnipotence to Him in the first place. 8. Words have denotative as well as connotative meaning, different associations and overtones. 'Mother' can be associated with feelings of respect and love to one person; overtones of punishment or harshness to another.

Our pundits have utilized all the above methods extensively to promote their beliefs. We call them ingenious ideas, misunderstandings or tricks, depending on our views. But word play is no substitutes for truth and wisdom. George Orwell said, "Allowing the twisting and misuse of words makes it impossible to examine the ideas they represent and dangerously obscures the truth." A wrong idea can sound right when presented skillfully by an orator. A good idea with powerful words can topple you off your feet. It is said that one of the best speeches in history, the Gettysburg address of Lincoln, was never reported verbatim because the reporters covering it were so carried away with the power of words that they forgot to write it while it was being delivered!

(B). Apart from all the wordy pitfalls, **Errors** creep into texts from many sources. Our texts were transmitted in memory before printing or paper was invented. Copyists, printers and editors have their own limitations and make errors. People also willfully alter texts. Interesting plays on words and myths catch people's imagination and become popular. Imperfections in language are also multifarious---in lack of clarity, conflicting statements, new words, local variations in meanings, unintended meanings, unstated principles, unimaginable situations; there is no end.

Misinterpretation? All Hindu saints and scholars have a grouse, sometimes genuine, that the other person misunderstands our scriptures. They have a point---up to a point. The plain fact is: 1. Any wrong statement can be presented in a favorable light, by people interested in doing that. 2. Any innocuous statement can be twisted. Look at the following two stories (the truth of which I will not guarantee):

1. During the war, Churchill and President Roosevelt once occupied a hotel suite in New York. A mix up by the staff lodged Churchill in Roosevelt's shower bath in the morning. When the president arrived for his own shower, the Prime Minister in all his naked glory was a sight to see. Next day, all the newspapers in America announced complete agreement between the two war leaders in a joint communiqué: "The Prime Minister of U.K. has nothing to hide from the President of the United States." 2. Before the Holy Pope was to visit America, his aids cautioned him to be extra careful and noncommittal while talking to clever journalists there. At New York airport a mischievous journalist asked: "Does His Holiness plan to visit the Red Light District in New York?" Remembering the advice well, His Holiness replied, "No comment." Next day a banner headline of the newspaper informed the readers: "His Holiness has a busy schedule in town today but he did not rule out a visit to the Red Light District."

That IS misinterpretation. Now, seriously, consider the Rigveda, the foremost of our most sacred scriptures. Nobody can understand it without commentaries. Fortunately we have several. The earliest available is by Yaaska (fifth century B.C.). He gives the names of no less than 17 predecessors whose explanations of the Vedas are often conflicting. They are so divergent that one of his predecessors, Kautsa, asserts in desperation: "The science of Vedic exposition is useless, as the Vedic hymns were obscure, unmeaning or mutually contradictory". Yaaska and Kautsa were not foreigners bent upon criticizing our scriptures; they were devout Hindus, scholars well versed in language and scriptures. If they arrived at such a sorry pass so early in history, what about you and me, after a lapse of thousands of years? If you can accuse them of not understanding the scriptures, can you not accuse anybody and everybody?

If you are a highly intelligent knowledgeable person and still you honestly misunderstand me, that is just possible. But if twenty people like you consistently misunderstand me, I must admit in all humility that I was vague, inconsistent, unwilling or unable to communicate. If several equally respectable scholarly saints interpret scriptures in their own separate ways, who is wrong? None. Although many ancient books and other beliefs too face this problem, it is easy to see that our Hindu scriptures have this difficulty elevated to lofty heights. Misunderstanding arises not because everyone is blunder prone. It is because the exposition is inconsistent. An honest blunder repeated over and over by worthy saints is not a blunder anymore. It is what our scriptures are and what they stand for. They are not compatible with something any more. That something may be logic or clarity or consistency. We need to acknowledge that, instead of continuing to blame each other for misinterpretation, as we have been doing.

Scholars have pointed out internal contradictions and ambiguities even in the Gita. It is one of the best and simplest in language and presentation. And yet, look at the numbers of varying interpretations! They were given by: 1. Shanker, Sridhar and Madhusudan Saraswati to prove the Non-Duality philosophy 2. Madhwacharya and Jayatirtha to promote the opposite, Duality. 3. Vallabha and Purushottama to promote Pure Non-Duality. 4. Yamunacharya, Ramanuj and Vedaantadesika to promote Special Non-Duality. 5. Aanandavardhana and Abhinavagupta to promote I-don't-know-what. And remember, this is only a partial list. Add to these the medieval commentaries like that by Gyandeva and modern ones like those from people like Tilak and Vinoba, all three of them in Marathi---just one of India's 16 languages. Again, please bear in mind that the major subject matter of the Gita is not an intricate concept like God---it is a highly practical and straightforward advice on how to lead life. If there can be so much variation in this, anybody can imagine how much controversy can occur in other complex ideas in Hindu theosophy.

Freud said: "The truths contained in religious doctrines are so distorted and systematically disguised that humanity cannot recognize them as truth."

Misinterpretation works both ways. If misinterpretation is used by a nonbeliever to question a scripture, it is used even more by a believer to extend and distort its meaning. This helps him to prove whatever he wants it to mean, not what it obviously means. People always try to substitute their own words and thoughts as scripture. Learned commentators see truth clearer than truth. Interpreters extract hidden meaning where there is none. Pundits, no less than lawyers, can be blinded by ego or self-interest. Gandhi said that in case of doubt, "the meaning grasped by the opponent must be taken as the true meaning." There are numerous genuine good hearted believers who simply cannot bring themselves round to believe that there can ever be another side to what the scripture says or what they believe it says. They will go to any length to defend, rationalize and elaborate the scriptural word to defend it. Their faith can create a dense fog of denial and a penchant for redefinition of words. A standardized terminology can be of some help here, but that is what Hindus have always lacked.

Every Hindu pundit, after duly complaining that the other guy has not understood the religious text correctly, proceeds to give his own interpretation. The unwritten assumption is: "If there is disagreement on a statement, it cannot possibly be that the scripture is wrong; I also cannot be wrong; it must be that the other guy does not understand." If a man does not agree with somebody, he can always accuse him of misinterpreting the texts. That kind of accusation in itself is meaningless because there is no objective standard---your guess is as good as mine, since there is no way to know what the original writer intended. More often than not, such accusations are sophisticated ways of wriggling out of untenable logical positions. Scholars utilize them perennially to justify their own beliefs and inflate their egos. They invent nuances, presumptions, spins, into something they call correct understanding. To emphasize one aspect and neglect the others is a popular and perennial game. But it is different from plain old honesty.

Out of context? Context and connotation are of course important. Ex: 1. Suppose you are seriously sick in bed and your girl friend casually says while departing, "See you soon", you may be happy. But if she happens to be working in a Funeral home as well, the same words have an opposite effect. 2. A vacationing young woman on a cruising ship told the captain, "You know, captain, I met my husband on your ship." The captain happily congratulated her. "How nice! Isn't that romantic?" The woman said, "But I thought he was home with the kids!" So the context can certainly be misunderstood.

But a popular stratagem to defend some indefensible theology is to accuse the other party of quoting the text "out of context". Suppose you quote a verse from a scripture. I disagree but have no good argument to counter it. So I accuse you of ignoring the context; the big story needs to be told; discussion gets broadened into peripheral issues; the main point is side tracked and my purpose is served admirably. This strategy almost never fails, because I can never quote the entire chapter and verse. When I disagree with what you say is stated in the scripture, I accuse you of lifting it out of context and embark on a lengthy explanation of how and why it is so stated. But the 'what' and the 'why' are two different issues. The 'what' refers to the idea, the 'why' refers to intention. The former is specific, the latter subjective, inferential and presumptive. But I thereby succeed in confusing the subject sufficiently, to bar a substantive discussion of the core issue—the 'what'.

Context means interpreting the overall sense of the subject considering the background. Yes, but this only begs the original question--context itself is interpreted differently by different people. If after considering the issue within its full context, my interpretation is different from yours, who is right? So the debate shifts back to square one---to misinterpretation. Scriptures often support both the opposite sides of a question equally forcefully---place of women, nature of the ultimate reality, etc. Everyone uses it as a stratagem to advance his own viewpoint. So why not accept the commonly understood standard dictionary meanings of words and examine what is said instead of getting diverted to why and when it was said? Judge the content first, go to 'why' and 'when' only if the content is ambiguous. Context must be kept in mind without losing the main issue in the labyrinth of too much detail. I say to the pundit: If context will not substantially alter the meaning, why divert into unnecessary detail? But if context will reverse the meaning, please explain that kind of meaning to me and admit the vagueness in your scripture.

Redefinition: If I quote any number, you can prove me wrong simply by adopting another definition: What percentage of Indians is poor? Depending on how we define 'poverty', this number can be made to vary hugely from 30 to 70 percent or even more. Unless we both subscribe to the same definition, the debate is futile. This is clear to all except our Hindu scholar-debaters. They revel in Redefinition of words. We Hindus have the world's foremost experts on the redefinition of fossilized words.

Pundits will interpret the simple word Tyaga (Renunciation) to mean renunciation, relinquishment, abdication, detachment, repudiation, rejection, aloofness, non-involvement---each one as will suit his purpose. Sanyasa means leaving home to become a recluse. A Hindu pundit enlightened us this way: "If you only leave your home and hearth, it is not Tyaga (renunciation). It is abdication. Tyaga should be accompanied with the spirit of Sanyasa. You must distinguish between renunciation and relinquishment. Renunciation is liberty from worldly passions, real detachment of the soul from its surroundings. You can be a Sanyasi even in your own home. Like a lotus in a pond. Surrounded by water but untouched by it." Great, is it not? But the catch is that the common word 'renunciation' has been redefined, adapted, utilized to suit the speaker's own purpose to promote his own ideas. He may be right, he may be wrong, but that surely is not what we commonly understand by the word in normal course. Notice the meaning of the word 'renounce' in the following life situations: 1. I renounce my right to sue. 2. Nehru renounced his wealth for the nation. Does the word mean what the pundit says it means? It does not stop there. The pundit says you cannot renounce anything. Why? Because nothing in this world is yours---everything belongs to God. How can you renounce something that is not yours in the first place? Well, even Karl Marx did not advocate abolition of private property to this extent. But our pundits can beat Marx and Adam Smith both. To define, redefine and twist the meanings of words is the strong weapon our philosophers have invented, used and perfected. Redefinition of words can actually result in abuse of language.

(A) Krishna advocates Karma (Action) Yoga in the Gita and pleads very strongly and clearly that Karma is good, everybody must perform his Karma and it is the duty and so on. Mahavir propounds that Karma is the root of all evil, the impurity that is attached to the soul, the cause of the bondage of the soul and must be burnt or destroyed to gain salvation. Obviously there is an unbridgeable gap. How do we reconcile these two opposing lines of reasoning? The only way out is to propose that the simple word 'Karma' means two different things to these two Gods. (B) Yoga has been defined in two famous, authoritative and influential works as (1) Skill in actions and (2) Restraining or controlling the disposition of the mind. These meanings are so very different from each other that it is astonishing that both are simultaneously accepted and quoted so often. (3) A scholar saint recently explained to me, "Yoga is communion with the whole." "Intellect is not the same as Intelligence."

It is difficult to define abstract nouns in precise terms. But that is exactly the reason---all the more reason---why at least a workable agreed definition is essential to start with. Don't the dictionaries define abstract nouns? When a concept is intricate, why should the mind have to sort out unnecessary semantic confusion? When you are discussing something, you need to be clear what it is that you are talking about in the first place---chalk or cheese? Imagine the anarchy if every lawyer in every law court were free to define the word 'murder' in his own way. In Hindu thought LASER does not mean the usual Light Amplification by Stimulated Emission of Radiation. It means Lie Amplification by Sustained Enunciation of Redefinition. It sounds absurd; but it is amazing to see how many Hindu philosophers wriggle out of intractable theosophical problems through the simple expedient of amending, refining, defining, redefining, bending, stretching, changing, or questioning the meanings of simple words. But we must give the dictionary the first chance; and only when it fails, common sense the second. Every Hindu pundit must be compelled to define important words <u>before</u> he starts a debate, <u>not during</u> the debate. Lincoln said, "If I call a dog's tail a leg, how many legs does the dog have? Five? No, four. Because calling a tail a leg does not make it a leg."

In short, interpretational wars are a futile pursuit. Scholars have interpreted the scriptures. The need now is to change them, to update them, to make them consistent with altered times, newer disciplines and knowledge wherever that is feasible. And have the honesty and courage to reject them wherever not.

Our Theosophical Literature: Without deep blind faith, it is impossible for modern men of reason to read, let alone understand or trust, the outdated and contradictory vast ancient religious texts of the

Hindus. Our excellence in poetry, grammar and phonetics applied to religious and philosophical themes had the following distinctively undesirable features:

1. We see a lot of **Metaphors**. A metaphor illustrates an idea; it does not prove it. It has limitations in truth. Shri Sai Baba used a hand stone grinder, a common Indian household appliance. A devotee describes the action thus: "The upper stone slab is Action, the lower one is Devotion, the handle is Knowledge; and people's sins are ground to dust by Baba with the help of all three." What a great metaphor! Let me alter it thus: "The upper stone slab is hypocrisy, the lower one is credulity, the handle is oratory; and people's common sense is ground to dust by clever manipulators with the help of all three." Metaphors are easy to manipulate. Powerful poetry can conceal deficiency in logic. Versification of an idea is not its verification. Hindu scholars are fond of imputing metaphors of their own where they do not exist in the original. Relating the story of Rama breaking the bow, a preacher inserted four different metaphors of his own: The bow is the ego and Rama is the wise man. The wise man overpowers his ego. Great idea, but did Valmiki say so? No. Another idea was: Just as Rama could unite with Sita only when the bow was broken, the soul can unite with God only when worldly bonds are broken. Did Valmiki say so or did he even imply it? No. But the oratory, the power, the piety were so great that the listeners were terribly impressed. There is nothing wrong if you teach people. But people take it all---your personal viewpoint---as gospel truth which it certainly is not. As a poet describes all poets, "We are the music (or myth?) makers; we are the dreamers of dreams."

2. **Ambivalence** is considered a merit, not a limitation. We tend to think that lack of clarity is the highest form of scholarship, especially in theological matters. But an ambiguous confusing signal is more dangerous than no signal at all. We like euphemism and oxymoron; we are mighty impressed with a paradox and a play on words. This can be good in poetry where great poets utilize connotations skillfully with great results. But in social science where clarity of thought is important, this is a drawback. We don't need spin when we seek facts or truth. Hindu theosophists have an advanced degree in obfuscation. They dwell in a wonderland where language is an elaborate artifice for the purpose of speaking nonsense. A lot of the blame for this fuzzy philosophy rests on our penchant for believing in high-sounding metaphysics provided it is sufficiently vague. Odd as it may seem, a lack of comprehension is sort of gripping, attracting, awe inspiring to our Hindu minds. Lack of specificity and precision in expression are major traits of our scriptures. As an indirect consequence, it has developed into major traits in our life.

Charlie Chaplin told Einstein: "People like me because they understand me; they like you because they don't understand you." Our theosophical writing is a black hole from which no light can escape. Imagine an operating manual for your domestic appliance written the way our scriptures are written! You will have an urge to trash the manual if not the appliance itself. If a software program were written that way, the computer would freeze and get locked every time. Try going into an unknown territory with vague route directions. Try to enforce a law with ambiguous wording. Precision and clarity are more pronounced in scientific disciplines which did not exist when religious texts were written. It is no wonder that almost all religious authors were good poets and most of their literature is poetry.

We have too many apparently profound statements going unchallenged. The Upanishadas say: "This is perfect (or full, or infinite); that is perfect; when you take out the perfect from the perfect, still the perfect remains." Great thought, great poetry; but is it clear or unambiguous? Or precise? When the philosopher says God is not this, not that, not that, the question still remains: What then is It? Anybody can talk in negatives. But isn't positive more important than negative? Can anything be meaningful or real or true that has no positive attributes at all? When you have decided to embark upon a description of something, why say it is indescribable?

Many predictions of Nostradamus, the 16th century astrologer, seem to have come true. The truth is: His vague metaphors and ambiguous description can be stretched to apply to various situations. People apply the ideas to whatever fits their own circumstances. Now consider many statements in our scriptures and judge for yourself how many of them apply. Check out, for example, ideas of Satya Yuga and Kali

Yuga. Do they apply to the golden age of the Gupta period or to the present day in India? Or to India and America? To Gandhi or Hitler?

A king asked his astrologer whether his pregnant queen would deliver a son or daughter. A wrong prediction would guarantee a chopped head, he promised. The clever man wrote his forecast in Sanskrit on a piece of paper, sealed it in an envelope and asked that it be opened only after the birth. When they opened it, they found these words: "son no daughter." Put the comma where you like, either before the word "no", or after it. Ambiguity saved his head----though it may spin ours.

Symbolism abounds in our theosophical literature. The trouble is that while symbolism can be great poetry, it can also be a great enigma. Hindu theosophy allows you to attach any meaning you prefer not only to symbols and words, but also to the absence of words, to silence. Many funny stories are told about symbolic gestures----one of how poet Kalidasa in king Bhoja's court defeated a scholar without uttering a word; another story about how a Pope was vanquished in theosophical debate by a dumb Jew.

3. The unverifiable universe of psychobabble is **mixed with Myth**. From abstruse to absurd is a small leap. Nobody considers their epic heroes--Hercules, Zeus, Lucifer--as role models; but we Hindus do. An epic is in essence poetry, however grand or great. It is at most a partial truth. If many of our serious writings are epics in escapism, our epics themselves are a confection of glamour and make-believe. That Dwarika or Lanka was a city of gold lends glamour to the story. That stones will float in water if sanctified by the name of Rama is a make believe. Poets always enjoy such licenses and there is nothing wrong if we too preserve our license of a good degree of skepticism.

4. Ideas are wrapped in **Jargon-coated one-dimensional analysis**. It rarely covers all relevant dimensions of the problem. Opinions smuggled into a torrent of impressive material win through oratorical flourishes. Objectivity and evidence make their appearance less frequently than devotion and bias. Ex: The answers that Yudhisthira gave to the Maya Danava in the Mahabharat are good but other equally convincing or valid answers are possible. Ideas that are either unverifiable or partial are presented as universal truths. As holes in a wall are covered with art frames, gaps in logic are often covered with artful verbiage. Statements of unknown and unknowable meaning are punctuated with swarms of words like soul, soul meaning, soul pleasure, soul form and the like. Commentators, duly impressed, invest them with more meaning than they can bear. Even in simple matters, mystical meanings are implied, if not literally expressed. Many arguments have a dense jungle of seemingly scholastic prose that on close inspection does not have a single green plant of upright logic in it. The language is unnecessarily cumbersome.

Two distinguished economists were having coffee. One said, "We are short of sugar." The other learned man raised his eyebrows. "I don't know what you mean," he said. The first one explained, "Well, you know, the supply and demand algorithm of this vitally important consumer commodity has today reached a stage where it does not seem to be supportive of a proper inventory level at this particular center of consumption." The second economist beamed with understanding. "Oh, I see", he said, "Why didn't you say so simply in the first place?" Well, obfuscation has its advantages. "All the fish died" is simple but trite. Saying instead: "The biota displayed a hundred percent mortality response" sounds scholarly and scientific though it conveys the same meaning. My child does not recite the ABC's; he practices "oral enunciation of sequential alphabetical characters."

5. Names of authors and professions are interchanging. Many are not individuals but **generic names**: Manu means man, Bharat means Indian, Vyasa means editor. These are supposed to be authors of Manusmruti, Natyashastra and Mahabharat, respectively. Their specific identity is not established with any degree of certainty. Throughout the ages, dozens of persons bearing these names appear in literature. The periods of most are so uncertain that all we can do is approximate the truth by centuries. Most of our thinkers are little more than the name that attaches to certain hazy legends for the authenticity of which no one even bothers to argue. Ex: 60 saints bearing the name Vyasa have been counted. Vyasa is supposed to have written a part of the RigVeda, as well as the whole of Mahabharata, both works definitely separated by centuries in time. Vyasa is also the writer of, as well as a character in, the epic Mahabharata.

6. **Hyperbole** is a figure of speech in literature and enhances its power; but in philosophy and science it produces lack of proportion and inaccuracy. Big numbers are often mentioned in descriptions (60,000 sons of Sagara, 16000 wives of Krishna) which are obviously ridiculous, not just exaggerations. Grotesque representation of mythology at every stage is obvious. The Bhagavatam, the holy book revered by all Hindus is a good example. But it is preached routinely to devotees even in the USA today.

Hindu religious literature displays all the above literary features. They occur so frequently and consistently that they raise a reasonable question whether these are limitations only of literature or of the Indian mind of the time.

Shri Sankara Acharya wrote a brilliant commentary on Brahma Sutra. Shri Sureshacharya wrote a commentary to explain that commentary. Several highly respected teachers wrote several commentaries to explain, amend, refine, modify those commentaries on the commentaries. To save you the (impossible) effort of reading through them all, let me say this: It is all about fine philosophy, splitting hair, spinning superfine yarns, playing with words in evocative phrases, advancing unsubstantiated beliefs, justifying or contradicting each teacher's assumptions through earlier unsubstantiated assumptions----all through superfine poetry and quibbling with words.

Our Hindu scholars of old were threadbare in coat, bread, body and brain, ever dusting their old lexicons and texts. Many Gurus were no original enunciators of new principles but rather clever scholars with new spins, angles or hypotheses. Most were poets and authors. They wrote literature in addition to or mixed with philosophy. One of the things that have always made our philosophy so hauntingly powerful is its adaptability, its way of acquiring meaning beyond its wording----just as it is in poetry. Penchant for suggestive phrases and delirious generalizations is a merit in poetry but a drawback in philosophy. Oscar Wilde said, "Women have nothing to say but they say it charmingly." A pundit may only repeat a well worn age old truism but he says it charmingly. They have mastered the art of making it sound impressive through imparting to it pious ambiguity and metaphorical mysticism.

We mistook 'literature of power for literature of knowledge.' Inspirational quotes are not true in the strict sense. But that was the way we Hindus interpreted them and floundered as a result. Ex: "Knowledge is power" is inspirational but not always and quite so true in real life. A scholar is not a president or politician. Power is not knowledge. Plato's 'philosopher-king' is an ideal, not a reality. No other nation in this wide world has ever mistaken so much poetry for principle as we Hindus have done. No other nation also did what we Hindus did----mistaking mythology for history, etymology for anthropology, vagueness for mysticism and controversial arguments for eternal truths. We neglected the fact that mythology like folklore is highly susceptible to corruption; that etymology is mostly inference; that arguments cut both ways; that imaginative poetry is exactly that---an imagination.

Did our scholars not realize these things? Yes, some of them did, certainly, but they were outnumbered and neglected. People preferred juicy stories, play on words, interesting anecdotes and all these almost became slogans in course of time. Poetry is more effective in arresting and holding attention than dry truth in plain prose. Poetry is also easier to memorize and recall. Pithy sayings with a small grain of truth endure much longer in popular perceptions than do long winded prose passages with tons of truths. Many sayings can be interpreted exactly in reverse. As we pointed out earlier, if it is true that the early bird catches the worm, it is equally true that the early worm gets eaten up. So an early morning walk is a good idea? Well, I would not recommend a slogan for guidance in action.

Literal interpretation of ancient texts today is hazardous. When the Bible says, "Following Jesus' lead, the apostles were in one *Accord*," it certainly does not mean Honda Accord. When "God drove Adam and Eve out of the garden of Eden in a *Fury*", it certainly was not the Plymouth Fury. Do you interpret scripture rigidly according to its text as understood at the time it was adopted? Or do you interpret it as a flexible living document that should change with the times? Does it really mean now what it was supposed to convey at the time it was drafted? How can you be reasonably certain of what it really meant at the time?

If something can go wrong, it will. If anybody is free to rewrite, modify or add to the texts according to the prevailing predilections of his time, somebody will certainly do it. Ex: Can you believe a Bible story occurring in a Hindu Purana? The Hindu Bhavishya (Future) Purana tells the ancient Biblical stories of Adam and Abraham! Brahma, the creator of the universe is regarded as the author of Adi Purana. There is nothing definite about the period of the Puranas---anything from the Vedic times up to 1800 A.D. is surmised, based on indirect evidence and guesswork. Grounding principles firmly in clear texts is the best way to prevent people from imposing their casual personal views on everybody. Modifying them consciously to make them flexible enough to respond to changing times and needs of society is the best way to uphold them. We Hindus did neither.

Scriptures of all religions are outdated today, those of the Hindus much more so since they are the most ancient. Should the advancement of mankind be "rummaged for among old parchments or musty palm leaf records?" The Hindu Rigveda language is the Vedic Sanskrit which is very different from classical Panini Sanskrit that we know today. The Rigveda is close to Avesta (the Parsi scripture) of ancient Iran, in language as well as subject matter. Every Hindu needs to read the Vedas, if not for anything else, then at least for judging for himself how surprisingly contradictory, how meaningless sometimes our ancient religious texts can be in spite of convoluted efforts to explain them. Few Hindus are aware that their most sacred text directly from the mouth of God includes verses describing humor, battle, a gambler's situation, effects of alcohol, pornographic text and such other subjects. The Bible contains stories of masters and slaves, subjugation of women, death sentences for children who talk back to their parents and many outmoded laws and practices. The Koran reveals a God at once merciful and cruelly revengeful.

Theosophical fighting has arcane terms as weapons. People who call themselves divine are very fond of puzzling one another. If God really wanted us to follow the scriptures, he would have made them easier to understand! Scholars spend countless years to decipher the ancient scripts that refuse to reveal their secrets. They often miss the writing on the wall. Scholarship comes but wisdom lingers. Research is good but realism is vital. Hair splitting impresses the mind at the same time that it depresses common sense. The story of the Tower of Babel in the Genesis (11:4) says that God did not like certain people's arrogance. So he confused their language and sent them to earth. What it fails to mention is that these people became Hindu theologians!

A famous statement in the Upanishadas says: "That thou art". Shankara interpreted this statement to mean his Non-Duality (Adwaita). Madhava interpreted the same to mean exactly the opposite---Duality. Ramanuja interpreted it to prove Specific Non-Duality. Is it not crazy that a single statement of two simple words is interpreted so differently that entire philosophical systems can be based on them and millions of people have enough faith in each of them? What does all this say about differing interpretations, reliability of scriptures as guides, our credulity and so on? Where ideological viewpoints clash, the first casualty is language itself. Precision in language therefore is a prerequisite for precision in thought. The very fact that everything depends on what the meaning of a word or phrase is in itself captures the quality of Hindu debates. It is about verbal duels, not intelligent argument; about shadows, not substance; it is airiness, not essence; it is presumption, not practical sense.

From nomenclature to etymology to grammar, our religious literature splashes joyfully in the play and power of words. Please consider the above points and answer the following questions to yourself: How much trust can we place in our outdated, non-authenticated, ambiguous, contradictory, religious texts? Can we muster enough courage to stand up against faith and critically examine the precepts found in our holy books? Can we outgrow the cultural conditioning inflicted on our subconscious minds in our childhood? Above all, can we summon the intellectual honesty and capacity to do so? In brief, can we be rational?

17. DECAY OF COMMON SENSE
Aspects of an Ancient Religion

Please trust me when I say that the ideas in this book are by no means biased pronouncements of an ignorant foreigner dazed by western glamour. These are deeply reasoned conclusions of a student of Hindu philosophical thought. I am certainly not a decadent materialist who has lost his soul. I happen to be a vegetarian, ethical, non-violent Jain-Hindu; and this book is certainly not about finding fault with Hinduism. This book is about private cultural beliefs that damaged our public life and destroyed the Hindu nation---beliefs that still persist among the vast majority of our people and are firmly rooted in religion. If you happen to dislike some observations of mine, I respect your feeling and beg your pardon. But I refuse to admit limitations in ideas, pleasant or unpleasant.

Hinduism just does not work. Rituals and Limitless faith that often violate common sense dominate Hindu religion. Switching from one extreme to another comes easy and natural to it. Even its best scriptures expound ideas that are often only partially true from a restricted perspective, as we shall see using the Gita as an illustration. Lack of clear definition has been a prominent feature of Hinduism.

1. Hindu religion is highly **Ritualistic**. Ritual sometimes does help, as in the following story: Squirrels had overrun three churches. The devout bishop at the first church prayed but they won't go away. The kindly second one trapped and banished them; but no results. The third bishop, a ritual lover, baptized them all and the problem vanished!

Well, all religions have rituals; but our Hindu rituals are a class by themselves. Everyday throughout this vast country, thousands of quaint rituals and ceremonies are performed in homes, temples and public places on all kinds of occasions. People perform Poojas and sacrifices, ring bells, blow conch shells, observe silence, recite Mantras, pull chariots, apply saffron, take baths, give gods a bath and so on and on. We have piles upon piles of deadwood rituals so moribund that they are positively fossilized. The religious process takes precedence over religion itself. We chase the shadow and shun the substance; we are enchanted with the echo and forget the sound. A religion that is always ritual becomes never anything but mechanical. Religion becomes a thing of form instead of fact, of mechanical motion instead of principle or notion. Ritual gives us glasses at the expense of our eyesight. It cannot make us see real religion if we believe in one. It is a smokescreen to hide emptiness. Ritual is really our orthodoxy that is wrapped in rites within traditions, inside our religious looking outer shells. Ritual fills a vacuum, pervades the mind and preempts the need for hard thinking. Nothing is more troublesome than the hard work of thinking. People who are too lazy to think for themselves and too proud to let that fact be known do really love rituals. The ritual lover is like a blind man who on a dark night started walking in darkness with a lighted lantern in hand. He did not know when it got extinguished by the wind and continued to walk nevertheless.

The new hokum holds that rituals have nothing to do with religion and philosophy. But even a blind person can see that ritual has been an integral and inseparable part of the Hindu religious ethos ever since the sacrificial fires of the Vedas. Two of the four earliest Vedas are mainly concerned with laying down in minute detail how, when, where and by whom sacrifices should be performed.

Why should a priest advocate and recommend a lot of ceremony and ritual where he is needed and paid for? The question answers itself. But our blind faith in religion makes us blind to the obvious answer. It is the priests who preach us religion which they define as tons and tons of ritual where they are personally needed and paid for. These payments, sometimes called donations, in turn they define as something you part with, to get united with God of whom you already were a part in the first place. But can we blame anybody for refusing to cut off his own lifeline? Nobody can convert a cat to vegetarianism.

Some rituals and practices took creativity to come up with. If we had displayed such creativity in other fields like economics, we would have been much better off.

2. Hinduism is based on superabundant **Unbounded <u>faith</u>,** much more so than other religions. There is nothing wrong with faith in religion as such. But the big problem here is that it demands faith not only in the Vedas and in God, not only in Rama and Krishna, but also in rebirth, in the epics, myths, allegories, idols, customs and a whole lot of things some of which are good and some outright absurd. Anybody can eat a sweet candy or swallow a bitter pill; nobody can swallow a hundred bitter pills or a thousand candies however sweet. When you stretch the cords of reason beyond limit, they snap. But realism has never been a striking feature of the Hindu psyche.

3. Shifting from one **Extreme** to another like a pendulum comes naturally to Hinduism. For ex: 1. Vedic animal sacrifice was one extreme. Absolute non-violence is another, where killing of not only animals but also of insects and green vegetables was forbidden. Such extremist ideas weakened Hindu society so much so that the spineless Hindu society had little left by way of a backbone. 2. Realization of Supreme Reality through Knowledge on the one hand and Taantric practices (ash-cladden meditation in crematorium) on the other, surprise none among Hindus. 3. Controlling sensual pleasures was carried to such extremes that some Jain saints even today pull out their own hairs with their own hands. Devout Jains consider this a penance that generates great merit for the soul; and they celebrate the practice.

4. We Hindus believe that God is real, the **World is unreal**, an illusion--Virtual reality was not invented earlier—and what is permanent is real. Whatever is subject to change is not real. But why? Durability is not the same as reality or existence. To be does not mean to last for-ever. Change is the law, change itself is a reality. Nothing is permanent. Not even the concept of God. A rose will wither, the sun will die one day, love will rise and ebb. Does it mean therefore that the sun I see today, the rose I smell and the love I feel intensely today are not real today? If everything is changeable and unreal, it does not follow per se that something real has to exist. If God is absolutely unchanging and therefore the only reality, did he not change a wee bit when he created us out of himself? How are we a part of him, however small?

Our definition of reality itself is unreal. Three sinners were talking amid the hot burning fires of Hell. One said, 'I was a Christian but I committed adultery; that's why I ended up here in Hell.' The second man said, 'I was a Muslim and I ate pork, so I was sent here.' The third person said, 'I was a Hindu. This place is not hot. It is not Hell. It is not real. I am not here.'

Assuming that only a hypothetical reality is real will not help us advance in the actual world where we have to live. Let philosophers split hairs to define and find reality to their hearts' content. Philosophical obfuscation should not blind us, the real people, to the fact that practical reality is real and knowable; reason is efficacious and can arm us to live successfully on earth. We need to remind our theosophists that there is more to life than theosophy itself. We need to restore sanity to our perfect philosophizing. We need not let the perfect drive out the good. The world may or may not be good or real. Whatever it is, we have to deal with it. There is no choice, short of committing suicide. You will suffer grievously if you neglect it, even when you are a secluded ascetic in the Himalayas. If your entire philosophy, the principal heart and soul of your philosophy, is tailor made for ascetics only, your society will go to dogs--whether you call dogs a reality or a non-reality. This has actually happened. Our society has decayed---in reality.

There is very little one can do about the misfortune of being born in this world. We are already there, for good or bad. Even while hoping to be liberated, what is the sense in wasting this life? Why not make the best of even a bad bargain? Hinduism has neglected this eminently sensible approach. We admire a complex machine like a rocket or a computer. Why then should we denigrate the most complex, the most amazing, the most intricate machine we have---the human body? But our beliefs neglect, denigrate, detest the body and elevate the soul.

5. Hindu pundits seize upon ancient beliefs to emphasize **<u>One-sided conclusions.</u>** They assume that escape from this miserable world (Nirvana) is the only worthwhile goal. But is it the only way to look at the world? The world is not all evil. It is really an interesting mix of sun and shade. The magnificence of nature, the smile of an innocent child, the tenderness of true love, the touching faith of a true devotee--all of these--are of no account? Life can be real, life can be beautiful, life can be worthwhile to live. Scriptures say all pleasure is momentary. Yes, indeed, but so is pain. You savor the moment while it lasts.

And what good is the sunshine that is never tinged with a shadow any time? It would be a dull life if it were not for rain, thunder, lightening and of course, sunshine. Life can be looked at from various interesting perspectives. It is not necessary to assume that ours is the only angle that matters. What is left unsaid is often more important than what is said. We are shown only one side in a directed light.

Hindu philosophers make us feel quite sorry for having been born on this wretched planet. (They still celebrate birthdays). By declaring the world as a terrible disappointment, our scriptures teach us to relish the pleasure of despair. The feeling fascinates us. In an old movie, someone asks the hero, an angry young man: "What are you rebelling against?" He replies: "What have you got?" What is it in life that our holy men are running away from? Whatever life has got.

Our philosophers have a simple job: Find out what men like and make sure they hate it. Food? No; fasting is fun for the soul. Money? It's dirt. Emotions? Curb them. Sex? Too bad even to talk about. Knowledge? What's the use of worldly knowledge? Reason, rationality, intelligence? All useless because they can't reach God. You like sunshine? Well, the light of Brahma is brighter than a million suns. The scriptures teach me and I keep repeating, "I am a sinner, I am unworthy, I am ignorant." I am incessantly taught to respect others---the gurus, the elders, the ancients. Nothing wrong here; but how about a little respect for myself too? Not vanity, but healthy self-esteem, just for a little change! To me, there is something indescribably pathetic about religions that provoke self pity in man. To demean man is to dehumanize him. To rob him of reasonable self-esteem is to steal dignity from him. To convert the glorious mystery of living into an ignominious begging bowl of mercy of some supremo is a tragic error.

The Gita

After hundreds of commentaries glorifying the Gita for over two thousand years, would you like to take a fresh look at it from a slightly different angle?

The ideal person with a stable mind (Sthita-pragna) as per the Gita (2-56) is one who is "without sorrow in misery, without attachment in happiness, without love, fear or anger." Without sorrow? Okay. Without attachment? May be. Without love? Certainly not. How about love for my lovely innocent child? How about love for God or a saintly person? Why not love virtue? Not only love but a little appreciation, even infatuation, a kind of craziness if you will---these are in order and okay for me. That is really the spice of life. That is what makes life worth living. Can or should a young man love his wife without attachment or passion? Regarding anger, how about getting a little angry with a rapist, a tyrant, a Ravana? Many times anger is not an evil; it is really shameful not to get angry. We must not lose the gift of outrage against incompetence, evil, dirt or lethargy, for our own sake as well as society's sake.

Being a man of a steady mind is a great ideal, equanimity is usually an asset, but whom is it for? Is it for the householder common man, for a soldier or for a monk? It is certainly not for the common man because it is neither possible nor desirable for him to become such a thoroughly desiccated inert personality in real life. It is for the monk. But this point is rarely clarified in practice and this is assumed to be an ideal to aim at for all. Now consider this as an ideal, a goal in everyday life for the common man or for the soldier, like Arjuna. Serene even handedness in the face of clear contradictions is a weak strategy in life as well as in strife. It is not even practical wisdom. What kind of person will I be if I have neither joy nor sorrow nor love nor fear nor anger? Do I still remain a human---mobile, vibrant, alive? I may become anaesthetized, "a dreamless knave on shadows fed", as the poet (E.E.Cummings) put it. Assuming that a state of such supreme serenity is possible in practice, this kind of person will be devoid of a great deal that is precious in life, much that makes life worth living at all. Life would be mighty dull without all feeling, assuming that you can achieve it or desire it. You can be such a person only if you have exchanged hearts with a frozen Eskimo.

A kind of narcotic trans-séance that keeps us tranquil in turmoil and pacifist in penury is a negative, not a proactive, ideal. Imagine a man with exactly the opposite attributes---one who is naturally a little sad when misfortune strikes, who rejoices in happiness, who is not afraid of his natural emotions, who feels as well as he thinks. This is not a bad person at all. On the contrary, he is more natural, more realistic, more interesting, and perhaps even more successful in life.

The above is an example and I am not saying that what the Gita said is all wrong. I am only saying that it is possible and desirable to look at life from other equally valid perspectives. It is not necessary to accept anything as gospel truth simply because it is "written there in the scriptures."

Preaching **Non-attachment** to fruits of action (2-47) to winners is rather pointless; yet it is a great solace to losers. But only a defeated society constantly seeks solace. People with hope, ambition and vigor seek challenges, not solace. Such people need attachment to the fruit of their action, not detachment, unless they are ascetics. All actions in sport and war are based on attachment to fruits. Coaches and commanders rightly and effectively emphasize this. It is their job, duty and skill. No great achievement is possible without a passionate attachment, a single-minded pursuit, an intense submersion into whatever it is that you want to achieve. Non-attachment dilutes effort. A warrior's indifference to victory or defeat is only the flip side of a coin that includes absence of a motivation to win. Detachment from the fruits of action tends to result in negation of motivation. Whether we desire it or not, the negation will happen, because men need motivation. Absence of motivation produces indifference at best, renunciation at its worst and inaction quite often. So when non-attachment becomes an ideal, inaction becomes an option---at times a strong option, a preferred option. Long term it becomes a highly desired option and often the only option. The Gita indirectly leads to that option while purporting to preach Karma or Action without attachment to fruit.

Great ideas have great reverberations, some beneficial, others not; some intended, others not; some direct, others indirect---Nietze into Nazism; Hagel's materialism into Stalin's Marxism; Adam Smith's free trade into monopolistic capitalism. Vyas's Non-attachment indirectly promoted inactivity, passivity and fatalism in Hindu society. A culture of detachment in spirituality can easily translate into a culture of detachment from life. A sense of connectedness is vital for a society to prosper. In historical times, our society remained indifferent to and aloof from momentous events happening around it, accepting everything with supreme equanimity. But passivity can win no wars. Often it cannot procure peace too. The right course is to expect fruit, act, evaluate results and apply course correction if the fruit is not right.

Full consequences of our actions and inactions are impossible to predict. Both have their risks and rewards. But actions taken with a view to maximize desirable consequences are more likely to be more productive. Misfortunes will come. It is wrong to assume that they will come all the time. Though occasional disappointment is a part of life, we do have the power to shape a huge part of our destiny.

If I am a devout Hindu believer, I feel that Lord Krishna cannot be wrong. In fact, it is wrong to doubt his teaching. In that case, since the wrong consequences are there for everybody to see, the only explanation is that we misunderstood his teaching. This is possible. But remember the other possibilities too: 1. Did he himself say it? 2. Is it not possible that others amended or added to his speech? 3. Can a good idea get outdated after 5000 years? 4. What if other equally respected Gods said something different? 5. Misinterpretation works both ways (Ch. 16). 5. If a good principle produces wrong consequences---whether intended or unintended---we will do better if we examined it critically without assuming everything solely by faith.

Another famous stanza from the Gita (2-62) says: "Thinking constantly about sensory pleasures (Vishayas), man develops Attachment to them. Attachment leads to Desire, desire to Anger" and so on. Very largely true and expressed well. We should try not to think constantly about sensory pleasures. But think: Desire can also be produced through a biological instinct, not just because you constantly think about it. Hunger and sex will come, whether you think about them or not. Actually, if you ask a healthy young man not to think about sex, he will think even more about it---in spite of his best effort. Whether instinctive desire produces thought, or thought produces desire, is not a question like egg first or chicken first, although it sounds like one. In this case, the instinctive desire comes first. Thinking follows. Thinking can accentuate desire and it is surely wise to set limits to it as the Gita teaches. But desire certainly did not originate because of thinking. Hunger does not go away simply because you stop thinking about it. Happiness can result if: 1. desire never arises, 2. it is fulfilled, 3. it disappears from the mind, 4. mind itself disappears, or 5. desire is restrained. But insisting only on the last one of these five alternatives is one-sided presentation. All of the alternatives need to be taken into account realistically and exhaustively.

Does Desire produce Anger? Not always. Not necessarily so. A fulfilled desire does not produce anger. An unfulfilled desire may produce anger, though not always. An unfulfilled desire for food can cause more effort, submission, dependence, malnutrition or even death, depending on the specific situation.

Clearly, in an effort to inspire faith, all scriptures downplay the possibility of other alternative ideas like the above. The Gita is the best and the most modern of the important Hindu scriptures. If it can propound one-sided partial truths exemplified above, what can we say about other much more ancient scriptures? I am fully aware of the feelings of most Hindu believers here. I like the Gita myself, much more than the other Hindu scriptures but I refuse to close my eyes to limitations in ideas. Love for a faith should not rob anyone of his reason or common sense. I know I shall be accused of the usual charges of misinterpretation and talking out of context (Please see Ch. 16).

What were the two vast armies (about two million?) doing while the 700 verses of the Gita were being spoken? Just waiting? Cannot be. So the answer is that the Gita is indirect speech, not the direct word of God. Vyasa, the author, told Ganesha to write for us whatever Sanjaya told the king about what Krishna was supposed to have told Arjuna in battle. When was it written? Nobody knows for sure. At least three thousand years ago, around 1000 B.C. (Bhandarkar Institute, Pune), about a battle that took place another 200 years ago. When paper or ink was not invented. And then, it was orally transmitted.

Scholars have listed 60 authors of the name of Vyasa, the author of the Mahabharat that includes the Gita. The original book was named Jaya and contained 8000 verses only. Vaishampayana added to it and called it Bharata containing about 24,000 verses. It was expanded by several writers, chiefly Suti and Shaunak. In course of time it became the Mahabharat. The modern version we see today has several editions and contains anything from 82,000 to 1,20,000 verses. Almost every Hindu scripture has suffered this kind of fate. Each one had expansions, throw-ins, addendums, amendments, what have you. Verses were freely added by later versifiers. Language itself can change in thousands of years. And yet debates drag on perennially as to when these happened, whether these happened, what each word means, which parts are real, which ones are fake, and why it is so very important for us to believe each word of it.

The whole point is that scriptures are not authentic, specific or balanced; they represent partial truth from a certain restricted perspective. They too can be inappropriate, invalid or both in a lot of situations. Appeals to scriptures can be made to support completely different, sometimes contrary points of view. Scriptures can also be out of tune with the times. It is possible and desirable to look at them from different angles which may be more accurate in certain cases. Christians do not follow the precepts from the Bible ('Turn the other cheek') verbatim. Why should we not be selective about our precepts? Our naiveté prevents us from noticing such things. Our blind faith and childhood conditioning stop us from admitting them. Our passion for God and religion makes us defend them. In reality, we must look upon our scriptures not as some iconic masterpieces whose wisdom cannot be challenged but as a fallible faith of mortal men.

6. Hinduism has **no authoritative** or universally accepted **principle** or text or spokesman. Call it an umbrella, not a religion. Call it devolving or evolving. But it is always non-specific, subjective and changeable. Because it is amorphous, foggy, fuzzy or shapeless, it is flexible, labile, ductile, malleable, whatever. Also, there is no focus. Most Hindus believe in 10 incarnations of God, but the Bhagavatam (in 1-3) counts 22. Some say even 24. Christians have Ten Commandments. We have zero commandments, ten suggestions, twenty options, hundred amendments, and a thousand opinions. If you believe in the Bible and in Jesus, that is all you need to be called a Christian. If you do not believe in Mohammed, you are not a Muslim. It is that clear and straightforward. But a Hindu can believe that a (personal) God exists or he may not. He can worship Brahma, Vishnu or Mahesh. He can worship Sai Baba, Rama,

Krishna, Agni (Fire), Hanuman, Matajis (goddesses), Shiva Linga (take a pick) and he is still a Hindu. He can believe in the Gita or in the Vedas as the authoritative standard, or he may not. He may set Heaven, better birth or Liberation as his goal. He may profess Dwaita (Duality), Adwaita, mixed Adwaita or some other you never know or understand---he is still a Hindu. Long list? It can get even longer, but the point is that in each and every case, you can claim to be a devout Hindu. Hinduism includes everybody---idol worshippers and idol haters, advocates of strict nonviolence and defenders of animal sacrifice. The paths offered are so diverse, options so innumerable, choices are so bewildering, freedom so licentious. The most pampered person in the world, the American consumer, does not have so many flavors to choose from in his ice-cream.

This is the principal reason why Hindu religion is all things to all men. Different authors at different times have quoted from Hindu scriptures to prove their point that Hindu philosophy supports socialism, egalitarianism, rationalism, mysticism, Sati, beef eating----you name it. 'Seek and you will find', as the Bible says. A learned Hindu theologist reached Heaven. God Himself asked him, "Well, my son, expound a point of your philosophy to me for my pleasure." The learned man scratched his head and said, "My Lord, I cannot think of anything particular at the moment. But I will tell you what. If You expound a point of my theosophy to me, I will show you how to refute it." And God gave up. What with Duality, Non-Duality, Specific, Pure, Unique and Dual-Non-Duality, and much more to tackle, none can blame God if He did not dare to accept the bait.

The American ambassador to the UNO once quoted a story from Aesop's fables to prove his point. Replying to him, the Russian ambassador said, "If you will kindly return the story book I lent you last week, I shall quote a story with exactly the opposite conclusion." We Hindus hardly need to borrow books, we know them all by heart.

My friend's name is Raj. In a variety of documents he presented at the American consulate for a visa, a variety of names---Rajesh, Rajendra, Rajubhai---were printed and the Americans had a hard time figuring out that they were dealing with the same person. You can well imagine the sometimes hilarious, sometimes confusing, sometimes problematic and irritating situations that arise. We are certainly not famous for precision, consistency or specificity in daily life and it is no different in our theosophy.

Lack of definition in words and ideas is a serious problem in Hindu philosophy. Because they are not specified or even identified properly, Hinduism and its principles are vulnerable to a high level of uncertainty among its adherents as to their real meaning, purpose or practice. We cannot defend what we cannot define. We lose focus in faith and clarity in belief. We lose single mindedness in our precepts and practices. Flexibility of principles may be good in principle. In practice, it is a positive disadvantage in some situations when you wish you had a fulcrum in your faith and steel in your spine.

Everyone is free to interpret Hindu philosophy as he likes and everyone does. What we call liberalism or broad-mindedness in our religion is in truth a free wheeling license to believe in anything we like at the moment. Scholars have pointed out many contradictions and inconsistencies among the Vedas, the Gita and the Puranas. But every time the argument is: That is a misinterpretation; that is not an authoritative text/edition; that is not our correct scripture. But then what is? No meaningful description is ever possible. As a matter of fact, fogginess and lack of specificity is held out as a merit. Though a lot of ink has been spilled on the subject, there is no agreement even on whether a Hindu is defined by geographic, cultural, ethnic or religious parameters.

It certainly does not pay to be too rigid in rules. However, too much flexibility promotes confusion, disunity and anarchy. How can you form a belief based on an ever-changing ever-shifting statement of principle? Careful wording makes or mars an idea, as every poet, judge, diplomat or statesman knows. When even the basic issues are left too open, that can lead people into inability to discriminate between sense and nonsense. This kind of licentiousness added to our divisive caste system is a major factor in the inherent disunity in Hindu society.

In any country's constitution, the dividing line between personal freedom and individual licentious behavior is difficult to demarcate but very essential to define. Ordinary people will be better served and will feel more comfortable if detailed rules and guidelines are laid down at least on broad-based basic issues, instead of leaving all cases open to interpretation by clerics, courts or tradition. People will follow anyone they happen to like if there are no set criteria to go by. This is a royal road to a culture of blind faith and hero worship. We routinely confuse the message with the messenger. We neglect even good ideas from an unrecognized person; we never question a well-known person like Gandhi even when he is obviously wrong. We put blind trust in our leaders. When this trust is found wanting, we become cynical.

Hinduism can be called a kind of "Yes, but---" religion. Do you believe in God? Yes, but--you yourself are God. Do you believe in idol worship? Yes, but--an idol is only a symbol. Is spiritual knowledge absolutely necessary for salvation? Yes, but--you can also attain salvation by true devotion. Can devotion unite you with God? Yes, but--you do need good actions. Do good actions lead you to God? Yes, but--non-attachment is necessary. Is it good to renounce the world in search of God? Yes, but--a good householder can also attain God. Is Hinduism based on faith? Yes, but--it is scientific. Is Hinduism a religion? Yes, but--it is also a way of life. Can you ever talk of Hinduism without using the words "Yes, but--?" Yes, Yes, certainly we can, but--.Do I want to give more examples of this kind? Yes, but—

Too little choice is rigidity. Too much is pandemonium. We must either presume that scriptures need no definition or else we must attempt after all to define them. The former is faith in fuzziness, the latter is logic. Broad terms and principles have to be well-defined and clearly laid down. We don't need rigidity in ideas but we do need definition. We don't need fanatic certainty but we do need specificity and clarity. None of the other theosophies require men to understand a bit of everything and indulge in the wholesale crossing of barriers. We must not confuse rigidity with definition. Rigidity is lack of flexibility; definition is clarity or lack of ambiguity. What is needed is flexibility coupled with clarity. Islam is rigid and definitive. Hinduism is non-rigid and non-definitive. The former is wrong about the former, the latter is wrong about the latter. Civilization and common sense will appreciate non-rigidity and good definition in both. Proper flexibility after careful definition is certainly not impossible to achieve.

Rigidity in religion as in Islam is not good but it will at least define what you are. It is clear. It is effective. It is decisive. It works. Why does Islam work better than Hinduism in practical terms? Partly because too much choice or fuzziness in ideas confuses the simple mind. And most people in the world have simple minds. They prefer the comfort of going by the book to the effort of using their discretion. A clear simple message and unique objective is the first requirement for effective action. "Kill the infidels" is a simple, short and effective command. "You must fight your holy war of duty, but you should not expect the fruit of your actions" may be good philosophy; but it is not simple, clear or effective as a directive. It needs to be explained. War of duty needs to be defined. And what happens if your opponent too is fighting his own brand of holy war against yours? If all is fair in love and war, it is the KISS (Keep It Simple, Stupid!) that is the key to success in both.

Sword in one hand and the holy Koran in the other, Islamic armies conquered half the known world, in a couple of centuries after Mohammed. A seventeen year boy led the Islamic army to conquer Sind in 712 A.D. for its first foray into Hindu India. It was the first of many more victories to come to a rigidly simplistic, highly motivated and hugely effective religion over a complicated, wavering, uncertain Hindu philosophy.

You cannot discuss theology without consistency in logic. And if you have no standard or authoritative text of the subject under discussion, what will you apply your logic to, consistent or otherwise? For our religious precepts, we need to have 1. A clear well authorized universally agreed set of terms and well-defined basic principles and 2. Proper flexibility in details of those principles with well defined limits. Both these needs, though difficult, are not mutually exclusive. Actually, the former is a prerequisite for the latter. Clarity and definition can help reform. You cannot reform if you are not clear about what it is that you intend to reform. A position on a graph is meaningful only if the frame of reference is defined, known and agreed upon.

Enough about problems in Hindu religion. Other problems can be listed but this book is not about making an exhaustive list of faults in Hinduism. Eminent Hindus themselves have pointed them out.

The important thing is that no reformer has traced them enough to the real root---Destruction of plain old Common sense by Religion---to draw clear conclusions; and so none succeeded in making any long lasting real impact. It is amazing to see that a religion steeped in symbols and symbolism is today unable to recognize the symbols of its own downfall. These are: 1. The common believer easily drawn to uncommonly divergent beliefs. 2. The downtrodden converting easily to other religions. 3. The rational getting fed up with its ritualism, blind faith and magical myth.

Intelligent people can differ in their views. But assuming that the certainty of our uncertainties is the best possible arrangement in the world is self-defeating behavior. Arid scholasticism, baseless generalizations and assumed truths are mistaken for universal theosophical truths in our religion. Encrustations of superstition, routine moralistic platitudes and wishy-washy piety are respected as sainthood. Our holy scholars are what someone described as "extra chromosome conservatives." Our common sense has been corroded by Faith to such an extent that a profound scholar believes in the feasibility one man's soul entering another dead man's body and reverting back after a time to his original body. He even cited scriptural and other references to me to prove his belief! The time has come to question our competence, if not our sanity.

Many of my good friends argue: "Hinduism is misinterpreted by many. It did not preach the evils we see in it today." Well, perhaps it did not; perhaps it did. That kind of debate will never end. Everyone calls his opponents misguided. Some call America misguided; America called Taliban misguided; Taliban called Buddhists misguided (and broke the Buddha statues); Buddha called the Vedas misguided. But think: 1. There surely is some such thing as unintended consequences. None can foresee all the future effects of a set of beliefs or actions. If the consequences are clearly disastrous, why not change course and rectify? What is the point in waiting for a tragedy to happen? Also: 2. If most people misunderstand most parts of Hinduism most of the time, is it not possible that something is seriously wrong?

What is the difference between education and brain-washing? The former exposes one to facts and also to differing opinions; the latter erases someone's opinions and replaces them with different beliefs. Brain-washing can occur through intensive repetition of one sided belief. A washed brain is filled with opinions but they are someone else's opinions. We need to think hard whether the exposure of Hindu society to a repetition of unquestioned beliefs for the last thousands of years can be called faith based education or brain-washing.

Religion is too serious a matter to be left entirely to professional priests and flamboyant philosophers. The tragic results of doing so have been demonstrated several times for several religions over a span of several centuries. We Hindus like to think that we respect philosophy. In fact we respect possessors of occult power whom we call Rishis, saints, know-alls, Gurus and so on. Lofty sentiment walks hand in hand with triviality in us Hindus. V.S. Naipaul, the Nobel laureate, says: "No other country I knew had so many layers of wretchedness.--The bias and the fantasies of Indian society--difficult to break through--Small people, big talk, small doings--Philosophy of the devitalized"--(Literary Occasions—A.A.Knopf, New York).

I know I will be denounced as a self-hating Indian because I have the consummate gall and utter chutzpa to say the obvious. But the unpleasant truth has to be told. And the time to tell that truth is: Now. That truth, plainly, is this: Hinduism is outdated, spineless and needs transformation. No 'ands', 'ifs' and 'buts'. No splitting hairs. No beating around the bush. We strayed too far from plain common sense. It is time to go back. Civilizations are built with rational rules, not with speculative sermons. Societies based on sound common sense principles advance much more than those based on decaying debris of presumptive faith. Debate should not be necessary. Hinduism does not work. It is a religion of losers. Its results have been shameful for several centuries. Everybody knows it. It has got to be fixed. Whatever the price to fix this foundation stone of our culture should be paid.

18. FAITH UNLIMITED?
Or Rationalism Resurrected?

We need to be aware of limitations of both, faith and rationality. With our inherent limitations, we humans have to make decisions based on a balance of best probabilities. This needs Reason--even in matters of faith. The critical difference between rationality and religious faith is not just about the conclusions reached, but even more so about the methods used to arrive at those conclusions. Openness to correction differentiates rationality from faith. Capacity to suspend one's judgment when necessary without speculating is given to only a few among us. We must resist the temptation to describe the indescribable or to speculate about unanswerable questions like meaning of life.

A brilliant student of philosophy struggled about the intractable problem of existence--Descartes' famous dictum "I think. Therefore I am"--for the whole night but could not arrive at a good conclusion. Early next morning, in his night pajama and slippers, hair disheveled, he knocked at his professor's door. "Professor, sir", he said, "Do I exist?" The good professor, himself half asleep, replied, "Who is asking?"

Apart from such philosophical quibbling about nature of truth, reasonable people agree that: 1. Human knowledge is limited in scope. Truths that are conclusively provable are few. 2. Still we need to make decisions in life based on probability and judgment. Samuel Butler said, "Life is the art of drawing sufficient conclusions from insufficient premises." 3. The only certainty in life is that there are no certainties. Based on the certainty of this uncertainty, how should we make our decisions?

The dictionary defines faith as belief that does not rest on logical proof or material evidence. The probability of its being valid is extremely low, though some beliefs may prove correct merely by surmise. I may believe an earthquake will come next year and it may even occur. But without a basis in any natural verifiable laws, my belief is faith, not logic or truth. There are few criteria by which to judge abstract beliefs. Too many pious persons claim communications with God. Webster defines rationalism as "the practice of guiding one's actions and opinions solely by what seems reasonable." Reason is "the power to think, or intellect". A rational man makes decisions on a balance of best probabilities based on reasoned judgment. Will the sun rise tomorrow? The maximum certainty we can have is only this: Based on natural laws and past observations, there is a very high degree of probability that the sun will rise tomorrow. If this is the case with the most obvious event like sunrise, what can we say about abstract belief?

For an intellectually honest person, there is no escape from rationality even in matters of faith. Interfaith and intrafaith, both kinds of decisions require a struggle drawing conclusions based on insufficient, unknowable, indeterminate data using reason or rational judgment, because reason is all we have, however imperfect. Since the supernatural or metaphysical is beyond verification, natural laws or past observations, it is futile to say that it has a high probability of being true. The supernatural can be good (angels, heaven, God), or it can be bad (witches, hell, Satan), depending on my faith; but it has close to zero probability of being logically true. It is not only not provable, it is also not plausible. Whether possible or not, it is almost certainly not probable. We must learn to distinguish among all these.

Irrespective of who propounded it, a theory is acceptable by a rationalist only if verification even by opponents also supports the theory. Faith, on the contrary, depends entirely on one authoritative personality. While Reason is willing to change belief in the light of changed data, Faith hopes to alter or question the data and will not change its belief. In spite of overwhelming evidence in support, Christians of deep faith did not accept gravity and evolution because the Bible says something different. But sooner or later, even the Pope has to accept inexorable natural laws like gravity, especially when His Holiness may accidentally slip and sustain a fall. During renaissance and reformation, Bruno was burnt; Martin Luther and Galileo were ostracized; protracted battles were fought between blind faith and skepticism to establish rationality. Rationalism so won is too precious a commodity for mankind to lose it again.

My wife and I decided to drive inter-city, since a train ride was costlier. Then we saw a bad weather forecast and considered a train. Next came a train accident somewhere. So we may be better off driving after all, and who knows, the weather may even improve. Then I got a severe headache. Should I drive? My wife was exasperated. "For Heaven's sake, why don't you make up your mind, once for all?" She says.

To change course as evidence changes is right but frustrating for most minds. As nature abhors vacuum, people abhor uncertainty. The rare capacity to suspend our judgment when no clear answers are available is a very valuable mental asset but it is often frustrating. Man gets a vague feeling of indecisiveness, insecurity and uneasiness. Emotional need for the illusion of definitive truth is deeply embedded in our psyche. What a common man does not know, he tends to imagine, assume or hypothesize. But a rational man knows what he knows and is not unduly disturbed by his natural inability to know everything. Desire to acquire indubitable knowledge pushes people into strange assumptions. That is why many intelligent people believe in God, priests and devils although they would be wisely skeptical about believing in astrologers, meteorologists and politicians.

The four blind men 'looking' at an elephant in the popular story are not the only ones who are blind--we are all blind. Our inherent limitations made us so. We can only see in parts---half the surface of the moon, a small part of a logical argument, a small part of philosophical truth, a small part of our own 'self'. One man who is not comfortable with partial truths will believe in some assumed truths and cling to them, however absurd they might be. Another man who is capable of being at peace with partial truths will presume nothing even while striving to know more and more. The first is a man of religion and faith. The second is a man of science and reason. Both are seekers of truth, dissatisfied with ignorance, striving for certainty in this imperfect world. But both have to learn to go beyond the need for absolute certainty.

Faith is a great asset in certain situations like war as Islam proved in the middle ages. But modern wars are fought with a lot more technology, diplomacy and sophistication. These are possible with reason, not with faith. For normal men in normal life, in the overwhelming majority of situations in practice, reason triumphs. Galileo---a devout (though persecuted) priest and pioneer scientist---said, "I don't feel obliged to believe that the same God who has endowed us with sense, reason and intellect has intended us to forego their use." He was jailed by the then Pope but finally exonerated by Pope John Paul 2 as late as 1992.

Those parts of life that cannot be understood can very well be left alone with a humble admission of the limited capacity of our tiny brains, without making weird assumptions. As time passes, as we refine our techniques of science and logic, the oases of knowledge will expand to overcome the deserts of ignorance. The moon to us was a goddess, an old woman with a spinning wheel or a piece of cheese. Now man walks on it; brings a piece of it to earth. The Sun God was a wonder; now we can measure its size, distance and temperature. If I don't know, being embarrassed to say 'I don't know' is a sign of immaturity. Richard Feynman, a Nobel Laureate, said: "It is better to live not knowing than to have wrong answers."

A man of blind faith trusts his neighbor; a man of pure intellect builds a fence; a man of reason maintains a good fence while he continues to trust his neighbor. A man of pure faith believes in a prophet; a man of pure intellect denies Him; a man of reason maintains a healthy dose of skepticism in either case. Who has the best chance to survive and prosper in the competitive struggle that is life? Obviously, the third kind. We may take Fancy for a companion but must follow Reason as our guide.

Academic fascination with unanswerable questions is exceedingly bad training for making decisions in life, let alone quick or correct decisions. To spin the truth is to juggle around a troubling situation until it is impossible to figure out what is going on. The epidemic of spin can drive everybody to despair without a conclusion or a decision. Somebody has said: 'A fool can ask more questions than a wise man can answer.' He can also ask more questions than he needs to know the answers of. If curiosity can kill a cat, our curiosity about the next world killed our will to live in this world. If something is unknowable, why pretend to know it? If an infinitesimally small creature has natural limitations in knowing the infinite universe, why not honestly accept the limitation and try to live with it even while continuing to strive to extend the horizons of knowledge? Can we not learn to occasionally stop creating a Unified Field Theory out of everything that happens and just let it happen? Experiencing without interpreting. Enjoying without understanding. Rejoicing without regretting.

Steven Weinberg the scientist said: "The more the universe seems comprehensible, the more it also seems pointless." With all the progress in science and philosophy, some questions will always remain. Not merely because these two are inadequate but also because of the nature of the questions and also the way we ask them. When we ask what the life force (or the soul or consciousness) is, we forget that we make a number of assumptions: 1. That there is a clear line of demarcation between living and nonliving organisms, 2. That brain, mind and soul are three distinct and independent entities, 3. That simple answers can be found for very complex issues and so on. Similarly, when we ask what the meaning of life is, we forget that we are making a number of unwarranted assumptions: That everything must have a meaning; That it can be discovered; That we are capable enough to find it; That the exercise is worthwhile and essential. And we momentarily lose sight of the fact that meaning of anything essentially is that which we ourselves assign to it. Actually, words have meaning, events have none. Events have a meaning, cause or purpose only if they are created by living organisms. To ask for the meaning of life is to assume an answer while purporting to ask a question.

19. THE IRRATIONAL RATIONALISTS
The Importance of Being Non-Intelligent

Hindu theosophy assigns intelligence a much lower place than faith and thereby undermines it indirectly and imperceptibly, even when it ostensibly pays lip-service to intelligence. Unquestionable faith in gurus, scriptures, saints and mythology is routinely advocated, emphasized and assumed. Skepticism is considered highly undesirable. Absurd myths are preached, defended and believed under various pretexts. Miracle stories encourage irrationality that becomes a habit of the mind in the populace. Irrational attitudes imparted to children become entrenched through life. It is not easy growing up intelligent in India. There is nothing more debilitating to a society than irrationality spiced and legitimized by popular culture. We revel in speculation. Most adults cannot think clearly, precisely or to the point. Life in India has enough examples of all these. If you find these statements too broad, please read on.

Three doctors traveling in a car heard a loud thud of a bursting tire. One got down, saw the collapsed tube and opined, "A flat tire." The second doctor inspected the damage very carefully and said, "In my opinion it is a flat tire." The third doctor, after surveying the damage in detail and conferring with the other two, gravely remarked, "Looks like a flat tire. Let us conduct some tests and find out."

Well, let us conduct some tests on our irrationality. Not that it is not obvious. But most of our people find it too drastic to confront, too depressing to the ego, and therefore too derogatory to admit. It is strange but true that many obvious issues are not necessarily obvious in life until they are spelled out.

Some of my good Indian friends in America believe that their respected Guru had attained ultimate spiritual knowledge when he was waiting for a train at a lonely railway platform in India. Now, seated on a high chair, the Guru would touch a kneeling devotee's forehead with the big toe of his right foot and recite Mantras. This ritual was supposed to transfer ultimate spiritual knowledge to the devotee and was designed to confer quick liberation of the soul in a couple of future births. My friends asked me to kneel down and grab the opportunity to obtain divine "knowledge". When I refused, they concluded that it was my 'intelligence' that obstructed me; it was my big handicap in the way of attaining spiritual knowledge; and spiritual knowledge is all that is really important to a pious Hindu mind.

The above is no isolated case. It is a typical illustration of what religion expects you to do--suspend your intelligence. It is widely believed by pious people in India that intelligence is a hindrance in matters of religion. To them reason or even skepticism is not only undesirable; it is an unmitigated evil. They have a visceral distrust of intellect. They are impressed and awed by superior intelligence but in the heart of their hearts they do not really trust or like an intelligent person. We have a strong tradition that sees mental derangement itself as somehow holy when accompanied by kindness and humility. In our culture, he is a sincerely pious good man who is nearly terminally naïve.

Intelligence is something that raised man above all others species and established him at the top of the evolutionary pyramid of life. How can it be a handicap? When theology requires logic, and logic needs intelligence, how can intelligence be a handicap even for spiritual knowledge? What they advocate indirectly is to keep thinking away and accept whatever they preach--all the mumbo jumbo, the myths, the assumptions, the contradictions and all. The ancient saints, after all, cannot be wrong, so the belief goes.

In the Upanishadas, the scholar saint Yajnavalkya says to Gargi, the disciple, "Ask not too much." But it is not often that our theosophy and religion denounce intellect so directly, openly and clearly. They do it indirectly, insidiously, imperceptibly, even while ostensibly paying lip service to intelligence. They quietly subordinate intelligence or subvert it. They do not overtly oppose intellect; they covertly undermine it. Often they purport to encourage a devotee to ask questions. The answers in most cases are based on faith only. What is the worst possible word of abuse a saint can use in a holy scripture? The sacred Gita uses the adjective "vyabhicharini (adulterous)" for skeptical intellect. To a Hindu mind, nurtured for centuries on lofty ideals of a pure woman like the holy Sita, no adjective is imaginable that is more despicable than this.

An intelligent child in India faces an uphill battle from day one. A child is born with a sound brain. The problem is how to keep it. Under our irrational cultural environment, smart kids can fail; those less smart can degenerate still lower. Their innate common sense experiences a relentlessly downward pull from our popular culture that can turn talented Toms into average Joes. If the child has a genius in him, the genius keeps hiding; it grows wary of him. We know innumerable instances of children, positively brilliant at school, failing to make impact in later lives. Instead of assuming answers, we need to investigate the causes and implications of letting god given talents wither away into oblivion. We need to analyze what kinds of stress, circumstance or countervailing cultural influence---in addition to material deficiencies---society exercised over such persons to neutralize their brilliance.

It is not easy growing up intelligent in India. Intelligent people in India find themselves adrift in a sea of simplistics, homeless in the neighborhood of naiveté, exiled in their own town. If you happen to have a rational bent of mind you are condemned to living a lie most of your life. You have to live with heaps of hype and hypocrisy. Not only live with them. You have to learn to do them yourself to avoid being isolated or outcast. India has the extraordinary gift of banishing her most worthwhile talent because while her home is jammed with original minds, originality is never at home here. But cultures that teach that intelligence is bad are eventually forced to live with cultures with bad intelligence. Cultures that imply that intelligence is less desirable or less acceptable develop in course of time a culture that in itself grows undesirable or unacceptable. Our backwardness is the inevitable consequence of our downright refusal to use our brains.

Myths: My son had no children. A learned well-wisher advised him to start reading Harivansh Purana (a holy Hindu book) at home. He said he knew two families who got children through its daily reading, but faith was a pre-requisite for success. My friend's five year old son was watching a video showing Krishna as a child of four years killing a huge ugly monster. The son asked, "Dad, how can a small child kill a monster?" My friend had a difficult time explaining that Krishna was God and God can do anything. Another child of six asked while listening to the Hanuman story: "How can a monkey carry a mountain and fly?" Well, because he was a devotee of God Rama. But then, we see monsters also flying! We tell stories and promote myths that even an ordinary child finds it difficult to swallow. Our adults are incapable of asking common sense questions like these innocent children. But a culture that teaches its children that myths are rational eventually creates a society that rationalizes myths and trivializes the truth.

If children are taught to blindly accept mindless claims without examining them, they will be equally undiscerning when they reach voting age. Raised in a culture that systematically bans common sense, they will produce an undiscerning democracy like ours (Ch. 4). In the popularization of pious predilections of our culture, we routinely make fact-defying leaps of logic. Yet it is not necessary to promote naiveté in order to promote religion. It is not necessary to rationalize naiveté in order to look intelligent either. Myths make us stupid one-track minds. Myths can be durable. They can overpower the mind. Our religious literature overflows with myths and stories that are mere anecdotes more amusing than plausible, more shallow than sensible.

Apologists for Hinduism say: "We use stories and myths only to teach a principle or drive home a point. Common people need them to understand religion." Firstly, they don't. Secondly, if some people are really so dumb, it is all the more reason why these stories should not be told. When a learned man makes incredible statements, people are misled and confused because such people trust him. Thirdly, this defense is similar to the false defense of creators of violence in films or TV. They offer violence, promote it, market it, encourage it, expand it more and more till people get hooked to it and then blame people for liking it. Though people may occasionally like violence, they don't really demand nor need violence; it is the marketers who get them accustomed to it. But to purveyors of pious myths, a mass audience is its own justification. The argument that the existence of customers justifies the product does not distinguish preachers from drug peddlers. It is the worst kind of antisocial marketing technique. They create an artificial need and then fill it and call it service. Please consider the following points:

1. Many myths have no point to illustrate and no principle to teach. Saint Narada flying in the sky with a musical instrument in hand does not teach any great truth. 2. Myths promote irrational attitudes. People's minds get trained in non-reason. 3. They stupefy the mind and act like habit forming drugs. Like TV, they entertain but convert you into a passive audience, barring you from thinking for yourself. Think: How does Gandhari help her blind husband by voluntarily blinding herself for life? There are better ways of demonstrating a woman's devotion to her husband---if at all that kind of demonstration is needed.

4. When an otherwise acceptable truth is sought to be propped up by a myth, skepticism about the myth can result in a corresponding skepticism about the truth. Credibility suffers. Why can't our heroes just be great men without being unbelievable? I can believe that Bhishma or Parashurama (in Mahabharat) were great men. I can not believe that the former could control death and the latter is for ever immortal. The high level of credibility that you wish to create in me gets eroded when you tell me the myths.

5. The negative side of even useful myths lies in not being aware of the myths and allowing them to seem real. They become rigid and calcified. They create an environment where entertainment makes dissent unlikely and reason undesirable.

But the pundits have a reply to all this: Believe whatever you can according to the level of faith you have, they say. But a leap of faith cannot be in stages. Either you believe it or you don't. Either you have a logical attitude or you have faith. When you are free to accept one part and reject another part of the same sacred story, you are free to accept one part and reject another part of the same principle as well. You don't know what you will end up with. You develop doubt, split personality, equivocation, indecisiveness, lack of direction, either any or all of these at various times. These are responsible for a lot of problems we see today in India.

A biography of the scholarly Sankara Acharya includes the following stories: 1. A crocodile would release young Sankar's foot only when his reluctant mother agreed to permit him to become a monk. 2. He asked an untouchable to get out of his way but the lowly man taught the great teacher that the same soul resides in both 'you and me'. 3. His debating opponent's wife asked him a question about sex. Sankara, a celibate for life, entered the body of a recently dead king, enjoyed sex-life for a month, returned to his original body and then gave the correct answer. Now please think. How much of this nonsense can you believe however good a Hindu you may be?

Our invisible insanity knows no bounds. We relate stories of our gods fighting among themselves to assert their egos, Indra having 1000 eyes (Bhagavatam), one arrow capable of destroying the entire earth, human beings who never die (Ashvatthama in Mahabharat), saints who always curse (Durvasa), monkeys that fly to the sun (Hanuman), birds that talk (Jatayu), and so on and on without end. The child in me asks: How is it possible? The wise pundits reply: Everything is possible, because they are gods. Or god's devotees. Okay, you have faith, you just believe it all. But Marich was a monster---he assumed the form of a golden deer, tempted Sita and deceived a real God, Rama. Nectar was obtained from the salty seas by churning them. How can you churn the ocean? Yes, you can, if you use the Shesha Naga (serpent god) as a rope to wrap around the mountain Meru surrounded by the sea. But don't the same scriptures say that Shesha Naga constantly carries and supports the earth over his head? How did he give up the globe to churn the ocean that again is a part of the globe itself? Only children will ask such questions. Adults are supposed to swallow them and have faith in all the stories that are dished out in the name of our holy religion.

Actually we have been justifying the unjustifiable for so long that we can no longer tell the difference. Even if we can, we have lost our power to justify the justifiable as well. It turns out that some stories are offensive to intellect but they are also comforting. They wrap life in the archetypal tastiness of fairy tale where everything is either black or white and magical. Their reassuring simplicity makes complicated understanding unnecessary. They permit people to identify appearances with realities, and so exempt them from any further mental or emotional effort. They keep familiar things simple. But can we say this is adult stuff for mature men?

Mythical stories might or might not have been useful in ancient ignorant times. Today they are an anachronism. It is no accident that the most ancient religion in the world, Hinduism, is super-saturated with myths; that Christianity (32A.D.) has fewer myths; Islam (632 A.D.) has still less; and Sikhism (sixteenth century A.D.) has almost no myths at all. The older the religion, the more the myths.

Most Hindu families---even governments---hold Satya Narayana Pooja. Its story is silly and concocted. (Please excuse my understatement). Yet we not only listen to it in large numbers but also like to have repeat performances of it day in and day out. The devotion is infectious, the faith is touching, but the absurdities are monstrous. Every sect of Hindu society has a tradition of telling similar stories in one form or the other. We would all be better off if competition to win the minds of men were not based on who could best make them swallow immense absurdities without a murmur of protest. To adapt a famous line from Winston Churchill, let me put it this way: Never in the history of human affairs, was so much absurdity believed so passionately by so many for so long, with consequences so disastrous.

Confronted with indefensible stories, these merchants of myth land try to wriggle out of their dilemma by telling us to ignore myths and concentrate on the higher philosophical plane. Fine. But such fanciful stories are an integral part of the Hindu religious ethos and cannot be separated. Most have their roots in the earlier scriptures, even in the Upanishadas. You cannot ignore the Ramayana, the Mahabharat, all the Puranas, the Bhagavatam and a vast collection of religious literature assembled over centuries that all Hindus devoutly believe in. Can a doctor be allowed to ignore the serious side effects of a medicine that he prescribes? No. Our saints prescribe a medicine with a myth, to cure our diseases and save our souls. But when challenged, they ask us to ignore the effects of their prescriptions--the growth of irrationality and promotion of blind faith. Often they ask us to ignore the medicine itself.

The typical Hindu mind has developed a strange fascination for miracles of all brands without blinking an eyelid. We Hindus cannot present a philosophy without making it incredible through an unlikely story. Nothing enhances the incredibility of a story like we Hindus telling it. We cannot talk of God without making him sound unbelievable. We cannot even make a Hindi movie without making it ludicrously unnatural, even when we steal the plot! A headlong retreat from realism has made escapism for us an end in itself. The line between fantasy and realism continues to remain blurred forever in our minds. This chronic disease of irrationality is caused by a beautiful butterfly called spiritual faith.

In my personal experience, I have found this quite often: Tell an obviously incredible story, rumor or speculation (even on a non-religious topic) to two kinds of people---1. staunch believers and 2. weak believers or non-believers. More people from the first group will believe it than from the second group. Among the former group, faith in spiritual matters has somehow induced faith in all matters.

Putting aside everything that might excite laughter by its absurdity or detestation by its profanity, it is impossible to conceive anything more derogatory to gods than the stories told us by our preachers. Our creator God sits on a lotus flower. Vishnu, the supreme god, lies down at the bottom of the ocean, on a bed of the serpent god, his feet being massaged by a dutiful wife, Laxmi, the goddess of wealth. Our great God, the destroyer, has three eyes, dances with a snake around his neck and the moon on his forehead. Our gods belong to a hierarchy, higher or lower. They have a degree, greater or lesser. Our stories trivialize our gods, make a caricature of them and represent them as harboring all the vices that men are advised to shun. No other religion has ever brought down the gods to such a sorry pass or degraded them more. Hindus deify big men. In the process they some times demonize the concept of God and subject it to ridicule. Ex: Hindus of Nepal consider their king--any king--an incarnation of Lord Vishnu. When the crown prince shoots down his father and then shoots himself, the king dies immediately; the prince is in a coma but attains the throne for two days till he also dies. A murderer of one Vishnu ascends Vishnu's throne for two days until a third Vishnu takes over. See the problems of incarnations of God?

The masters of meaningless trash ask us to consider the stories as metaphors and parables; and believe only in the message they give. But if the literal word itself is senseless, how can the meaning be meaningful? And many stories are not parables. We believe in the Mahabharat that includes the holy Gita as an integral part of it. None can believe the following fantastic story in it:--Vyasa, the author himself, is the bearded saint who dutifully impregnated three widowed queens. One went pale with fear during sex with him and gave birth to Paandu (meaning pale). Another queen closed her eyes and so gave birth to the blind Dhritarashtra. The third escaped and sent in her maid to the holy man. Why such adultery with queens? Because the king was impotent and died without an heir to the throne. It would take a genius to call such a story anything but crazy. But we had innumerable wise owls who not only believed and explained it, but also justified the actions.

Our Puranas overflow with one dimensional characters, one sided truths and exotic moody actions. Should our Hindu epics be considered history, scripture or poetry (or all combined) that we are free to interpret as per our expediency? Did any pundit honestly and clearly spell out whether and which Puranas should be considered our scriptures? And which parts of them are acceptable and which are not? Not so far.

Apart from stories, consider some of the ideas that are a part and parcel of Hindu thought. Everything in India is sacred---statues, rivers, monkeys, plants, saffron, mouse, cows, cow-dung, cow-urine, conch-shells, you name it. Everything except man. Man can be despicable, dispensable, untouchable or worse. Believing that God resides in everything and everything is a small part of God has resulted in this situation. Hindus proclaim that it is impossible to describe God adequately. A reasonable person would find it impossible to describe this kind of belief adequately.

It is mind-boggling. We are caught in the grip of our culture's anti mind myths. We grow up with mystical mumbo-jumbo constantly streaming into our ears. We inhale it from the air. We subconsciously absorb the dominant ideas taught. We adopt the assumptions of our generation while we are growing up. We do not realize the noxious effect irrational culture has on our upbringing. There is nothing more debilitating to a society than irrationality spiced and legitimized by popular culture. When entire populations are nourished on such myths since their childhoods for centuries on end, you expect and obtain huge masses of naïve people swallowing great fantasies. They get permanently set in irrational modes of thought before they grow old enough to realize it.

Cultural notions are not innate; they are implanted. Babies are born with blank minds. The incessant inculcation of the incomprehensible into the receptive innocent minds by the inane, works wonders. In our culture, simpletons do not grow like grass; they are processed for conversion wholesale in mass production factories during their growing years. When you repeat and practice something--physical or mental--often enough, it becomes a habit. The habit of irrationality practiced daily becomes instinct. Instinct becomes ingrained. We have done certain mental drills so often that everyone falls in line with the practiced ease of an actor who has been playing the same role for years. Someone called our life "a habit disturbed by a few thoughts." Since habit is stronger than reason, it is extremely difficult to unlearn what you have learnt in your most impressionable years. Even when we are able to consciously discard the wrong ideas that we were taught in childhood, they lie buried deep in the subconscious or unconscious mind. Most of us have trouble shedding these unacknowledged assumptions and unknown irrationalities when we grow up. The irrationalism lasts us a lifetime. Men cannot outgrow the compulsions of their birth and culture. "Cultures can get set like hard concrete."

Other more obvious conditions like poverty and malnutrition add to all the solid cultural blocks to reinforce irrationality. Irrationality has ruled our minds so long that it is a wonder there is any rationality left. We have almost automated non-reason. We thus have a good explanation of why an overwhelming majority of the Indian population displays such irrational tendencies in reacting to the problems of life. And these irrational modes of thought are at the very root of our downfall.

Nature versus Nurture: We all know how natural selection operates in the evolution of species. We do not normally realize that it operates at the psychological and cultural levels as well. We need not enter into scientific controversies regarding nature versus nurture except to mention the significant fact that experiences and notions acquired during childhood can determine how the person will behave for the rest of his life. According to the theory of Neural Darwinism, our brain at birth is a result of biological evolution and genetic inheritance. As we acquire experiences, another process of evolution begins. Those experiences cause certain pathways in the brain to be augmented and others to be abandoned. Our brains develop, based on rewards and punishments that come. Our consciousness is unique, adaptable and highly amenable to cultural influences because it results from a learning process rather than from a logical program. The more we learn, the more complex our consciousness becomes and the more subtle our values. A scholar states thus: "Positive reinforcements of responses by social environment serve to select and perpetuate behaviors, values and ideas; those not so reinforced tend to disappear over time." This is natural selection in action in the cultural sphere. This is how, over a period of several centuries, philosophical ideas like Sankhya and others almost disappeared, once the Vedanta ideas became popular in our society. History tends to progressively strengthen traditional dominant perceptions through societal sanction and reinforcement.

The short take on all this is that a person is not a slave to his genes or biology. The brain is constantly interacting with the environment. Anybody raising young kids already knows what a great deal of knowledge, attitude, belief and thinking skills adults impart to children in their most impressionable years. Children greedily and naturally swallow whatever they are taught, including myths, good and bad, rational and irrational. It is brain conditioning, plain and simple.

An elephant trainer in a circus said the following: "The tiny chains on the elephant's legs cannot hold the big animal in place. But we put the chains on the animals when they are babies when they cannot break them. As they grow older and larger, they continue to believe that the chains can hold them. It is not the chain that holds them. It is their belief that it does that keeps them from breaking free." This is what happens to children. They grow up with various "chains" given to them by their parents---chains of anger, guilt, shame, sin, spirit, faith or God as also the chains of morality, obedience, rationality or irrationality. They bind them for ever.

Now consider what effects the irrational attitudes we impart to our children will have on them and on society, especially when this is multiplied on a massive scale for centuries on end, from generation to generation, as it happened in India. Remember also that there were no countervailing influences of rationalism in the form of science or secularism in education---because almost all education was family or religion based in a comparatively isolated society. Irrationality won by default, not by design. Rationalism was drowned out in torrents of faith.

Eric Fromm, a famous psychologist, has explained the influence of childhood conditioning on the subconscious mind. Such conditioned minds are not programmed to process evidence; they simply keep repeating the same ideas as if they have a microchip malfunction.

Our preconceived notions are so powerful that our minds block out any incongruity and override our senses. Subconscious bias cannot be ruled out by will power. Researchers in any field have to get trained in openness of conclusions and willingness for course corrections. Medical scientists use the gold standard of double blind experiment to rule out bias. No new medicine is ever approved until it is proven under this kind of testing. If trained scientists need to guard against such bias, imagine the situation with laymen. Mankind needed centuries of mental gymnastics to develop such hallmarks of a rational mind.

Scientific Religion? Nowadays it has become fashionable to make tall claims about scientific nature of Hindu religion, to include a sprinkling of modern scientific words (Black holes, Quantum physics) to impress the educated reader, and then merrily present the most controversial assumptions as universal truths. Every saintly person willing to violate elementary rules of reason must frame himself as a scientific preacher of Hindu theology. He certainly knows what people need today and which side the bread is buttered. In India, he will espouse faith, ethics and devotion. In America, he will emphasize intelligence, science and knowledge. Marketing of spirit never grew so subtle, so sophisticated, so customer driven and focused. If this were science, I don't know what traditional faith is. Gurus quote the famous Einstein equation "$E=MC^2$." If E represents the Enormity of damage that pseudo-science can inflict, M symbolizes the number of myths propagated and C stands for the Credulity of the common man, then Einstein may well be right after all!

We Hindus like to think of ourselves as rationalists. Well, in that case, we must be the most irrational rationalists in the world. The Strategic Air Command is the most lethal war-machine of the dreaded US Air power. Its headquarters displayed a sign: "Peace is our profession." A mischievous member scrawled a subtitle below it: "Bombing is only a hobby." Our Hindus display a sign: "Reason is our religion." A suitable subtitle should be: "Credulity is compulsory."

Blind faith feigning historic or scientific truth is more difficult to overcome than simple faith by itself. Superstition with scientific pretensions does more harm than pure superstition itself. Clever scholars can twist and cite any number of similar looking ideas from both scripture and science to claim that they are the same. They are an affront equally to science and to good sense. A few examples:

1. The fact that E. Schrödinger (Quantum physicist) showed interest in Vedanta, is implicitly cited as proof of the truth of Vedanta. Well, we do have many people studying many things at many levels, but I don't know what that fact alone proves. I read the Bible and liked it without converting to Christianity.

2. A Hindu scholar in America stated: "Vedic deities are to be correctly viewed as cognitive centers of the mind." The operative words here are "correctly viewed" to conform to whatever the speaker intends to opine. But it is certainly interesting to try to view the principal deity in the Vedas, the great thousand eyed Indra, the king of the gods, Vajra in hand, Shachi by his side, always afraid of demons, always on the run, as a cognitive mind center, whatever that may mean.

3. Another profound statement: "The Vedic texts speak of biological rhythms and a reality that has many parallels with the insights of the Quantum theory." What a wonderful combination of biology, physics, Vedanta and mumbo-jumbo! If Reality were propagated in discrete particles of energy called quanta, and spirituality could be proved like equations in calculus, will it not be a great idea? Will it not be equally wonderful if all parallel lines and insights could meet and prove to us that they are no different although they may appear so? Well, if physics is fuzziness, mathematics is metaphysics, and quantum theory is a bunch of quizzical quixotic ideas only, then the above scholars richly deserve a Nobel Prize for revealing their eternal and ultimate insights to us.

If imitation is the highest form of flattery, religion claiming to be scientific is the highest tribute that faith could pay to reason. Religion's problem is organic to its being a faith based dreamy outfit. It is also its defining characteristic. It is the nature of the animal. You have a better chance of finding a nonviolent tiger than a scientific religion. Those applying a science label on any religion probably never heard the word oxymoron. It is time they stopped inflicting their kind cruelty on innocent masses.

The caliber of our intellectual life leaves much to be desired. Europeans often taught us our sacred language and were authoritative experts in Sanskrit literature. We did have a few rationalist thinkers in India but they never made any headway. We had our share of brilliant minds (recent examples at random are D. D. Kosambi, Laxmanshastri Joshi, D. P. Chattopadhyaya, Agarkar, M.N.Roy), but the country always ignored them---the very names sound so unfamiliar to the general public. Even a famous person like Nehru, educated in England, encouraged by Gandhi, with a sensitive modern mind, with all his advantages, could not overcome the inertia and the orthodoxy of our masses. But average minds that appeal to emotions and assume high moralistic pedestals become popular. A pious looking Rama Rao becomes a hugely popular Chief Minister; his intellectual son-in-law Chandra Babu Naidu has to struggle even to get elected. We need to ask ourselves why we do not appreciate or like intellect or intellectuals.

Looking for rationality in the minds of most of the Indian population is like searching for a Robinson Crusoe in the island of Manhattan. In our cultural warehouse, silly ideas inconspicuously occupied large spaces and had long shelf-life. We got into such a mindset that eroded logic and reason long ago. Our irrationality is securely wrapped in layers upon layers of traditions inside a plethora of customs and rituals. Our culture is like a giant tree. Its roots are a vast invisible underground maze of outdated beliefs. These roots are nourished by innumerable streams of irrational ideas emanating from an ancient religion. In a vicious chain, myths produce irrational mindsets; irrational mindsets induce and sustain more myths.

Faith supports both. The great danger of poverty, intellectual as well as economic, is that it feeds on itself, although the former is not as obvious as the latter. Bad attitudes always feed on themselves. So the overwhelmingly irrational predilections of the Indian population should surprise nobody.

Bread alone will not nourish well, but it is a basic necessity. Similarly, reason cannot answer each and every question--real or imagined--but it is an indispensable basic necessity. Our Hindu Faith-preachers don't realize that a population unaccustomed to rationality does not need a sermon on limitations of rationality or intellect. It is silly to argue against bread and preach vitamin supplements to a severely hungry man who needs bread. Let him eat first. We can then point out the drawbacks of carbohydrates or limitations of rational thought. I need basic math before I hear a learned exposition on the limitations of differential calculus. When I cannot walk, a guide does not need to tell me disadvantages of marathon competition. So rationalism even with its limitations is a desirable, nay, an indispensable goal. Especially for the Indian population.

We Hindus find it almost impossible to restrict faith within reasonable limits. Faith makes for imbalance and lopsidedness. Like in a Jain who will not eat potatoes, a Hindu who will bathe in a dirty river or will believe in sanctity of cow urine. Most of our people---even some scientists---do not possess the genuinely scientific bent of mind or rational attitudes. But these are so necessary for success in the modern world. Apart from myths backed by religion, our irrational thinking has acclimatized our Hindu minds to various other kinds of myths too. We entertain quite a few myths about ourselves: We believe that we are peaceful and non-materialistic, when we may just be weak and poor. We must examine how far all such petting on our own backs is justified. Common perceptions do not always correspond to objective reality.

Common sense has been starved to death in India for want of nourishment. The still small voice of reason is drowned in the beating of bell, cymbal and drum. It cannot rise above the din of blowing of conch shells and chanting of Mantras and slogans. The rational mind gets distraught, distracted and lost in the massive maze of monstrous myths. Common sense cannot breathe, surrounded in reams of ritual; and it dies a natural death in tons of timeless tradition. The brutality of our beliefs has scarred our souls intellectually, emotionally and aesthetically. The unacknowledged effects of theosophical conundrums have added to the sum total of our irrationality. It is a sad, sad, sad, sad story of a mad, mad, mad, mad world.

Personally, I found it quite difficult to convince a lot of common Indians about the importance of punctuality, about the need to often wash hands with soap, about eating with spoons rather than with fingers, and so on. These are minor issues but illustrations of irrational thinking and unreasonable action are found at all levels in many areas of everyday life. Some examples of less than rational attitudes, although they may or may not 'prove' anything, may be of interest as straws in the wind:

1. A weather report in a local Indian newspaper describes in vivid detail the effects of a very cold wave on a particular day. It lacks the most important detail—the actual temperature. It is not a slip; it is a frequent omission by this reporter and editor. I am amazed almost everyday at the disparity between the intellectual caliber displayed by most Indian writers in Indian newspapers on the one hand and American commentators in America on the other hand. With few exceptions the Indian commentaries hardly ever provide the depth of coverage and the freshness of ideas that we see daily in American media. The superficiality, the staleness, the stereotyping we see in a majority of local Indian press commentaries is amazing. By the way, it is essential for anyone desirous of getting a good perspective on India to read local Indian papers in the vernacular languages. These provide a real insight into what India is really like and what Indians think, unlike the English papers in Delhi or Bombay, which are not that poor.

2. Huge sections of the population believe in astrology and honestly consider it a science. Some years ago Hindu astrologers predicted dire consequences for the world because eight planets were coming together on a particular day. It is difficult to imagine today the excitement it generated all over the country, the dark forebodings of doom and gloom, the agitated minds, the attempts to avoid disaster through worship, sacrifices, donations, the nonstop mass chanting of Mantras and all. A recent news item: The

University Grants Commission proposes to start graduate courses in Astrology in Indian universities. This is the highest body of eminent intellectuals controlling higher education in the country. If these gentlemen can be so superstitious as to believe in astrology, I can forecast (without being an astrologer) that even God will not be able to save this country. If they decided to do this only due to political pressure, their timidity and sycophancy leave no hope for India to be saved. I beg no pardon for my understatement.

3. In a most modern manufacturing plant in India, I saw a temple of Melody Maataa--a Mother goddess few have heard of. Workers wanted that. Can anybody count how many Mother Goddesses are worshipped in various parts of India? More important, does any preacher-scholar-saint ever clearly oppose such anti-religious superstitions?

4. I don't want to describe the stupid things Devout Hindus do when, during an eclipse, two devil planets are believed to swallow the sun or the moon.

5. A man claimed he lived on sunlight for 411 days without food. Photosynthesis without chlorophyll? We don't know. He got a lot of adulation and publicity.

6. The famous magician, P.C. Sirkar, once met Shri Sai Baba, the spiritualist whose followers are counted in millions. The Baba, as is his reputation, waved his arm and produced from nowhere a piece of a popular Bengali sweet. Sirkar said he would rather have another sweet; and he too waved his hand, produced it from nowhere and respectfully offered it to the Sai Baba. He said to Baba, 'We both perform the same acts. The only difference between us is that I am honest enough to call myself a magician.'

7. One of the principal causes of our poverty is our low productivity. At a middle management level in India, I wasted almost half my working time affixing signatures to papers that I had no time, inclination or need even to read. Working in America at a comparable level, I was required to spend hardly a few minutes for any routine daily signatures. Could we not simplify our procedures in India? No. Part of it was the law; part of it was routine and rigid hierarchy. In India, my small office of ten clerks was ably assisted by three office-boys performing vital tasks---one fetching drinking water, one turning over the papers when the officer was signing them and the third----well, management practices in India will need a separate book. But please trust me: mine was considered one of the best managed companies in my area in India!

8. A few years ago we heard stories of the idol of Lord Ganesh actually drinking milk. The wonderful "scientific" theories advanced and believed by educated people as well as common men would dazzle any real world scientist and put him to shame.

9. Our indigenous system of medicine dominated the health field for centuries. While pulse reading is important, it is the height of gullibility to believe that most complex diseases like cancer or typhoid can be diagnosed with pulse reading only. Recently a Vaidya himself had the courage to admit in public that this is a sham to impress the public. How long did the sham last? Only a couple of thousands of years.

10. A 'possessed' guy claims clairvoyance. He facilitates people connecting and talking with the souls of their dead relatives. All the while he asserts that his capacity is science based—he does not believe in myths, he says he denounces miracles. And people believe it all! Our people's obsessive fixation with most things supernatural---souls, angels, ghosts, gods, Brahma, everything---amazes nobody in India.

11. Keeping insanitation alive, non-hygiene widespread, drinking water infected and foods adulterated, we show magnanimity in building ultra-modern hospitals. Don't we need to build more public toilettes than hospitals? I saw a city in India where the faint smell of chlorine gas from a chemical plant was routine. In another city, foul smell from a sewage treatment plant constantly filled the air. I can name both the cities, since I happened to visit them both. And these were not just random incidents.

How debate is conducted on important issues of public policy tells us a lot about the psychology of the public. Regarding equality for women in public life: In America, they discuss breaking the corporate glass ceiling, preventing overt and covert discrimination and stopping sexual harassment in the workplace. In India we discuss about reservation quotas for women, we raise slogans in mass processions and hold up the working of parliament. The sounds are deafening, the fury is passionate, the stance of political parties is hypocritical and any action is often shelved. Superficiality rules the roost. We don't trust experts;

everyone thinks he is an expert. In contrast, in America, even minor questions like controlling deer population get thorough public debate and discussion with both sides represented, often side by side, to facilitate a comparative evaluation. As for important issues of public policy, one has to live and work in America for a long time to appreciate how deeply, how much in detail, with what passion and yet with how much tolerance the issues are decided.

Truth be told, most of our standard intellectual responses to debatable issues are, well, standard. And that, precisely, is the problem. There is no attempt at original thinking, information gathering or processing, forget about interpreting correctly. All that we see are stereotyped, stale reactions expressed in arresting words but hollow to the core. We shout a lot of slogans. What is worse, we think slogans. It is interesting to watch how even the educated and intelligent Indians discuss serious issues in groups. A real life discussion, condensed for space, went essentially as follows in a group where nobody really believed in the caste system:

A: We Hindus are not united as Muslims are. Is caste a factor?

T: Even Muslims have castes. I once met a---. (Is the order of magnitude in castes the same in both?)---- We should not blame ourselves. -- Examples---

K: Even Christians have many differences. ----Examples, anecdotes---

V: Caste differences are too much with us. I have seen even during natural disasters.

T: There are no caste differences in the Kumbha Mela.-----

P: Some people have the habit of criticizing Hindu religion unnecessarily.--they call us polytheists and idolators. (diversion) We are neither. Westerners call us these and we sheepishly agree. -- (wounded pride?)

V: What are you trying to say? --------- (Hot words)

B: Quarreling about unity is not the way to promote it. (compromise?)--quotation---

P: Ganesh was a uniter between Shiva and Vishnu. (unverifiable mythology)---

A: I am sorry to start the topic inadvertently. (frustration at futility of discussion)

Now consider carefully: What was achieved in the discussion? A lot of sound, little light, no conclusion. The short answer to the initial question may be simply: "yes" (or "no"); but no one really answered it. Our intellectuals are fond of splitting hair even when they are basically in agreement with each other. Look at the quality and relevance of the arguments; the wounded pride against assumed criticism; guesswork from mythology; eagerness to relate anecdotes. People will make up in irrelevance what they lack in substance, wasting precious time. When X discusses events, Y dwells on motives and Z dilates on causes. When the question is 'whether', people will dilate on 'why'. They cannot see different orders of magnitude--What percentage of Hindus practice caste differences and what percentage of Muslims or Christians? Why mention a drop of water when talking about a torrent? Somebody will have nothing to say, but he will insist on saying it anyway. Another will insist on relating anecdotes in lengthy detail. All the above were highly respected scholarly individuals, three of them Ph.D.[s] This kind of exchanges is quite typical of what goes on in intellectual circles among our people. It is impossible and exasperating to discuss a serious issue meaningfully in most Indian groups. If you ever attended meetings in America, you will surely realize the contrast.

This is only a random illustration and my purpose is only to illustrate the trends that are noticeable so frequently in Indian gatherings. We have many individually brilliant people and the trend of discussion could have been different in any specific case. But we do observe that our people find it difficult to focus on the real topic, most are fond of anecdotal statements and are fond of arguing minor egoistic detail even when they are essentially in agreement on the main issue.

Cars do not make as much sense in India as in America for various reasons. In an overpopulated country with rudimentary infrastructure of roads, paucity of imported fuel and sky-high air pollution, the sensible way is expansion of public transportation and encouragement to bicycles. Yet we know how many new models of cars have been coming up in recent years. A blind imitation of rich nations is the order of the day, illustrating our inability to think for ourselves. I am not against cars; they cannot be avoided.

But with all our constraints, should we not discuss the matter threadbare in depth and then decide? How does it help to put the cart before the horse; or to put car making before road building?

We had huge debates on Prohibition. America started prohibition in 1920 and abandoned it as a failure in 1934. Did we learn anything from their experience? Are we fond of reinventing the wheel? Victorian morality is dead in the west but we go on arguing passionately, not realizing how it is linked with industrialization, urbanization, liberation of women and their new found economic independence. Do we not tend to fish only in shallow waters?

Cow slaughter is a difficult issue in India. Without taking a judgmental position, I would like simply to ask the following: Is the war waged in the name of morality, animal health, public health, food, or fighting faiths? What makes one animal good and another bad? Is the problem in cruelty, abuse, illegality or economics? Have we found out a rational way to explain which animals should be banned for killing and for which reasons? Does it help anybody to make such an important issue an emotional one? Intelligent people find answers to such questions and then decide policy. Irrational people try to force the issue one way or the other through slogans, processions, street fights or sentimental outbursts.

We cannot distinguish symbols from real substance, whether it is idol worship or economic policy. Gandhi used Khaadi, the cloth from hand spun yarn, as a weapon of public awakening, mass mobilization, and temporary employment relief for jobless people in the lowest rungs of the economic ladder. It was a symbol of rebellion against a foreign power. It has no long term economic meaning, whether he himself intended it or not. But foggy thinking has clouded the issue ever since. We used Khaadi as serious economic policy, as a competitor to modern industry and we propped it up with subsidies. In a misguided effort to protect jobs, government subsidized bad quality and inefficiency. Artificial props and gimmicks do not work. Reality does catch up. We know the debacle today--modern textile industry is critically wounded. After the mist shrouding our collective consciousness clears up with the passage of time, then and only then, do we realize that the goose that lays golden eggs does not store eggs where we thought it did.

We have problems with Pakistan. 1. Our statesmen repeat ad nauseum that India and USA are the two biggest democracies in the world. But big is not necessarily beautiful. It will be more productive to emphasize Pakistan's theocracy versus India's secularism. This is rarely done with effect. 2. In talking about state sponsored terrorism, why do we not emphasize non-Kashmir related terrorism? Kashmir may be arguable, the other one is not. Which approach will appeal more to the international community? 3. If the opponent harms us through covert acts, why is it that we cannot pay him back in his own coin? Perhaps our diplomacy needs to be more diplomatic and our intelligence services more intelligent.

The entire edifice of our actions and ideas is based on belief, assumption and faith--anything but disciplined thought. How can such people advance? Hindu society is highly receptive to silly behavior if it is in connection with God or religion. It accepts or rationalizes it as faith, devotion, or yearning for God. When we meet people who do not gladly suffer common sense, do we need to suffer them gladly or celebrate and honor them by elevating them to the level of piety? But we do have a love for unattainable grandiosity---world peace, ultimate knowledge, universal happiness. The heart and soul of our philosophy is just that---heart and soul, not brain. No reason, no balance. We need a better rationale for conclusions that are treated as self-evident. Literary adornment by imaginative interpreters or verbosity is no substitute for valid argument and analysis. Our thirst for clear unambiguous conclusions remains unquenched by nuanced close calls of word play. The entire landscape is cluttered with inconsistent and downright unbalanced actions.

An apple once fell down from a tree. A man had the genius to ask: Why? Why down, why not up? And the universal Law of Gravity revolutionized the world. Apples of health, wealth, power, progress, ambition, everything---fell away from the beautiful tree of our ancient culture, one by one, and disappeared. Nobody even noticed. None cared. None asked why.

Individual psychology to a considerable extent is a product of the social system, not just a matter of genes. Society and individuals react and influence each other in various ways. Individuals find it difficult to outgrow the culture they have been nurtured in. How can politicians or scientists deal with the country's problems when the ideological landscape is tilted in the direction of doing nothing, expecting nothing, and tolerating everything?

Remember what we discussed so far regarding our regression, cultural traits, our literature and our religion. The correlations are obvious and striking. They cannot be accidental. But can we think for ourselves? Can we think clearly? If we can, and we did not do it earlier, is it not time to do it now? It is best to admit---and I hope we can muster the courage to do it---that an intellectual gap exists and it is best to find ways to address it. Until we do that, India will not really advance into the modern world.

20. A CIRCLE THAT SPINS
The Logic Hinductive

The way Hindus have been accustomed to think and argue about their philosophical ideas is grandiloquent, yet circumlocutory and ambiguous. The culture that produced some of the greatest logicians in the distant past suffers today from illogical ideas and does not even know it. Hindu arguments using impressive words go round and round in circles. The practical result has been lack of clarity and directness in thought and action in most areas. This chapter demonstrates how. Examples include fasting, idol worship, burden of scholarship, lack of precision and more.

Logic is a strange discipline. Like statistics and bathing suits, it often reveals what is obvious and conceals what is interesting. The cynical Murphy's law on logic propounds: 'Logic is a scientific system of arriving at wrong conclusions with complete confidence.' It is often misused to argue on both sides of a controversial issue. A governor was accused of misusing his official helicopter for personal work. "What could I do," he said, "I had no other means of conveyance. My daughter was using my official car for her graduation party." Even God can be illogical. After death, a priest was consigned to hell while a taxi driver was sent to heaven. God explained His logic to the protesting priest, "When you preached, people slept; when the taxi driver drove, people prayed." But such issues are for expert logicians. They argue and argue and finally agree to disagree about the real sense of logical statements; but we common people have common sense. So we will use that. (I hope you will not ask me to define it logically).

Hindu philosophers have a peculiar set of logic. Let me illustrate: Say you are speaking with a Hindu scholar. The talk can proceed somewhat along the following lines:

Hindu Scholar: Hinduism is a scientific religion. (What is 'scientific'?)

YOU: Do you mean to say that its truths can be proved like scientific theories?

HS: Why do you need proofs for everything? (Question is side stepped)

YOU: Can you give an example to show its scientific basis?

HS: Yes, our sages said centuries ago that God resides even in the smallest of creatures and plants. Your scientists have only now found out that plants have life.

YOU: When people eat plants, do they eat a part of God? You sacrificed animals at the altar. That is no way to show respect to God.

HS: Don't look at what some ignorant people are doing. Look at the real substance. Our philosophy is great. We believe in immortality of the soul. (Diversion)

YOU: Yes, you do, but no other religion believes in rebirth. Whom shall I believe in? I want to believe in all. But they preach many contradictory ideas.

HS: All are paths to God. Put your faith in whomever you trust. (Faith, not reason)

YOU: But faith is not science. Faith is religion. You first said Hinduism is scientific.

HS: Hinduism is not a religion; it is a way of life. (Remember how this talk started? We are back to square one).

-----And so it goes on. Most discussions move this way. They can use different forms or different words but in essence, they always go round and round in circles. In Hindu logic, the shortest distance between any two points is never a straight line—it is a circle; sometimes even an oval.

Deductive and Inductive Logic are well-known. But the third branch is what I may call Hinductive logic! It is a distinctive contribution of Hinduism to world philosophy and needs to be explained. It is based neither on deduction nor on induction, but rather on circumlocution. It constitutes a distinctive art form in itself. Strange as it may seem, its bright light was not a Hindu but a chemist named Kekule. It is said that he saw a serpent in a dream, moving round and round to catch its own tail. (This gave him the brilliant idea of a ring structure for Benzene, the basic aromatic chemical.)

You can never catch a Hindu philosopher by his (coat) tail. Nor can he catch the tail of his own argument in the Hinductive brand of logic. The argument may be self-contradictory but it keeps moving. It changes direction constantly and so moves in circles when it moves at all. It may not advance but it remains in motion; it may jump tracks but it is sustained. Question: What will be the distance covered in five minutes at a speed of a hundred yards per minute? Answer: 500 yards, if it is a running horse. Zero, if it is a running (Hinductive) argument, going in a circle. A Hindu lost his faith once and became an atheist. His new belief was: There is no God and Krishna is His incarnation.

Only a small fraction of our important beliefs is based on reasoned argument or disciplined logic. Hinductive logic can go directly from an unwarranted assumption to a preconceived conclusion. Facts are molded to make them servants of ideology----bend them, amend them, reinterpret them, invent them, exaggerate them, but by all means make them acceptable. Stylistic circularity creates an illusion of logical grandeur. The striking feature of our logic is the logic of Alice in Wonderland, where matters are as they are, because it is said that they are.

Idol worship: Our pundits show remarkable plasticity as per convenience. Example: A scholarly saint will go to a temple daily, often not eating food without first having Darshana (sight) of the idol of his God. He will give a ritual bath to the God. (Why does God need a cold shower?) He will dress up the idol, decorate it with jewels, fall at its feet, in short, he will make a lot of fuss around the idol as if the idol is the real God incarnate. When in a discussion he cannot defend idol worship, he will say idol is only a symbol; and that a layman needs a concrete symbol to visualize or conceptualize God. But he is not a layman. He is a scholar, he meditates, he preaches that knowledge alone can lead to God. Still he performs all these rituals. Some excuses deserve points for creativity but most often they are bad logic; or intellectually dishonest attempts to defend the indefensible.

Our learned men can be quick change artists like the pharmacist in the following story: A woman asked him for arsenic to kill her unfaithful husband. He replied, "Sorry, I can't sell you poison even if your husband is cheating." The woman then pulls out a picture of her husband embracing the very pharmacist's wife. He turns pale and replies, "Oh, I did not realize that you had a prescription!"

Idol worship lies at the root of a lot of ritual and perversion in Hinduism. How do billions of non-Hindus carry on without idols as symbols? Are Hindus less imaginative and less able to focus on the abstract? If yes, why Meditation? If no, why encourage idol worship? Why do the best of Hindu scholars and saints need idols as symbols of God? Do they make all the fuss over idols just for a show in the interest of the common people? We argue eloquently that substance is more important than symbol. Yet in fact, we treat symbol as the real substance. We spend trillions on statues and temples when millions of people die like dogs in the streets. All this for a symbol? Our malleable logic defends hypocrisy and glorifies symbolic actions. Idolatry---chasing shadows and symbols---has penetrated and pervaded our consciousness, our outlook, our intelligence and our attitudes. And this has caused more harm to India than the mere ritual of idol worship by itself.

Our logic is a process where a simple clear truth gets so twisted out of shape that a stone cold sober person could think he was drunk. Circumlocution, presumptive adaptation, abundant equivocation and imaginative redefinition are the weapons used with abandon. An untruth is repeated so often that it goes unchallenged. Certain phrases through mindless repetition become cant that bewitches us. We are a nation of nitwits. We like spoon-fed slogans. If one states one's legends often enough, loud enough, long enough, they become gospel truth to the gullible. Nobody ever invented a weapon more efficient than our lunatic logic.

The tragedy of India today is not its problems. The real tragedy is the inability of its opinion makers to think clearly about things that any western teenager with average intelligence will understand in an instant. Some of these things are: A society whose best brains are concerned more and more with the quality of the soul rather than the quality of its military or government is not likely to win wars. Also, a society whose intellectuals are unwilling or unable to appreciate such an obvious fact is least likely to advance in the world in any field.

Let us see some concrete examples of warped logic in practice. Some Hindus eat tastier and more interesting food on a fasting day than on a normal day. How do they justify this? "Well, everybody should act as per his capacity and faith." Other Hindus cannot eat anything at all. How do they justify extremely strict fasting? "Well, it purifies the soul, burns the sins", and so on. How do they justify eight, ten, thirty, even a hundred consecutive strict fasts? "Well, to die fasting is the sure way to liberation of soul". How do they justify asking growing young children to fast? Are they not too young to understand spirituality? Does it not hurt their bodies and minds? "Well, it strengthens their minds. Spirit is more important than flesh. They are lucky to get a religious bent of mind from earlier births". But don't the scriptures say that without spiritual knowledge, none can get salvation? How about malnutrition? How about pregnant mothers fasting? "Well, fasting actually is good for health, that is a scientifically proved fact; but you believers in western materialism will never understand!" End of argument.

Every year thousands of people, especially Jains, including kids and pregnant women, undertake such extreme form of fasting---not a grain of food----for eight or more consecutive days. They are honored by taking them out in processions on overcrowded public roads in animal drawn carriages. Group dances in the middle of the traffic and noisy music bands are a regular accompaniment to the processions. It is a proven fact that without morning breakfast, children are not able to concentrate at school and do not learn well. In American schools breakfast programs are considered desirable as academic support. Studies have shown connections between malnutrition in children, lower IQ scores and arrested social and emotional development. But in a poor country with millions of half fed undernourished children, we commit the sin of encouraging children to skip all meals for several days in the name of religion. We never realize the fact that starving the body can starve the mind, whether it saves the soul or not. Starvation even in adults has not only physiological but also psychological repercussions. Self flagellation, depression, binge eating, anorexia and bulimia---all have been recorded.

Many apologists of our glorious culture will not even admit the fact of the inferior status of women in Hindu society. They will defend Rama's action in asking the devoted Sita to enter a fire just to prove to the wide world that she was chaste. Even after she passed the ordeal successfully, Rama banished the unsuspecting pregnant wife to a forest based on a crazy man's stray overheard remark. As if a casual remark can dictate state policy! He did not accept her for the second time too, after 12 more years in the forest! She had to ask the earth finally to swallow her. And all this while, the great man professes his eternal love for her! Coming from an incarnation of God, all these actions are so very repugnant to common sense that only the Hinductive brand of logic can defend the indefensible. We say that Rama was an incarnation of God. But when we cannot defend his actions, we say he was a human after all! We evaluate his actions alternatively as human or as divine, depending on our expediency. Faith trumps reason, devotion trumps common sense. Warped logic concocts specious arguments to justify, even glorify, a divine man's wrong decisions.

Our cultural enthusiasts believe so passionately in the equality of the sexes that they went to unusual lengths to demonstrate their beliefs. Like branding her impure for several weeks after she delivered a child. Like prohibiting her from reciting a sacred Mantra. Like shaving off her hair when her husband died. Like disqualifying her for salvation simply because she is a woman. A most popular Hindu blessing to good women means : May your husband outlive you !

We are taught to live with opposite and contradictory messages. Everywhere we look, we see statements that are circular and self-defeating. Consider the interpretations of the Gita. One day we listen to (Shankar) a story advocating spiritual Knowledge or the search for truth (Gyan Yoga) as the only sure way to God. The next day we hear (Vallabha) that love for and Devotion to God is better than all the dry scriptures of philosophers and learned men. Next you hear a sermon (Tilak), emphasizing good Actions in contrast to either knowledge or devotion. All three routes are preached by highly respected personalities with great oratorical flourish. Westernized Hindu scholars like to call the Gita intellectual, to make it sound appealing to modern minds. All scholars can and do quote extensively and impressively from scripture and insist that only their interpretation is right.

If you are bold or silly enough to ask for clarity, compromisers set to work. Their reply is quite standard and predictable: 'There is no contradiction. All routes are good in their own place; you choose what suits you.' If I had the capacity to make such fine choices, why did I come to you for guidance in the first place? And if you, the most learned scholars, argue so violently among yourselves and cannot arrive at a conclusion, how can a common man like me decide such philosophical issues? At the end of all discussion, search for guidance and for truth, if a man is finally to choose whatever suits him, what is the point of it all, anyway? Mental gymnastics? Endless equivocation? The common man is back to square one, from where he started. And yet all orators emphatically declare that our Hindu scriptures give clear and practical guidelines for common people to lead their everyday life. Any doubt is parried with general assurances that the guru is highly learned, divinely blessed and hence infallibly right; and the doubter gets consequently consigned to the category of a childish ignoramus.

Should a doctor prescribe a specific medicine to a patient after checking on him, or should he ask him to take whatever it is that suits him? Are all medicines the same? If I decide that only the Devotional path suits me, am I not prone to neglect good conduct, effective action or good inquiry? What will be the overall effect on a society the vast majority of whose members concentrate on singing devotional hymns, performing worship and ritual day in and day out?

They declare that 'all paths lead to God; you can mix them too; in any proportion you like.' But if Right path is essential, how can all paths be Right? Do all paths in real life lead to the same place? Among those that lead to the same place, are all equal? As a matter of fact, Knowledge and Devotion are not complementary paths to God, as popularly believed. The former assumes Non-Duality and the latter its exact opposite--Duality. Just think. If I am a part of God, I cannot worship or pray to essentially myself; and I cannot ask for favors or grace being done to myself by myself. Being a part of God is different from becoming God. Attaining God is different from pleasing Him.

When two intelligent and honest persons are able to argue on both sides of a controversial problem, we can safely assume that the problem is far from settled and that the jury is still out. Can we privately pick and choose a few from among antiquated dictums and suppress doubts about the rest? Religion surely is not a restaurant menu---you select the dish you like. If you are free to selectively pick up what you like in your religion and reject the rest, it is easy to imagine where it will all end. It will end in a free for all. That is exactly what has happened with Hinduism. We treated our religious principles like a restaurant menu, we circumnavigated around what did not suit our taste, we got rid of good ideas and we retained bad traditions. We pick and choose; we feign modernity and progress; and congratulate ourselves on our own broadmindedness.

But not only the paths are different, the goals too are different. Concept of Liberation as a goal varies a lot. Aurobindo's goal is to attain what he calls 'supra-mental consciousness' through Perfect Yoga. Rajneesh aims at dissolution of bonds and inhibitions. Ramakrishna, Raman Maharshi, Mahesh yogi, Krishnamoorthy, all preach different paths as well as different definitions of Liberation.

It is convenient and expedient in the spirit of rambunctious Hinduism simply to let people believe what they want. It does not hurt. It makes you appear broadminded, magnanimous and liberal. It covers all eventualities. There is only a small problem: You don't know where you stand. Forever you remain perplexed, split, unable to act decisively. Like the pleasantly confused, wavering, blushing Hindu bride when she meets her future husband for the first time, as described most beautifully by the great Kalidasa: "She (Parvati) did not go and she did not tarry." Well, we Hindus cannot go. Neither can we tarry. We dither and hesitate. We waver and vacillate. We dilly-dally and can never act decisively. That is our history.

What kind of effect can an inconsistent logic produce on us? Assume that you are a devout Hindu, a scientist at NASA. At home in the morning, you chant your Mantras which may refer to anything like the Shesha Naga holding the earth on his head; or Lord Vishnu lying at the bottom of the sea. You believe in the myths and truths of your religion with more or less passion. When you arrive at the office, it is satellites and rockets that you deal with. You have to hang your beliefs on a peg outside the office, along with your jacket. You don the robes of science and reason. In the evening you again pray or listen to a discourse on the Moon god, Rahu and Ketu and all. Can you do all these? Can you put your brains on rational and irrational modes alternately and switch them On/Off at will? Obviously not, but you will have to do it.

Something similar has been happening for centuries to all Hindus. Life calls for practical common sense actions in real life. Religion calls the world an illusion. Imagine the cognitive crippling required for otherwise intelligent people to juggle such logical incompatibilities. This sort of daily dichotomy produces a certain kind of confusion and duality. People develop split personality, even hypocrisy, unknown to themselves. Why do we see so much hypocrisy in Indian life? The short answer is: Because hypocrisy is ingrained in us through unreal contradictory philosophy. Examples: 1. You are the soul that feels no pain, so forget pain. But pain is a reality to you. 2. Respect the Guru. But you happen to hate him personally for some reason. 3. Money is always bad. But you need money and love it. Synthetic sermon and deceptive devotion elevated to high pedestals have created a therapeutic society in India.

We criticize Hindi films but watch them anyway. An intelligent Indian dissociates himself from stupid mythical stories but listens to them anyway. Not only does he listen, he relates the same stories to credulous audiences, not believing in the stories himself. I personally know several such intelligent persons, some Ph. D.s in modern science. They treat their audiences as adults treat kids. It escapes their attention that the audience itself is often educated and intelligent and that irrationalism breeds more irrationalism and a lot of cynicism as well. The hypocrisy, the inconsistency, the wrong logic, are all justified on specious grounds, too difficult for any outsider to appreciate, let alone agree. Often the words of Hindus, who believe themselves to be rational, are similar to what somebody has humorously said: "I am an atheist, thank God." Their actions reflect the Hinductive logic of a man caught speeding: "I am speeding now because I am late to court on another speeding ticket I got earlier."

As a matter of record, out of the six well known Darshanas (schools of philosophy) in Hindu thought, the Poorva Mimansa advocates householder status and the other five argue in favor of monk hood. As a matter of common sense, the idea of dividing life into four Ashramas preached in Hinduism is rudimentary and impractical. This is not only my view; it is also the view of some progressive Hindu saints.

Mention absurd myths and the pundit will ask us to neglect them. Mention Detachment and he will say it is superfluous; what is needed is real Vairagya. Talk of Vairagya and he will say "not bad, but it is only an instrument. We need virtue. Virtue? Action? Devotion? Not enough. Knowledge? Yes, but only about the soul. Soul? Not different from Brahma. Brahma? Well, who can describe Him? You must realize Him yourself. How? By thinking, concentrating, meditating. Meditating in the din of life? Well, detach yourself---And it goes back to where it started from, to continue all over again. Round and round. Like the eternal cycles of birth and death. Like a merry go round. Until it leaves the ground and soars into the limitless sky of endless babble.

More examples of contradictory or circumlocutory arguments may be superfluous. We observe everyday a lot of orthodoxy feigning as faith and faith feigning as logic. A lot of childhood conditioning comes out in the garb of deep philosophical thought. But inconsistent logic masquerading as flexible philosophy is more dangerous than plain old silliness itself. Silliness masquerading as scholarship is more dangerous than plain old stupidity itself. The scarecrow in the famous childrens' story of The Wizard of Oz wants a brain but instead gets a degree. We still need to learn the art of differentiating between the two.

Our scholars are prisoners of their erudition. Scholarship crushes wisdom under its weight. A good scholar can support almost any Hindu principle or practice with a suitable quote from the limitless unauthenticated Hindu literature. Another scholar can do the same for exactly the opposite principle or practice. Examples are: position of women, origin of castes, cow-worship, beef eating. Both the learned men then accuse each other of misconstruing, quoting out of context and worse. The main purpose--- action, conclusion or decision---often gets side-tracked or lost in a torrent of words.

A hilarious story relates how four scholarly pundits arrived at a crematorium; adopted a donkey and a camel as their own brothers; tied them both up securely to each other by their tails, thus starting a loud braying kick-out circus---all this, while supporting their actions through real quotations from real scriptures they had learnt in Sanskrit. Too many years of punditry can be hazardous to one's neurological health. The poet Ogden Nash put it thus: "Here's a good rule of thumb; too clever is dumb." Children play this game: Speak this aloud---Question: How much wood a wood-chucker would chuck, if he would chuck wood all day? Answer: Too much. A similar question can be: How much wisdom a pundit would pluck, if he would pluck our scriptures all his life? The answer is: Not enough. Even if he struck a lot of luck.

We always allowed our scholarship to blot out our intelligence. We mistake scholarship for intelligence. We forget that a database has no discrimination and an encyclopedia has no cerebral cortex. Data collection is diligence, not intelligence; a dictionary is a compilation, not a creation. But our culture has always placed scholarship on a much higher pedestal than intelligence and originality, without clarifying the essential difference. We do not realize that one can be a genius without being a hero; one can be right without being popular; and one can be intelligent without being a scholar. A scholar should not necessarily be presumed to be very intelligent, simply because he has accumulated a lot of information. A silly man can become a scholar sometimes if he has other assets like memory and perseverance. When the learned act dumb, the dumb can look learned. It is well-known that India has the highest number of blind, poor, diseased people in the world. One can safely add one more item to the list: Learned simpletons.

We need to achieve a little more precision and logic in our descriptions and names too. For example, we mimic ideas and call them research. Our industries import and copy foreign technology and call it progress. We mistake fame for talent; submissiveness for goodness; and authoritarianism for authority. We practice orthodoxy and call it our cultural heritage. We have a blind belief and we call it faith. We imagine ourselves to be good simply because we are decent. We think we have an open mind when it is merely vacant. We disguise decadence as spirituality. We practice self-absorption and call it self-knowledge or soul knowledge. We often assign wrong names in wrong places. Like in the case of a hefty bearded gentleman who was walking his three big dogs in a garden. A stranger inquired about their names. He was informed that their names were Ajay Singh, Vijay Singh and Digvijay Singh (all meaning victorious or unvanquished). The stranger, quite impressed, asked, "And what is your good name, sir?" The gentleman replied, "They call me Tommy."

21. THE MOTH-EATEN MIRAGE
How Is Hinduism Different?

If all religions are irrational, how is it that Hindus and Muslims alone remained backward? It is a reasonable question to ask. If our religion held us back and another religion like Christianity worked differently, we must look into the differences. It is no use saying that all religions suffer from the same faults that we do---some do, some don't. As they say in common talk, the devil is in the detail. Hindu religion is very much different from other religions. Hindus promote fantasy, inequality and self-centeredness. They unreasonably subordinate all values to promote one value. They harbor extremist ideas. They are blissfully unaware of contradictions in their own ideas. Hinduism has huge store-houses of such infirmities. Their quantity also affects quality, and in the end, the effects produced on society.

Can we say that some religions are less irrational than others? Comparisons are odious but inevitable in the practical world. Hinduism froze ideologically in the ancient ignorant ages; the Muslim world froze in the irrational Dark Age; Christians ended their freeze at the end of the Middle age. It is clear to any student of comparative religion that Islam is the most ironclad, least flexible, uncompromising and demanding on its followers, as witness the punishments prescribed for apostasy and infidels. Catholics, though traditional, tolerate discussion without compromising much in their beliefs. Protestants tend to discuss and often accept modern ideas, as witness the controversies on divorce and birth control. Hinduism will discuss everything, accept nothing, reject nothing, and will continue for ever not knowing where it arrived because it did not know where it started from in the first place!

Now look who are the most advanced in today's world. Not the Islamic countries. Not India. It is Europe and America, all Christian countries. Again in Europe itself, which countries have been the most dominant and powerful during the last couple of centuries? All protestant countries like England and Germany, not the orthodox Catholic nations like Spain and Portugal. In the American continents, USA and Canada--both Protestant Christian countries—are world leaders, but the Latin American Roman Catholic countries are poor and backward. Japan reformed and modernized Buddhism; Tibet did not. How different both these countries are today! Kamal Ata-Turk modernized Turkey, differentiating it from fundamentalist Islamic Sunni nations like Saudi Arabia. And the difference is there for the whole world to see. Am I generalizing too much? Perhaps; but it does show which way the wind is blowing. The fact is difficult to ignore that only those religions that have pragmatic, dynamic, proactive and reformist ideas are in step with modern progress and prosperity. Those that remained orthodox were left behind. Advancement of a society appears to vary directly with its ability to change its beliefs with changing times.

A supervisor told Jane, his habitually late comer employee, that she was setting a bad example to her coworkers. Instead of correcting herself, she said, "Does not Mary also come late? Is there another door I can use to enter the office?" Faced with serious problems, we Hindus too ask: "Isn't there another religion also like us? Is there another way we can find to hide our infirmities?" Islam shares with Hinduism many backward-looking self-justifying attitudes and to that extent Muslims too have remained antimodern and backward. Hindus in India today need to be quite clear as to which direction they want to go. Do they wish to remain like the backward Muslim society when they assert that Islam displays the same faults as Hinduism does? Or, do they want to change themselves and compete with the advanced societies?

We must have a sense of proportion in viewing differences. I am richer than my neighbor and Bill Gates is richer than I am. Are both differences of the same order of magnitude? No. But if I claim that Bill Gates and I are both rich, I must be less than a reasonable person. When we Hindus claim that other religions are also ritualistic, mythical or irrational, we are displaying something much less than reason. Yet this is one of the most frequently heard arguments in popular parlance.

Actually Hinduism is very different from all other religions in several respects, quantitatively, if not qualitatively. The quantity—the extent and the degree---can affect the quality too. An experienced banker was teaching an apprentice: "If a client owes you 100 dollars, it is his problem; if he owes you a million, it is your problem." Size matters---whether it is the size of shoes, debts, waves, beliefs or fantasies. In real life, there is almost nothing we use, see, wear or eat whose suitability for its purpose is not affected by its size or magnitude. Plato emphasized the "qualitative expression of quantitative law" two millennia ago. When quantitative difference is great, quality itself changes. Ex: Physicists know it well that in the electromagnetic spectrum, X-Rays, Gamma rays, visible light and radio waves appear entirely different to a common man but essentially they are all the same in nature and are represented by the same wave function. The only real difference among them is the difference in their wavelengths. The shorter wavelength of X-Rays makes them more penetrating than the radio waves. Quantitative difference in wavelength creates a huge difference in quality and use.

Too much of anything is not only not good; it can also be bizarre and often harmful. All religions have myths and fantasies; but Hinduism has many more. All religions are illogical but Hinduism is extraordinarily so. All societies have inequalities like racism, even apartheid, but Hindu untouchability is in a class by itself and it continued too long. All religions harbor a few contradictions within themselves but Hinduism is entirely engulfed in contradictions of its own making. These quantitative differences have resulted in real big differences in the effects they produce on their respective societies. I invested money in two of the same family of mutual funds. Both held more or less the same stocks but the varying mix produced widely divergent results. The mix of values propounded by Hindu religion is very different from the mix propounded by other religions. So the results produced vary widely. The prevalence of irrationality, the preponderance of mythology, levels of abstractions, imbalance--all these are very much higher in Hindu religion than in any other. The difference is mainly of degree but the degree is so great that it results in a difference in kind.

That goes for the quantity. Now let us look at the quality. Some of the essential qualitative differences can be summarized as follows.

1. We saw earlier that Hinduism revels in **Fantasy**. More than any other. Most Bible stories like the Good Samaritan and the Prodigal Son are down to earth, practical and believable. Hindu stories like how Lord Ganesh acquired the elephant head are not so. Ancient Greeks and Romans had a few silly stories comparable to ours, but all of them have outlived them long ago. We still cling to them, love to repeat them and want to relate them to our children even in America, under the specious plea that we have the dire need to preserve our culture. Mythology served a useful need when man was an ignorant child in the infancy of civilization. But it is not wise to continue to be a kid all your life. Adults must realize that the best way to confront evil is not through the childlike chanting of Mantras (like Hanuman Chalisa), but through strength and hard work. The few stories I have cited are no isolated examples. Make a list of Hindu stories and the Koran and Bible stories and you will see the difference in the quality and the numbers immediately. Of course, our stories have merits as good stories. But so have Anderson's fairy tales.

How do we illustrate and promote the moral precept of Truth? We have popular stories like those of Harish Chandra and Yudhisthira. Y was such a model of truthfulness that his chariot-wheels always ran about a foot above the surface of the earth, in air. (We already had magnetic levitation before the Japanese ran a train on it! But how about the horses of the chariot?) Once, during a battle, Y had to speak a half-truth, not exactly a lie. That day onwards, his chariot (horses and all) came down to earth forever. Great story, but credible? Only if you have unbounded naivete and faith. Now, it so happens that the 'immoral' Americans too advocate truth and they too have stories. The most famous is about George Washington as a boy. He cut a tree and admitted it. As simple as that. Credible? Very much so. Right or wrong, it is very much practical, possible and probable. It does not need a leap of faith. Our story sounds attractive but it is too esoteric and arcane. The other story is simple but it is credible, convincing. Which would a modern intelligent man like to believe in?

If the same principle can be illustrated without recourse to myth or miracle, it is much better to do so. But we have made it a matter of principle to kill good principles with bad stories. If there is a grotesque way to present a good principle, Hinduism will give itself a hernia trying to find it. We call it illustration and example; in reality it is crudeness and credulity. When we make a habit of it throughout the country, through centuries, and don't bat an eyelid while relating it or hearing it, it is not wrong to ask whether this is faith, credulity, silliness or worse. Hinduism can surely be better than it shows. Our love of fantasy has not remained confined to stories. It has permeated our life and culture. We never notice the fundamental disconnect between life and fantasy. We have a well-marked strain of romanticism in our mindsets. Unreal situations, impractical pursuits, fanciful ideas---all have a strange attraction for our minds. Witness mass popularity of astrology, Hindi films, herbal therapies and a lot of our writings too.

A popular belief in Hindu society is that our scriptures map out a practical way to live life. This is true only for a small minority of them; and only as far as primary ethics is concerned; and that is very welcome indeed. But does the map include what we care about, what we need most to be successful and competitive in the modern age? Communist Russia did not show places of worship in their maps. Hindu India showed nothing but worship in its map of life.

2. We Hindus hardly, if ever, notice **Contradictions** in theosophies. Our religion preaches renunciation, self-denial, control of sensual pleasures. On the other hand, religious practice is supposed to produce and always promises wealth, pleasure, and power. Study the stories accompanying any vows or Pooja (worship). They all promise the very things religion asks you to shun. They tempt you with all possible pleasures of this world as well as the next. In the famous Upanishada story of Nachiketa, the God of Death tempts the boy Nachiketa with a Heaven full of sensual pleasures including beautiful women, riding chariots, sweet music and so on. Swami Vivekanand, a great Hindu saint said, "What are these Heaven ideas but simply modifications of this non-sensical priest craft?" Very well said and true. But the idea of Heaven occurs not only in the Puranas but also in the Upanishadas, whom the great man has praised profusely and justifiably as the quintessence of Hindu thought.

Try to make sense of the words in any Aarati (worship with a lighted lamp in a dish) in a Hindu temple. You will see the most striking evidence of the self-corruption of theosophical culture, hype and hyperbole. A popular Aarati describes a goddess as "the mother of the whole universe, the supreme ruling power." Anybody who worships even once is promised liberation from all sins, achievement of health, wealth and happiness, simply as a reward for singing and clapping. We cannot verify promises of the next world, but it is fairly easy to verify such promises of this world. We don't do even that. We trust, we hope, we pray; and what happens? We continue to be poor and miserable in the face of all promises to the contrary. Any person with the most elementary common sense would say it does not make sense. But we? Well, we are Hindu.

We never notice the contradictions. We believe it all. Our curious logic is similar to the following statement: "I don't believe in astrology because I am a Virgoan; and according to the science of astrology, Virgoans don't believe in astrology." If words do mean anything to us, we should be the first to experience the contradiction between asceticism and acquisitiveness because the former is preached and the latter is promised and practiced. Promising the world to those whom we teach the futility of the world is a crazy idea but it comes quite naturally to us.

Words in Hinduism have ceased to mean anything at all. Words lose all meaning or drown all sense in pious verbosity. Promises and blessings are routinely given when nothing is seriously meant, expected or achieved. Expressing a magnanimous desire for world peace has become a routine exercise devoid of significance or seriousness. We are magnanimous in big things that never happen but stingy in small things that happen daily. A Hindu who has petty quarrels with his family all the time, feels magnanimous when he chants "The whole world is a family." Before devout Hindus start eating a noisy group meal, they recite a prayer: "Om, ---Peace (or Silence), Peace, Peace".

3. **Inequality** of status among castes, sexes, and individuals is routinely denied but actively advocated and preached by Hindu scriptures and saints. Indra-Matang dialogue in the Mahabharat is as clear as

127

a crystal in laying down that a Brahmin must be considered superior by reason of his birth, not by way of intellect or penance. Manu said the same thing. The caste system and untouchability arose as a direct result of such theories. No other religion or society ever elevated inequality among men (or even among its gods!) to such a high pedestal, with such disastrous consequences.

4. The **Self-centered Introvert** Hindu was no match for two aggressive proselytizing religions in history---Christianity and Islam. The former was a driving force for colonization, the latter for conquest. In those days when religious expansion and conversion were the order of the day, Hindus fell far behind, whether they call them themselves good or not. Individuals won, self-absorption ruled, community lost.

5. **Imbalance**: We Hindus lack balance in ideas, though we may preach it in words. Our one-track minds lack Discrimination. Should we always speak the truth? Yes, certainly, most people will reflexively answer. But the indisputably correct answer is: "Certainly not." It is good, not bad, to tell a lie to a criminal to save a good man. When a child starts learning, it is helpful to lie to him with words of encouragement although he may not be doing so well. When an ounce of untruth is the only way to ensure tons of truths to prevail in the end, will you not opt for the ounce? Truth yes, but truth at any cost? Truth under all circumstances? To the exclusion of everything else? The Indian mind conditioned by Indian culture instinctively and unequivocally answers: 'Yes.' It sounds heroic. But the right answer, the reasonable answer, the practical answer for success in life is: Well, it all depends. We cannot and should not always tell the truth, not only for worldly success, but also from logical, emotional or moral considerations.

Reasonable people do not subordinate all values to any single value, whether it is truth, freedom, alms giving, health, safety or virtue. Expanding one freedom can restrict another kind of freedom. Alms giving can be wrong under certain circumstances. Health maniacs can endanger health. Safety at all cost can be unbearably costly. No right is absolute, no duty is a one-way street and no virtue is an unadulterated good. Balancing competing values is a mark of intelligence. Losing all other values to uphold just one value is a sure sign of a one track simplistic mind. We Hindus own that mind.

Our Karna gives alms at all cost, even when he knows he is being framed by his enemy's father. King Shibi kills himself to save a pigeon who sought his protection. Seth Sagarsha kills his only son to feed a crazy monk. They may all sound heroic but do they display an intelligent, discriminating, balanced mind? No. They subordinate all values to only one single value, that too of a dubious nature. That is not real life. Life is all about deciding priorities and making intelligent choices; choosing a lesser evil or a greater good. It is always about a direct or indirect cost benefit analysis, a judgment, a discriminating choice. It is hardly about a simple choice between good and evil. To choose one path or one value at any cost is like a child who will not let go of his favorite toy at any cost, whether or not a better, safer toy is available or not.

In the dawn of civilization when life was much simpler, when basic values in society were being established, emphasizing one value may have a certain need and attraction. Today it is a positive evil. In fiction these stories sound great. In fact they are silly. Stories of one-sided values can make us blind to the other side of truth. We do not have the critical minds to penetrate the skewed morals they preach.

The defining character of the Hindu mind throughout the ages has been its unbalanced one-track approach to the problems of life, lack of proportion and absence of good judgment. We are not trained to make correct discretionary choices. Rama, our eternal role model, exemplifies a single minded devotion to one virtue at the cost of all other virtues. The internecine quarrels of our Rajput rulers showed that they adamantly upheld one virtue at the cost of everything else. This started with characters like Bhishma, our highly respected ideal hero. If he (see Ch. 9) had not paid one-sided attention to a single virtue to the exclusion of everything else, he could have prevented the Mahabharat war. We hear innumerable Hindu preachers eulogizing Bhishma day in and day out; but does anyone have the courage, the good sense, the balance, to point this out? No. Instead they will give you a dozen pretexts and explanations for his entirely unjustified action (siding with evil) and inaction (insult to Draupadi).

The perennial question whether ends justify the means is in essence a question of balancing competing values. If I have no alternative but to steal in order to save my sick hungry mother, the basic question is what to choose between non-theft and filial love, which are both virtues I believe in. Any simplistic answer advocating either virtue to the exclusion of the other will be wrong. If you like democracy and secularism, faced with a difficult choice between an autocratic secular state and a democratic theocratic state, which one would you choose? It depends. Life is full of difficult questions of this type. Like children, we Hindus are also unable to understand the incompatibility of many desires----truth and self-interest; non-violence and power; self-sacrifice and wealth.

The virtue of emphasizing one virtue to the neglect of all others is its simplicity. Saying "It depends" requires a lot of mental gymnastics. Common people don't relish mental gymnastics. That is how one-track thinking becomes popular. In the heat of battle, single-minded devotion is helpful. Yet it is a fatal flaw in practical life and in a thought process. But we Hindus chose the worst of both worlds: We are eternal equivocators in war (like Arjun---'should I fight?') but over-simplifiers in philosophy (like Yudhisthira---truth only). We need the reverse for success in both. Belief in truth at any cost compels us to adhere always to a single rhetorical standard about the inviolability of that high principle. That, in plain English, is impracticable. And that is exactly why we Indians are "the most hypocritical people in the world." That is not my view; that is exactly what one of the ex-prime ministers of India (M. Desai) said.

Though we chose truth as a simple example above, the same kind of considerations apply to other values. Renunciation and generosity are virtues. But not unqualified virtues that justify the renunciation of all other virtues. When a king empties the entire treasury to donate to an ascetic, he also renounces his duty as a good ruler. We get a heroic donor, a hauntingly beautiful classic poem (Raghuvansham) from the master poet in Sanskrit and a warped view of values in life. The overemphasis our culture placed on renunciation and sacrifice resulted in sacrifice of many other desired values. We also in the end sacrificed our hopes, health, reason, and so on. Most stories in our scriptures are examples of disproportionate response and lack of balance. Mitigating circumstances, balanced judgment and proportional response are hardly considered; more to the point, such a one-sided response is considered ideal.

Our culture is nurtured with underground streams of this kind of extremist thinking that is shrouded well in attractive idealistic verbiage. We are extremists in many respects though we will deny it vehemently. Nonviolence is a good principle. Gandhi said so, Jesus said so, my mother said so. But nonviolence at any cost? To a Ravana? To a mosquito? No way. Sometimes it is good to kill the killers. You can call it virtue, moral superiority or idealism. I prefer to call it imbalance, silliness, moral exhibitionism, naiveté or worse. This kind of attitude has made a virtue of our not being able to see the forest for the individual tree. We, the presumably broad-minded and moderate Hindus, need moderation in the pursuit of extremes. Lack of balance in everything is a sure sign of lack of maturity and may be of low intellect. We always miss a thoughtful and nuanced expression of our values. The primitively traditional Hindu mind exposed to one-sided ideologues for centuries has grown accustomed to thinking in grooves, in single tracks, unable to see the other side. Our culture and religion are clearly responsible for this.

We have learnt many things from Hindu scriptures. But balance is not one of them. We have too much of history, too much of theosophy, too much of too many things. What we don't have is balance. And reason. Our philosophy is slanted, heavily unbalanced, and therefore unreasonable. Since reasonable and balanced thinking is the crux of rationality, you miss rationality and gain everything else. What does it profit a man if he gains the whole world and loses his own power to think for himself? When a man loses balance, he moves a little closer to a simple-minded love of the quick fix. To take opposing factors into account and devise a reasonable and fair solution is a sign of superior intelligence. We display this rarely.

We have grown incapable of balance; our exaggerations feed on themselves; ritual ever widens; the circle of non-reason ever expands. We need to seriously ask ourselves a simple question: Why is it that our beliefs are priceless and worthless at the same time? The simple answer to that simple question is: Simply because they lack balance. And in life, balance is everything. If virtue is the mean between two extremes (Aristotle) and if the middle path is the right path (Buddha), then the mean or the middle is best arrived at, not by facile judgments or overstatements, but by a process of rational thought and discrimination.

We think lack of balance is idealism of sorts. We also think that overreacting to events to espouse the other extreme is the best way of responding to them. We don't grasp that nothing in life is pure black or pure white----we always have different shades, tones and intensities of gray or brown. But we espouse values that are color blind. The truth is that all truths are half truths----there is hardly an unalloyed truth in life. When we shall realize this, we shall graduate into the adult world of mature men from our juvenile world of 'good-guy-bad-guy' kid stories.

With a good helping of sincerity and talking from a high moral pedestal in India, you can sell just about anything to anybody if you mention just enough truth to make it barely plausible—and this even to those who know better. "You need not tell them falsehoods, just tell them incomplete truth, appeal to their moral good sense and to their emotions, not to their minds. You can easily get them to view any vastly complicated matter entirely through simplistic colored glasses of your choice. What they will see may not be false but what they will miss will be crucial."

Our highly respected preachers hold discourses so often. They relate the same old mythical stories with oratorical flourish. Each saint impresses with his own interpretation, which in most cases is a well-worn cliché suitable for children learning basic morality with a little dose of common sense. Stories that are obviously indefensible, romantic, mythical or even plain statements are called metaphors or allegories, to be interpreted at will (Ex: Breaking the bow page 79). Few among the audience can look beyond words to examine the real ideas behind them. None can or will question the idea even when it is one-sided or unreasonable because people are too polite to contradict such famously pious saints. So the cycle goes on.

Throughout this book we have listed and analyzed how orthodox ancient Hinduism, much more than any other religion, promoted beliefs, attitudes and practices that hindered India's progress---many beliefs like fatalism, several negative attitudes like detachment from real life and innumerable practices like casteism. All these acting in conjunction for several centuries weakened our society and kept it backward and poor. Think of all the issues we discussed so far and then ask yourself: Perhaps, just perchance, is it possible that constant defeat, disaster, backwardness, poverty, constantly falling way behind in the race of life---all these---are God's way of telling people that they harbinger too much irrationality in themselves? Those of us who are accustomed to watching frequent displays of public frenzy in India already know that something does not jive. Something is amiss. Something just does not connect. How can we find out? Let us look at psychometrics next.

22. DEATH OF REASON
Measuring the Immeasurable

Examining different components of intelligence like critical faculty and clarity of thinking, this chapter will illustrate a very unpleasant reality: Although lots of individuals are quite brilliant, we Hindus as a group in a statistical sense, display several characteristics of arrested mass intelligence. Centuries of compounded growth in non-reason robbed us of our rationality. Disuse damaged our intellect.

Two psychologists wrote a famous but controversial American best seller in the nineties: The Bell Curve. Their interesting new conclusions on the testing of intelligence in various ethnic groups were highly debatable but revealing. They said in effect that in psychological testing, black and Hispanic groups displayed lower Intelligence Quotients than white Caucasians. Since neurobiology and genetics are clear and emphatic that there is no innate natural difference in mental faculty among human groups, this observed difference must be a difference arising out of culture and nurture. In spite of great advances in designing intelligence tests, we have not yet reached a point where we can use psychometrics with enough confidence as to its validity and applicability under varying conditions. Scientists in this highly specialized discipline warn us to use and interpret these tests with utmost reservations. Those of us with less impressive scientific credentials will therefore have to fall back upon more conventional methods of judgment.

We do know children who appear to be normal but whose genes for neurological development work improperly. We also know adults normal in every respect but for their inability to think logically or quickly. We also see educated people who are knowledgeable but not especially intelligent. It is almost impossible today to quantify or measure such small differences. Nevertheless everyone knows a retarded person when he meets one. We subjectively but instinctively grade and evaluate people. There is more than a grain of truth in such instinctive evaluations. And we could not be much wrong most of the time; otherwise we could not select a better lawyer or doctor; or a university could not select better students.

How do we judge a person in daily life? It would have helped if God had written the word 'stupid' on the forehead of even the silliest among us. But He left it to us to find out. We talk to a man, observe his words, actions, decisions, everything, and instinctively make an evaluation in our own minds regarding his mental caliber. It is a subjective process, so we can be wrong or right in our judgment. Others may have a contrary opinion too. Even then there are certain points on which most of us will generally agree even on this controversial subject of measuring intellect: 1. Group psychology is different from individual psychology. Statistical concepts play an important role in groups. My group may be intelligent as a whole, but I can be a model of stupidity. 2. Although intelligence is difficult to measure and still more difficult to interpret, we need to start with some kind of comparable scale to adopt and use in order to discuss it meaningfully with clarity and precision. IQ is such a scale and we will use it here for discussion and comparison only, keeping well in mind its limitations. 3. As the common saying goes, stupid is as stupid does. We can often obtain fairly realistic conclusions from the way men think, act and behave.

Discussing intelligence any time is hazardous, tactless and damaging. Praise can enhance self-esteem or vanity; criticism can hurt as nothing else can. But if criticism does not deliver sobering news, reality eventually will. For every self-deception, there is a moment when reality bites. Self awareness is often a prerequisite for self-improvement. Books like the Bell Curve perform the thankless task of telling some people how far short of normal they fall; and how all men and all societies are not found equal in mental capacity. It remains an awkward fact although there may not be many people rash enough to utter it because of the likely misunderstandings about its causes---genetic or cultural. All cultures are not created equal. Even if cultures were equal, the way men respond to their cultural environment is never identical. Because of all these reasons, groups and cultures have different behavioral and intellectual characteristics.

Actually people know all this instinctively. Although they argue against a book like the above one, people in the privacy of their homes do say that it has more or less some truth in it.

Intelligence is complex, difficult to define accurately and experts do not agree among themselves. It is not a single ability but a successful convergence of many cognitive functions. Conceptualization, Retention, Reasoning and Judgment are required attributes of intelligence. Without entering into technicalities, some of the characteristics or components of intelligence can be described as follows: 1. Critical faculty or Skepticism. 2. Ability to focus on real issues, without diversion or distraction. 3. Ability to differentiate between the chaff and the grain. 4. Verbal or language skills. 5. Conceptual skills. 6. Memory 7. Hand-motor coordination. 8. Quantitative and logical reasoning. 9. Quicker grasping. 10. Ability to think independently / originality / refusal to follow the herd. 11. Imagination. 12. Clarity of thought or lack of confused thinking.

It is best to approach irrationality in society as a systemic problem and not as a genetic one. Our genes give us the potential to make us intelligent but nurture and culture influence our brains from the day we are born and help transform our genetic potential into intelligence. Environment creates profound differences, not in innate intelligence, but in the practical manifestation and application of intelligence to the problems of life. The relative importance of genetics and culture is not clearly established but it is universally agreed that physical and cultural environments (malnutrition, childhood) play a tremendously important role in development of our intelligence. Genetics need not concern us here for two reasons: 1. We cannot measure the IQ of a child as soon as he is born. 2. Even if we could, there is nothing much we could do to change the genes, apart from praying and eugenics, both of which have not been enormously effective so far for humans. When we compare demographic segments for intelligence, it is therefore best in practice to concentrate on the influence of upbringing on intelligence.

1. Let us now start with the first component of intelligence we listed above, namely, skepticism or **Critical faculty**. In the hierarchy of cognitive skills, critical thinking occupies a high rank. It takes razor sharp intellect to penetrate beyond partisan rhetoric. Simply put, we the credulous Indians have it to a very limited degree. Not in an individual or personal sense but in a group sense, overall. In earlier chapters we summoned ample evidence to demonstrate our traditional mindsets, credulity and uncritical acceptance of presumed theories, stories and sermons. Our inability to sift the truth from the rhetoric originated in the field of our theosophy; we became acclimatized to it over the centuries; and now it manifests itself almost daily in our public life: Our politicians take us for a ride and we believe them. Our enemies cheat us and we are surprised. Our poets use fantastic hyperbole and we take them as gospel truth. Our theosophists describe mirages and we run after them. We have become uncritical zombies and hero worshippers.

2. Let us take the last component or characteristic of intelligence in the above list---**Clarity** of thinking or lack of confused thinking. Do we display this faculty in our public and private dealings? No. I shall give a couple of illustrations.

The original problem of Reservations for Backward classes arose from the age-old exploitation of the lower castes. Before this was adequately addressed, we started talking about reservations based on economic backwardness which is a different issue. Both the issues are complicated enough in themselves. Then came the idea of reservations for women---another complex subject. Can you tackle all these together at the same time? In the state of Gujarat, just for example, backward classes constitute 45 to 55 percent of the population, depending on how you define them. In a country like India, economic backwardness is difficult even to define---let alone estimate---accurately and to everybody's satisfaction. Women are naturally around 50 percent in both categories. How do you make a formula taking all these three categories into account, without converting the majority into a disadvantaged minority? What happens where a backward class person is economically strong and also happens to be a woman? How do you make a practical formula? How do you make it acceptable to all peoples and parties? A state government now talks about reservations for Muslims too. No party has truthfully and honestly addressed these issues in detail and nobody has the honesty, the will or the capacity to think clearly on the problems involved. Yet parliament sessions come to a halt in slogan shouting, pandemonium, fist fights and worse. Did we learn something from how the USA handles what they call affirmative action issues? Not yet.

Our confused thinking is evident on the public questions of cow slaughter, prohibition, economic subsidies and many others. In private life our ideas on celibacy, money and nonattachment are classics in contradictions and fuzziness. Observe carefully when people talk in India: Staunch defenders of democracy will question the competence of the electorate. A writer will praise and criticize democracy in the same breath without finding it necessary to define his own co-ordinates on the complex graph of democracy versus autocracy. Many cannot distinguish between faith and loyalty, values and truths, folklore and history, personal belief and truth. An agitation directed against untouchables starts at the statue of Gandhi, the champion of untouchables. Corruption is conducted and condemned in the same breath. The confused thinking, the lack of clarity, the ambivalence, are evident and omnipresent.

Confused thought breeds confused action. Minds must not be cluttered with irrelevant clichés. But ours are. Sometimes the mere act and speed of making a decision are of critical importance. Confused thought puts brakes on speed. In order to go beyond classic Hamlet type inaction, one needs a certain sharp clear reasoning that a Hindu mind has always been unable to summon. Ideological, intellectual, moral confusion has engulfed us in mazes of our own minds. We find it difficult to think clearly. But clarity of thought is a very important component of intelligence.

3. A third characteristic of intelligence is **Ability to Focus** on real issues or to go to the heart of the problem without getting diverted. Most of us Indians are deficient in this faculty as we saw earlier in Ch. 21 on Logic. We find it impossible to remain focused on relevant issues. People talk at a tangent. You talk of chalk, they talk of cheese. They beat about the bush and you beat a hasty retreat---if they let you.

It will be cumbersome and unnecessary to go into a lengthy discussion of our mental infirmities with respect to every other component of intelligence listed above. It is fairly clear, though a little bit unpleasant, that we are found wanting in most of them. How did we as a society manage to banish such characteristics of intelligent behavior? And this, in spite of our not infrequent individual brilliance? But many persons individually can be bright and yet collectively unwise. A good example is the militaristic Japanese at Pearl Harbor. It took two atom bombs to cure them of their collective madness.

To state the bland truth directly and clearly: We display several characteristics of arrested mass intelligence. This does not mean that all of us are dumb or that none of us is smart. Some of us are individually brilliant; many of us are just average; but the population as a whole, including the teeming millions, not as individuals, but as a group in the statistical sense, <u>displays</u> a lower median and mean IQ on the normalized distribution curve. A representative group of a million average people from advanced countries will in all probability be found to be more intelligent than a similar group from India. Just as a few rich men cannot change the statistics of India's real poverty, a few brilliant individuals cannot compensate for the inexorable irrationality of the masses. The brilliant minority is held back by the massive gravitational pull exerted by the inertia of the huge masses.

The above is only a hypothesis, not a proof---there can be no proof. Such matters are difficult to measure or prove, as we saw. We just have to look at the totality of evidence, make an assessment and find reasons for these problems. But in life what is now proved was once only theorized. Above all, we need to summon the honesty and courage to face the truth however unpalatable it may be. A good question to ask is: Where did this massive intellectual inertia come from?

Physical as well as mental abnormalities in a man or in a society can be nonfatal and can still be subtle and devastating. The subtlety can be too small to be detectable and yet the abnormality may be real. Such a man or society may yet survive but in a devastated state, as our society has been surviving. You may not even call it an abnormality or depreciation. Call it a characteristic or specificity or preponderance. Do we have any such irrational preponderance? The present state of our knowledge does not lead us to a strictly scientific conclusion. However, a little bit of judicious assessment may do no harm and may even suggest possible avenues of research in sociology and psychology.

Though a small deficiency in intellect in an individual may not be disastrous, such collective deficiency accumulated for prolonged periods in a population can be critical, even catastrophic. As we saw earlier, our society has gone through several such catastrophes in history. Though no direct linkage can ever be proved, it is certainly worth looking into whether centuries of unrestricted irrational environment could have played havoc with our minds. This is an effect known as compounding.

Suppose I earn a 10 % compounded interest on an initial investment of 100 dollars and you earn only one percent more or 11 %. If no additional capital is provided, adding only the compounded interest into the account, I shall have 11739 dollars at the end of 50 years and you will have 18456 dollars, almost 57 percent more than what I shall have. The same numbers after 100 years will be 1,378,061 and 3,406,417 dollars respectively. You will have almost two and a half times of what I shall have. The striking part is that 100 dollars grew to more than three million dollars after 100 years. That is the power of compounding. Einstein said, "The greatest mathematical discovery of all time is the power of compounding." What this illustrates is that: 1. Small initial differences in numbers when compounded over long time periods become surprisingly large. 2. The longer the period, the larger the difference. So the small differences need to be investigated and not treated as insignificant.

Suppose people in Group A have a median IQ of 98 and Group B have a median IQ of 95---not much of a difference in real practical terms, considering that IQ can go as high as 160 in a genius and as low as 50 in a retarded person. Now raise both numbers---0.98 and 0.95---to a power of 50 each. The result? 0.364 for A and 0.077 for B. The result in A is 4.7 times or almost five times as high as that in the case of B. The same numbers will be 0.133 and 0.006 after 100 years. Result A is now 22 times of result B. The small initial difference grows into a very big divergence in 100 years. Again, that is compounding.

This illustration proves nothing in itself regarding IQ as such. What it suggests is that seemingly insignificant initial differences between two human groups can multiply into overwhelming differences when transmitted over many generations. (In weather this is called the Butterfly effect.) Therefore these merit investigation, not indifference. Compounding may or may not work here as a recessive genetic disorder in a genetic sense but it is certainly significant in a nurturing, environmental implicating sense. IQ is too complex to be subjected to rigorous mathematical tools like standard deviation and statistically significant variations. This is not surprising. But we need to be aware of the exponential compounding effect of cultural influences on our rationality even where they are not easily perceptible.

98.4 percent of the genes in man are identical with those in the common chimpanzee. What a difference less than two percent variation has made between the two species! Physicists found that if the electric charge on the proton had been only a tiny fraction less, the universe as we know it today would not have existed. Tiny differences in some things, including intelligence, can prove to be critically important!

Many difficulties and problems in everyday life appear to be so common that we do not normally think of them as problems of low intelligence. Yet they are. Two children fell down from a sixth floor window and died. Safety problem? Yes. Negligence? Probably. But consider that a little bit of anticipation, thinking ahead, visualizing possibilities, would have prevented the tragedy by the simple expedient of a window screen or a few protecting bars. Failure to anticipate possible problems can be a sign of just a little lower level of intelligence. A little bit of common sense intellect can often save lives. Two friends decide on a rendezvous, but they neglect to specify precisely either the time or the place in sufficient detail. Anybody can imagine the confusion and the resulting heartburn. Imagine such situations in wartime---a missing bolt in an aero-engine, imprecise location co-ordinates of a submarine, failure to anticipate a leak in a fuel line. Modern war movies often demonstrate such incidents dramatically.

Faith is certainly not stupidity; but a lot of stupidity passes as faith in Hindu society. A woman described a clearly unbelievable incident like an idol of her God bathing or drinking milk or talking to her in person. Personal stories of this kind are a lot more common in India than in other societies. We generally let them pass saying that the person has abundant faith. Do we ever pause to think that probably she is telling a plain lie or just displaying a lower level of intellect? A man often blames his own luck, laziness, negligence or innocence for his own failures; but he would not face the simple fact that those who succeed more often than he does may perchance have better brains. We are all too polite to brand anybody as less than intelligent, so we often call him naïve or gullible or devoted. The real problem oftentimes is silliness. We know that traces of heavy metals like lead and mercury can do irreparable harm to our brains. But in India for two thousand years, concoctions of these metals in indigenous Ayurvedic medicine were believed to cure diseases and impart youth, even immortality. Such beliefs are not unique to us, but their persistence and widespread acceptance are.

We need to think seriously why our society as a whole measures up to a little less than intelligent in our private and public thinking and action.

The old adage 'Use it or lose it' applies as much to our brains as it does to our bodies. Intellectually demanding activities like reading, chess and crossword puzzles delay the onset of Alzheimer's disease. Innovative effort like starting a new hobby or learning a new language in old age has a beneficial effect on the brain. Conversely, passivity or ritualistic activities like watching TV have adverse effect on brainpower. In India tradition, monotony and ritual protect people from using their brainpower. They save them from mental effort and promote intellectual laziness. Disuse damages their intellect.

The causes of our collective mental depreciation lie buried deep in our culture and our upbringing. Both have been decisively influenced by our religious beliefs and practices. Pettiness, peevishness and obsession with trivialities are a constant refrain of everyday life in India. We cannot see the big picture. We get bogged down in petty detail when quick decisions are needed on broad issues. The dominant Hindu philosophy of conformity, withdrawal and detachment is not the best way to promote intellect or action. A closer look at the tangled web of our redoubtable ancient philosophy is in order.

23. THREE HIMALAYAN BLUNDERS
Fields of Dreams in Philosophy

We need to reexamine many ancient ideas in Hindu philosophy in modern context with strong laser lights of realistic reasoning. Our saints had mastered the techniques of mind conditioning and faith strengthening in the garb of reason. Beliefs and practices designed to promote faith were cleverly popularized as logical truths. Preoccupation of entire society with spirituality suitable only for individuals and monks had disastrous long term consequences, intended as well as unintended. Centuries of abstract philosophizing robbed us of our common sense and reason. Individuals were contented; religion prospered; society weakened. Popularly assumed truths in Hinduism----illusionary world, permanent reality, Liberation, Rebirth, realization of God and many others----are at most one-sided truths, more didactic than logically proven.

Hindu society committed three historical blunders of Himalayan proportions in the philosophical field: (A) We mistook poetry for philosophy. These two are very different from each other. Poetry is literature of power; philosophy is literature of knowledge. We discussed this earlier in detail in chapter 16 on "Poetry or Philosophy?" (B) We lost balance. Virtues and values need to be carefully compared, weighed and balanced. In our over-abundant zeal to promote certain values, we forgot that promoting one virtue at the cost of another is not a virtue. This we discussed in the earlier chapter 21 subtitled "How is Hinduism different?" (C) We extrapolated private philosophy for single individuals to apply automatically to entire groups---1. Personal ethics applied to the political state and 2. Spirituality suitable for single individuals and priests applied to huge masses of common people. We discussed ethics applied to the political state earlier in chapter 12 on "Surfeit of Spirituality" under the heading of 'Victory or Virtue'. The second point (C2) will be clarified here, along with some other unrealistic ideas in Hindu philosophy.

Groups are different from individuals. Our society failed to distinguish between the needs of a few seekers of spirituality and the needs of the overwhelming masses of common people. For a householder, we prescribed certain virtues---like distaste for money---that in essence were meant for ascetics or priests. Absorbed in abstractions of little relevance to the common man, our saints bombarded the entire population with minute nuances of metaphysics. Expecting society to strive for ideals worthy of ascetics only, is the least feasible way for it to advance in this world. After all, what percentage of the population is ascetics splitting fine hairs in search of Brahma? If a wonder medicine is good enough only for one-millionth part of mankind, why prescribe it to one and all? If a road is meant to serve the needs of only a couple of special persons in the entire city, why waste a vast amount of society's precious resources to construct it, pave it, maintain it, promote it, as the only way---real or unreal, good or bad?

Many individuals in personal life benefit from good religion practiced sensibly. Society too benefited from it in ancient times. But today in group settings, its costs far outweigh its benefits (Ch.11). What was good for individuals is no longer good for society any more as we have seen throughout the earlier chapters. Exclusive self-centeredness is selfish, narcissist and harmful even for an individual, even in religious matters. The above kinds of mass blunders abound at every step in our philosophy. Therefore we need to examine the axioms of our philosophy in a little more detail.

Human history is not inevitable. It is determined by choices we make. Arnold Toynbee, the historian, said that the way any society responds to its challenges decides its ultimate fate. How did we respond to the challenges of history? The Aryans faced innumerable challenges---as can be seen from the Ramayana. They faced them well and overcame the opposition of the non-Aryans in a vast unexplored tropical land. That was a glorious period for their society at the time. The challenge from the Greek invasion received a magnificent response in the form of the Mauryan empire. The Shak, Kushan and Huns faced the might of the Guptas like Vikramaditya. That was about 1500 years ago. But that was almost the end. We could not respond to the challenges we faced later on, with only a couple of exceptions. Why? What changed?

Our well-intentioned philosophies started producing their natural long term consequences. Philosophy begets all sorts of odd outcomes, intended as well as unintended: Nietze into Nazism, Hagel's materialism into Marx's and Stalin's communism, Vyasa's nonattachment (to fruits of action) into lack of ambition. Preaching virtues like contentment made us a tolerating virtuous society but not an achieving advancing society. We stagnated as we aged. High sounding philosophizing robbed our society of its innate common sense. Our biggest strength, our philosophy, became our biggest chain, holding us back. Our society lost its vitality; our culture lost its creativity; our religion got mired in myths and mindless ritual. Fanciful and speculative, romantic, hypothetical ideas obtained a permanent foothold in people's minds. Concentrating solely on the manipulation of abstractions, we found it difficult to manipulate the tangibles.

Philosophy is an abstract pursuit of the mind that can, when overemphasized, alienate society from concrete action. Allergy to fresh ideas can be shrouded well in so called eternal truths. Social psyche can become twisted by putting popular twists on ancient screwy ideas. For hundreds of years, our philosophy was trapped in a single track. Scriptures full of conflicting doctrine were used to justify narrow tradition, oppression and orthodoxy. Even today, the most diverse popular philosophical schools in India can still represent a narrow spectrum of universal interest, just as it did centuries ago. Half the intellectuals hold ideas separating them by centuries from the modern world. The most advanced ideologues among the enlightened intellectuals lag behind by scores of years. Parts of India look light years away from modernity.

Years of unrealistic philosophizing robbed us of our rationality and made us easy prey to marauding aliens. Our responses to our defeats grew out of theology rather than strategy, unconnected to the threats we faced. (In direct contrast, others like the founding fathers of the American independence, were concerned less with the philosophy of Liberty and more with practical implementation of political liberty.) Centuries of alien occupation left us in cynicism, negativity and worse. Practices like celebrating suicide through fasting are examples of the awful legacy of our reluctance to question our misdirected philosophizing. On a giddy odyssey of self righteousness, we were so blinkered by 'arrogant ideological incompetence' in our philosophy that whenever we were defeated, we presumed that the problem was not in its message but in our methods of communication. So we redoubled our efforts at injecting our worn out clichés into our docile masses and in this we succeeded admirably. That was our self-defeating Toynbee response to the historic challenges we faced.

Even then, reality sometimes bites. Life's inexorable demands compel a few of us to introspect. The light of reason in a few unconventional intellects peeps out, piercing the dark clouds of metaphysical mist. But we brush them aside by asserting that they misinterpret our scriptures. It never occurs to our scholars that it is possible that our original message itself may be flawed, that it may help if we re-examined it instead of reasserting it mechanically ad nauseum. The pundits go on accusing one another of misinterpreting the message when the message itself needs a thorough overhaul.

We have been manipulated. Our minds, no less than our bodies, have been brutalized. Our minds are in a time warp, arrested in their development in an ancient age. Spirituality has monopolized our minds and brainwashed us. We have been altered to our core by a wide variety of sales pitches that encouraged us to neglect our self-interests. We have been imprisoned in a castle of sorts by the industry of the soul. We have been taught to believe in mirages. Image wins over substance. We believe as absolute reality what even a five year old boy might find odd as explanations of reality. If we can be taught to believe that the mirage is the truth, then our intellect is too malleable for our own good. That accounts for a thousand things we have been propagandized to believe for centuries.

To what extent can we say our beliefs are based on sound reasoning, not on faith? Consider selflessness or benevolence. A lot of our philosophy is a strong precept---almost a tirade---against selfishness (Ex: Gita). That is not wrong or bad. But selflessness is a value, neither a truth nor a philosophical argument. Self is a biological instinct; but selflessness or sharing needs to be taught to a child. To preach a value to overcome a basic biological instinct requires sound justifying philosophical arguments, not just the assertion of the desirable value. It also requires defining methodology and balancing counterpoints.

Our philosophy did a good job of preaching this value but neglected these other aspects. When survival becomes a stiff struggle in an overpopulated society, survival wins over morality; anxiety for family breeds greed; insecurity trumps virtue; and corruption multiplies. Natural instinct wins over taught values. How many of our intellectuals have realized or explained such facts while weeping routinely over spread of corruption in impoverished India?

Look at it from another angle. While we ostensibly advocate selflessness in impressive terms, we always preach liberation of soul as the only desirable goal to the exclusion of everything else. This is naturally a self-centered individualistic approach. It results in neglect of its effect on the community as a whole. Great temples surrounded by defecating children and diseased, deprived slums are a common sight in India. Lack of civic sense is all-pervading. Dirt and disease are tolerated. A high-minded supreme detachment from a sense of collective community responsibility is the indirect consequence of emphasis on personal spirituality. Contrast all this with other religions. Why do we need foreign Mother Theresas? No other religion has so much metaphysics and so little sense of physique or physics as we Hindus have.

My thesis is that a lot of limitations on our intellectual prowess---non-specificity, lack of clarity, romanticized thinking, unreal attitudes---have their deepest roots in our philosophy. A theosophy that has merrily proclaimed Maya (illusion) and Neti, Neti (Not this, Not this) cannot but produce fuzzy ideas and negative mindsets. A culture that revels in assumed abstractions only, is unlikely to achieve substantial concrete advancement in practical terms. A society that is accustomed to look starry eyed at the sky only, is very likely to miss the earth under its own feet. Sherlock Holmes, the famous detective, camping in a forest, woke up in the middle of the dark night and asked his companion, "My Dear Watson, what do you see?" Watson replied, "I see the beautiful stars, the vast expanse of the sky, the magnificence, the grandeur, the exquisite peace and bliss of the universe around us. But, what do you see?" Holmes said, "I see that somebody stole the tent from over our head while we slept."

In the underground tourist caves in America, every observer exercises his own imagination regarding the shapes he sees and finds what he likes to find. Truth is subjective. The One Ultimate Truth does not make sense; and absolute truth is absolute nonsense. Clearly, no one person has found the absolute truth so far in spite of fantastic claims to the contrary from time to time. No one did, no one can. And this is so in spite of all the prophets, popes, scientists, saints and stockbrokers. It is the same everywhere.

In Vedanta, only true knowledge will help, all else is superfluous. There is no way, really, to attain this ultimate spiritual knowledge. Because there are fifteen steps enumerated, all of them concerned with only one thing---concentrating your mind on your soul only, through various routines like Yama, Niyama, Yoga, Meditation----and so on. According to this theory, Brahma or God or Soul cannot be realized directly or even indirectly, but only non-directly (A-paroxa---not away from the eyes), whatever it means. Actually it means you go on thinking and thinking and thinking and--meditating and meditating and meditating and--concentrating and concentrating and concentrating--squatting on the floor, palms clasped, eyes closed, mind focused, right there, at the tip of your own nose--or is it, at the center of your own forehead?

There it is---the ultimate truth. It is philosophical quibbling of the first order, as a real road to real knowledge. As a matter of fact it is a little tough thinking about your soul all day. It is like a carpenter thinking all day only about Fermat's theorem in Mathematics. But of course, you must have faith and be pure at heart. Like that naked king in the story, who thought he was wearing divine clothes visible only to the pure hearted. The plain truth is that the inscrutable mystique that surrounds solitary meditation fosters a fantasy of divine knowledge. If I stare too long at the shadows on the wall, my mind gets deceived into believing that they are forms. A microscopic mist of metaphysical mystic surrounds my sight and makes me presume that I am blinded by the brilliant divine light coming from my soul. Self hypnosis cannot be any different. Auto-suggestion cannot be more automatic. Mind training and brain washing can never be more effective. Autonomous nervous system and blood flow to certain specific parts of the brain can never be controlled more efficiently. The malady of self delusion is incurable.

The Gita (2-62) says: "Thinking constantly of sensual pleasures (Vishayas), man develops attachment to them; attachment leads to desire". The same applies to the soul in meditation. Thinking constantly of the soul, man develops attachment to the idea of the soul. That attachment leads to a desire to know, to realize the soul. That is exactly what religion wants you to do. Whether this desire may or may not be good, it is desire, not knowledge. Desire to obtain knowledge is not knowledge.

Think of the Soul constantly and you will find It. Think constantly of Marilyn Monroe and you can sometimes see a beautiful maiden in a dream or fantasy. When you meditate and go on repeating Mantras to yourself about the great properties of the soul, you are not proving anything about the existence of the soul; you are only trying to reassure yourself that what you have been assuming all along IS the truth. You hype an idea of your own creation. You persist with yourself "I am the soul. I am Brahma." So you obtain self-realization, you obtain eternal bliss, you obtain what you think is the Light. There is only a small problem. It is not knowledge. It is faith, pure and simple, unalloyed and unadulterated.

It is your own assumed belief repeated a million times to yourself, by yourself, for yourself. It is coaxing, compelling and training your mind to receive, remember and accept whatever you want it to accept. Any psychologist can tell you that when the mind concentrates on an abstract image, it tends to produce what it expects and in a sense trains it to do. It is brain washing at its best---or worst. Best in terms of its effectiveness, may be good for an individual's health and peace of mind, but worst in terms of the consequences it produces on society when it becomes the highest ideal for all. It is mind conditioning of the first order, no different from what George Orwell described in his famous book---"1984". It is transferring your assumptions to the subconscious level so that they get permanently etched there. It is no different from memorizing or hypnotizing the mind. It is good old wine of faith packed in new bottles labeled as spiritual knowledge. And because you prefer to call it knowledge, you start making claims about its rationality, logic, sanctity, whatever you fancy. Illusion of ultimate knowledge effectively stops the search for any knowledge. Our self-made spiritualistic caves prove what Plato thought: "Prisoners in a cave might find shadows on the wall more real than the outside world."

The fact is that all such stratagems of theology have been utilized to generate and promote faith, to train the mind to believe the unbelievable, to gradually and imperceptibly coax the brain to regard faith as real truth. It is like a vastly successful strategy to make us faith-full and reason-less.

A will to believe cannot deliver true belief. But man has a wonderful capacity to rationalize his own assumed belief. He also has an emotional need to do so. This capacity and this need make him trust all the wrong labels. He accepts voodoo spiritualistic faith as true knowledge, the only knowledge, the ultimate truth, without so much as knowing or realizing what is happening in his own mind. A predisposition to believe one's own fantasies makes a very sweet sound indeed.

All questions in metaphysics boil down to one ultimate question: What is true knowledge? It is too complex, not at all easy to answer; and philosophers differ----sometimes violently. But all religions have a great answer that is simplicity itself: They say: Knowledge is what WE tell you. Ignorance is what other religions tell you. That is faith, pure and simple. If any religion ever was a science, then Hitler was a model democrat and Stalin was a capitalist tycoon.

Reflection by saints is itself worth reflecting on. Can mere thinking produce truth? If nobody ever tells anything to a child about stars, can he know what they are even if he is a genius? Can Rishis closing their eyes and reflecting in a forest always find the truth by themselves? Truth is not always revealed to a man ruminating or meditating in isolation although he may have occasional flashes, hallucinations, stupor or spells. He needs to check out, assess, interact and exchange ideas. Ideas are a slippery stuff, more slippery than a cake of wet soap. At the time of the Vedas, when paper was not invented, when even palm leaves had not yet been used, when all knowledge was transmitted by word of mouth, complex philosophical doctrines had a lot of practical limitations in enunciation, transmission and preservation. We started being trusting of our saints and ended up being credulous of their speculative philosophies. Our small traditionalist minds are incapable of appreciating such obvious facts. We fight over the shadows of misinterpretation and forget the substance of limitations in the message itself. Theorizing expands to fill a void of originality, talent or even mental effort.

It is simply amazing how much truth you can find if you stop guessing and start observing; if you stop speculating and start searching. Meditating cross-legged under a Pippal tree, eyes closed, may be an impressive way to try to find the light of truth. But observing the curvature of light rays in space during a solar eclipse is a better way to find the truth about light, as Einstein predicted and the astronomers found. People announcing their thumping certitude about the other world should be chastened by the history of false prognostications even in the current world. Thomas Watson was a chairman of IBM, the most renowned computer company. He reflected thus in 1943: "I think there is a world market for may be five computers." In another instance, John van Neuman, the inventor of the computer, said in 1949: "We have reached the limits of what is possible with computers." See the absurdity of reflecting or speculating even by these very knowledgeable persons? If this is the situation with hard boiled scientists, what can one say regarding predictions by many poets and receivers of revelations from God? What can one say about hordes of hibernating high priests in the Himalayas?

If truth can be found this way, why did Buddha and Mahavir find different truths? Why did Ramakrishna, Krishnamoorthy, Rajneesh, Raman, why did they all find different truths? There are fundamental differences in their philosophies (see chapter 15). The charm and attraction of our saintly philosophers are directly proportional to the skill with which they drown questions of principle sometimes in a torrent of verbal rhetoric and sometimes in an aura of mystifying silence.

A Rishi, a prophet, a poet, has a dreamy sequence of ideas. Ten Rishis describe it, twenty more comment on it. Most of them are mature old men with limitations natural to old age. All of them interpret and emphasize different aspects of the same idea. Each thinks the other misunderstands. It was hazy in the first place. Recall was difficult in the second place. Language had its own pitfalls. And interpretation? A lion seen in a dream can symbolize ferocity, power, victory, violence, blood, supremacy, anything or everything. Where is the sense in quarreling over interpretation alone? Manipulating language to cover harsh truths is not a new game.

Science and Faith: Some people say: We put faith in scientists and experts though we cannot understand them. Why not put faith in mystics? They are experts in their own field. There are several answers to this attractive but deceptive argument. 1. Nature's laws are inexorable, impersonal and objective. Mystic experience is varying, personal and subjective. Whom do you believe in, and why in him only, and not in the other? Differences in science become hypothesis for discussion, but not accepted as truths until universal acceptance is achieved. 2. In science these claims must be duplicated or verified by unbiased third parties before they are acceptable; not so in spirituality. 3. In science the conclusions are revised when better or newer ideas are available. Not so in spiritual matters. 4. There is no mystery in scientific matters; anyone with practice, training and intelligence can achieve success. In spiritual matters, there is no such openness or certainty. 5. I cannot understand Einstein if I do not know enough physics; similarly, I cannot understand soul if I have no preparation in penance, purity, devotion, whatever. That is quite true. But religion asks for 'self realization', not merely self-knowledge, understanding or training. Science expects you to understand Einstein; but spiritualism expects you to become an Einstein yourself.

A psycho patient had stomach-ache, a dream and a strange phobia that he had swallowed a mouse. The psychiatrist as a last resort arranged for a surgeon to operate upon him under anesthesia. When the patient woke up, they showed him a real mouse in a cage in the operation theater. They told him the mouse was removed from his stomach. The patient was convinced, satisfied and cured. All were happy. But the next week he came back and said, "How come that mouse was black? I had swallowed a white one."

No psychologist can ever explain or cure us of all the mystical mice we swallowed or believe we have swallowed in our lifetime. They come back haunting us at odd times, unannounced and unknown to us. We simply cannot let go of them. A lot of men carry a lot of loads of intractable conflicts, incompatible thoughts and unbearable traumas on their minds. A large number of cult leaders have claimed direct communication with or from God; and many of these have been exposed for what this was really due to---drugs, enzymes, pretensions, dreams, self delusion, self hypnosis, and so on. A killer of one man is called a murderer; a killer of thousands is glorified as a great commander or conqueror. A mystic with a few followers is called a cult leader; a mystic with a million followers is worshipped as a prophet.

Expert psychologists and ophthalmologists can explain many of the hallucinations, illusions, neurosis, psychosis, hallows, flashes and fixations people experience in real life; but we often call these things divine and keep the scientists away from them. In a hallucination, a man with no obvious symptoms sees ghost-like figures visiting him unexpectedly, even walking and talking with him. Doctors know the many possible causes--various mental disorders, drugs like beta-blockers, narcotics, certain anti-depressants, also alcohol withdrawal, delirium, depression and various brain diseases. As Freud and others after him have conclusively proved, the human central nervous system meshes ideas, emotions and imagination and occasionally produces nonorganic or functional diseases like hysteria. Neuroscientists have already demonstrated that applying a mild electric current to the right angular gyrus (just behind and above the right ear) induces an "out of body" experience in mildly epileptic patients.

When myth, mist and myopia come together, they can engulf whole societies in a shroud of easy belief, making them blind. Just think of what the racial myth and the nationalistic mist did to the German people--one of the most advanced and intelligent nations in the world--when they voted in a plebiscite in 1934 to vest sole executive power in Hitler. Nazism took over the nation. In a misty morning if you are driving your car with a foggy windshield and your eye-glasses are covered with moisture from your breath, can you drive well? Our society in India has been doing exactly this for centuries, with a thin invisible mist of spirituality constantly covering our sights. No wonder we cannot go fast enough, no wonder we crash at every turn, no wonder we cannot compete with other drivers with a clear vision. We Hindus have been running to grab a mirage that moves, a dream that deceives since ages.

Silliness sanctified does not become sense. But to some people, whatever sounds mystical, exists. Whatever they cannot understand, they presume it to be intuitively obvious. In the words of Mathew Arnold, we have cultivated a "passionate, turbulent, indomitable reaction against the despotism of fact."

The great Buddha abandoned everything to search for truth, for a cure to old age, disease and death. At the end of it all, did he find a cure? No. As he told a grieving Kisa Gotami, there is no cure, there is simply no way---death is inevitable. Accept death; accept life; live life the best way you can. At the end of all search, you realize the futility of all search. At the end of all knowledge, you know how little you know, how little you can know, how little you need to know, in order to live well.

Spiritualism promises three things: Doubtful welfare in a doubtful future world; Protection from the least likely threat; and Protection we would probably never need or use anyway. If a bird in hand is worth two in the bush; if present worth is higher than future worth; if it is a dumb idea to give up certainty in favor of uncertainty; then who will protect us from our own dumb ideas? It is certainly possible for ideas to be forbidding but foolish, stupendous but silly, wonderful but weird. And the silliness of our scholars and credulity of our audiences can simply reach the sky.

Noted physicist and world renowned scientist Swamiji so and so at his Ashram in the Himalayas explains how the Vedas proved Quantum physics. We believe him. Another, a Knower of Souls, Self realized Yogi---an engineer or doctor with impeccable high qualifications from foreign countries in another life---explains how the soul is pure light, energy, entropy or whatever. We are impressed. A third orator serves a delectable cocktail of morality, metaphysics and electromagnetic theory to Indian American audiences. We are completely overwhelmed. In each case, "there is not to reason why; there is not to make reply; there is but to" believe and buy (all their assumptions). After all, we are disciplined soldiers of spiritualism. We are Hindu.

They say the soul is higher energy, Kundalini, brilliant light, ultimate reality, pure consciousness--whatever sounds great and mystical. The Indian mind is lost in the labyrinth of spiritual sounding sound bites, searching for pure meaning. The net result? Perfect silly sense. They say God is impossible to describe. Still they describe him. Then they say He can only be described in negative terms and coin scores of negatives to do so (I counted 34 in one article). Then they say God is pure energy and the idea makes waves. They say take away the perfect from the perfect and still the perfect remains---just like what happens to the number zero (or infinity) in mathematics. Then they say He is like the sky and they attach impressive adjectives to the sky too. There, finally, there, they are perfectly right---the sky is nothingness, it is an illusion, it simply is not. Someone said about God: "He is a circle whose center is nowhere and whose circumference is everywhere." So also are many Hindu philosophical concepts. They are grand, grandiose, big and bloated; but have no definitive fulcrum, origin or dimension.

When we get to things we cannot talk about, we must learn to stop talking. When we get to things we cannot know, we must learn to stop professing knowledge. When we get to things we cannot see, we must learn to stop claiming divine vision.

All ideologies----be it communism, capitalism, spiritualism, Brahminism, or any other---suppress or exploit their minorities to some extent, even in open democracies. Some do it directly and openly, as communism did. Some do it indirectly, discreetly, imperceptibly, through mind conditioning, as Brahminism did. The former is obvious and can be easily seen and countered. The latter is insidious and difficult to visualize. To adapt the words of Rousseau expressed in another context: "The strongest theosophy is never strong enough to gain unequivocal acceptance, unless it transforms its strength into something morally right and converts belief in itself into a worldly duty". Duty in our language is Dharma; and Dharma is also religion. That is the Dharma that Hinduism, especially the Gita, preaches so well. At the heart of it all is how Dharma (theosophy) is transformed into ethics (duty) for better effective promotion and mass marketing. Hinduism did this well, so well in fact, that it successfully and completely obliterated the distinction between religion and ethics.

Technology can make us smarter but it cannot make us smart. It can extend our reach but it cannot teach us how to think. So modernization in the physical sense alone is not enough. We need to modernize our minds too. If our values are not clear, rational, and balanced; if they contradict natural instinct; if they are self defeating; no amount of technological progress will help us. A German author (Bonhoffer) says, "If you board the wrong train, it is no use running along the corridor in the opposite direction." If we are riding on wrong values, running around in any direction will not help.

To stem the tide of imbalance in our value system, to align our values with progress, to keep in step with the march of civilization, we need a revolution in our ancient values. We need new goals, new motivations, a new vision. If we cannot absolutely live without myths, we need new myths to live by--- myths that will reverse the course of history of our nation. No one person can provide these new myths or values. They will have to be rooted in human experience and reason, and not in supernaturalism nor in theological abstractions. We must take responsibility for our own destiny.

SECTION FOUR
THE CURE

24. MODERNIZE OR PERISH
Action for the Good Believers and Our Youth

A man had Parkinson's disease. He also had diabetes, arthritis and cataract. He carried a pacemaker too. He prayed to God, "Lord, please give me dementia so I will forget all the other stuff." We in India had poverty, backwardness and disease. We prayed for independence as a panacea for all these. The good Lord granted it, but that did not help us. Fortunately he also gave us our priests and politicians to boot; so that both of them can now make us forget all the other stuff!

Forgetting a disease is the least feasible way to cure it. Remembering ancient cures for chronic diseases is equally fruitless. Because we are not able to face reality, we unwittingly and habitually shove it under the carpet. An ostrich burying its head in the sand does not stop an approaching storm by trying to forget about it. Our society today is like a child who grew old but did not grow up. We don't hear adult conversation, only child talk on serious public issues. Our minds are mired in miracles, wired with witchcraft and sired by sycophants. Our reason is rooted in rudimentary beliefs and primitive practices that we like to call our proud culture and our unique religion. Only when the cataract covering our intellectual eye will be surgically removed by modernity, India will be a truly great nation.

We are perpetually fighting the last war---the war of establishing the first standards of civilization. When shall we stop refighting the same old battles? The war today is concerned more with competing with other civilized societies, rather than fighting the vestiges of uncivilized behavior. We don't need religion to teach us primary virtues like love for a brother and condemnation for the rapist (as in the Ramayana). We don't need religion to speculate about what life is. We are no children to need old props. Belief in many gods and speculative philosophies are nothing peculiar to us. Greeks, Romans, Egyptians---all had them. The big difference is that while everybody else has forgotten them and evolved, we prefer to repeat them, chew on them and refuse to recognize the absurdities in them. We need to be very clear about our cultural ideologue: Is it decadent or dignified? Is it pure or petrified? Is it perfect or does it need a change? A drift on such vital issues robs us of our future.

Mitch Albom says (in 'Tuesdays with Morie', a best seller): "You have to be strong enough to say**:** If the culture does not work, don't buy it. Create your own." Do we have that courage today to abandon old roles and rewrite old scripts that did not work? There is nothing to be ashamed of in a retreat in the war of values—brilliant retreats have won several wars in history. Unless we own up to our deficient values, we shall continue in futile attempts to pursue progress. We need to recast and expand our value system.

Goals can get disconnected from strategy; strategy from skills; and skills from leadership. Our society is like those people who lost their way in a desert and had to choose a leader to show them the way out. One leader offered a currently workable plan. The second leader offered the most eloquent condemnation of the desert and ways to avoid being lost in another setting. We chose the second. With us, another world wins, the current one loses. How can we escape the desert?

Somebody joked about his old dilapidated car: "The only thing that does not make sound in it is the horn." The only thing that does not have a ceiling in our culture is its myths. The things that do have a ceiling in it are numerous---adventure, effort, innovation, ambition, wealth, desire for progress. We circumscribed our own advancement. We are losing the race of life through self-sabotage. We must break out of this vicious circle now. "We have miles to go" before we stop.

We made wrong choices. We must change the error in those choices. It is foolish to let ourselves be bound by the chains of old irrational thought processes and keep ourselves permanently hitched to ancient ideas. These ideas were great in their own time; they are valid no more. They certainly have an honored place: That place is a pretty high pedestal on the bookshelf of history and that is where they must be consigned. Forever. That history itself is precious. It is the history of evolution of ideas, the history of our heritage of culture, the history of civilization itself. But let us not confuse history with a time machine that can take us back to our past. For the river of time flows only in one direction---from the steep mountains of the past towards the limitless expanse of the ocean of the future. It cannot flow backwards. And we cannot afford to look back or remain adrift forever.

The world has changed and is changing everyday, more and more, faster and faster, in wider and wider fields undreamt of before. When natural evolution is giving way to engineered evolution, it is silly on our part to stick to the so-called sacred statements of the past. The whole world exists outside of us, but we keep withdrawing inwards like a turtle. The world acts, reacts, runs, flies. We sit still---meditating, ruminating, pining for what is not. The world is inquisitive, learning, searching, researching, restless, dynamic. We are cool as a cucumber, content with what we are and proud of it all. How can we advance?

The economics Law of Diminishing Marginal Utility applies to many things including Religion and spirituality. Our religion had given us the best that we had in our culture in ancient ages. Now it is giving us the worst. India's greatest strength yesterday was spirituality; its greatest weakness today is spirituality. "Our sweetest songs are those that tell of saddest thought," as the poet said. Religion is not the solution to our problems. Religion IS the problem. Rather, obsession with religion is the principal problem. The irrationalism that religion generates and promotes in the minds of men is the basic problem. Propping up religion today means putting a problem in charge of a problem. It will not work.

From a Hindu intellectual in America, I heard a story of a buffalo reciting the Vedas. He believed it all, most fervently, without a shadow of a doubt, and wanted us too to believe in it. How can anybody, let alone an educated person, believe in such crazy folklore? Well, you can believe in anything, just anything, if you feel an emotional compulsion for religion at any price. Or, if your mind has been conditioned, brain washed, in the name of religious faith. Our scholars' naiveté touching the sky is a wonderful spectacle to behold. It is still a hallmark of our Hindu culture in this, the twenty first century after Christ. There is a strong reactionary group in India today trying to lead us to a strange historical philosophy that negates established facts. The most highly placed Hindu priest---the Shankaracharya of Puri, a very learned pious man---supports Sati and Untouchability in public and quotes scriptures in support. That is clearly against the Constitution of India as well as against common sense. But most of the so-called 'modern' intellectual believers remain silent in half consent.

By the way, Pope John Paul II in the year 2000, in a very unusual moment in the history of the church, asked for forgiveness for the sins of Roman Catholics through the ages, including wrongs inflicted upon Jews, women and minorities. Would anyone like to compare this against our practice of Sati and Untouchability? And the unrepentant attitude of our Shankaracharya even today?

We imitate modern looking cultural formats, crudely simplify them and claim them as novel, missing all the while the real heart and soul of the thing, as in the story of this farmer: A farmer was advised to modernize his marketing techniques, using automobile marketing as a model. When a car salesman came to buy a cow from him, the farmer quoted his cow-price as follows: Basic cow $998.95, Shipping and Handling $99.99, Two tone exterior $89.90, Extra stomach $98.50, Deluxe dual horns $95.50, Automatic fly-swatter $69.95, High output drain system $78.50, Auto fertilizer attachment $88.50, Farmer's suggested list price (total above) $1619.79, Additional dealer adjustments $109.95, Total list price including options (standard) $1729.74.

In truth, we don't need this kind of cosmetic modernization; we need REAL and immediate modernization. Real modernization is modernization of attitudes, beliefs and values. Modernization of agriculture, industry, institutions----everything else will follow automatically if we have genuine and deeply felt modernization of our minds.

A man asks his surgeon if he will be able to play the piano after his operation. When the surgeon says "Yes", the man says, "That is funny. I could not play it before." So modernization per se will not make us rational unless we ourselves learn to be rational.

That India is slowly changing is a fact that cannot be denied. But the change is too little, too late. If the Berlin wall happened to fall one brick at a time, could anybody claim it as his glorious achievement?

We are here after 250 years of contact with Europe. Still the change is local, superficial and involuntary. We dress in western modes but wear Indian culture on our sleeves and also deep within our hearts.

India prides itself on the talents of its young men in computer programming. How is it that it cannot visualize the irrational cultural preprogramming that the minds of its children have been receiving in so routine a fashion? Our ideological software was created 3000 years ago in the form of our culture. All that we are doing with it today is tinkering with it, if at all. The ideological software of the advanced countries of the world was created 300 years ago. With its help they are creating sophisticated new software and powerful novel hardware everyday. We are learned, they are intelligent. We chew and churn; they brew and burn. We are reproductive, they are creative. How can you ever compete with them?

Western Europe through democratic ideals led the world to break the chains of political tyranny. Now it is time for Asia to lead the world to break the bonds of religious tyranny in the new millennium. And India alone, with China, is capable of doing it.

Modern advanced nations are putting religion aside as an irrelevance in national life. A secular ideal is not disavowal of religion. It is a policy that personal religious belief will not be allowed to interfere with public policy. We will truly advance when we are ready to treat religion as an irrelevance in public life, with neither boasting nor apology, just as another little fact about ourselves. If I were the Prime Minister of India, People would be my God; Constitution my Gita; and Duty my Guru and guide. I would seek Heaven in the heartland of India and Moksha in the prosperity of its mesmerized masses. Till then Brahma will be a blasphemy and Ishwara an epiphany. God can wait if He wants to. Rationalism implies this ideal along with the others we discussed in this book. I fervently hope we can adopt it as a way of life.

To the good Hindu Believer

If you are not ready for pure rationalism and are a fervent believer in Hinduism, then also there is no insurmountable problem. My aim is not to rob you of your faith, however much you may agree or disagree with me. Yours can be the best religion in the world if you decide to follow it reasonably. Forget its fables and forgeries, convolutions and contradictions. The philosophy may not be proven (none is), but it is much better than most. Why? Because others believe in the miracles of revelation; you believe in the power of human consciousness. Others preach blind fanatic faith; you preach a tolerant ideal. Others teach submission to a supremo; you preach Karma. You had an edge in history, an original angle, a different perspective; yet you have squandered it all, most inadvertently. Simply because you got stuck in myth, mirage and miracle. You got entangled in elaborate ritual and tradition. You often allowed piety, like patriotism, to become the last refuge of the scoundrel. Abandon these and adopt modernity, reason and common sense if you want to win with your religion. Tap your moral energy for better, more useful, progressive ends to clean up not just yourself but your society. Ask yourself: Why did our society fall so low when we are so high in virtue?

You need not discuss whether to perform worship with your right hand or left. You need not continue to love the cobwebs that surrounded you in ancient times---holy stones, sacred threads, Ganga water, cow urine. You need not know about 16108 queens that Krishna metaphorically or mistakenly is supposed to have had. This relentless retelling of epic tales must stop if we wish to graduate into the rational world of mature adults---they have not been good for anybody except the storytellers. Meaningless, nonproductive, theoretical discussions on subjects like the age of the Vedas, or interpretation of scriptural stories and statements, serve no useful purpose. They are speculative. Even if correct, such discussions prove nothing. We do not automatically become great if the Vedas are more ancient than most people are willing to accept. Determining whether our ancestors ate beef or whether the Pre-Vedic Indians used horses cannot and should not be a factor in guiding us to decide our current policy on livestock. It is not necessary to split hairs on how and when and why caste system originated; it is enough to bury it well.

Faith should not preclude common sense. It is vitally important and outrageously overdue to break the Berlin wall of separation we have built between common sense and the common man's craving for theosophical truth. We can embrace the power of faith but we must not confuse naiveté with piety. What you believe about God or religion is a matter for your own conscience. But what effect your beliefs produce on society is going to affect the whole country. Religion as a virtue should not stand in the way of rational approach to the problems of practical life. Hindu religion will have to become more compact, clear and progressive before Time the Leveler steam-rolls it into oblivion.

Preaching Ramayana in and by itself does not constitute religion, whether the pious preacher is perched on mountain tops or trees or flies in air. Preaching abstention from smoking or alcohol is not religion when the preachers can commit murders to gain control over the wealth of religious trusts. Preaching elementary virtues and primitive values are good but society needs a lot better and a lot more to advance in the modern world. You can support your religion's influence from its innate strength, intrinsic value and exemplary role models rather than from myth, slogan and short cuts. If you don't, Murphy's law can take over. If we do not change, we will be changed. We are sitting on a volcano in the form of the India of today. It is just too risky to sit still. Today the downtrodden and the underprivileged leave Hinduism. Tomorrow the intelligent, the modern, the sensible, will start leaving.

Words and stories can be cited, turned and twisted at will to mean many contradictory things. We must abandon curdled rhetoric, banish the sterility of argument and shun the sheer littleness of semantic fetish. Even if it were feasible to understand and interpret the ancient literature correctly, it will have to be updated, amended, and modified extensively in the light of the completely changed times and places, as our scriptures themselves have preached us to do. Discussion will be a lot more beneficial if we did it for current problems of which there is no dearth.

If you are an intelligent believer in faith, my sincere request to you is to think dispassionately about the following: The conflict today is not about politics, morality or regionalism; the conflict is essentially about modernity. It is about tension between a developed section of human society that is succeeding at modernization and an underdeveloped one that is failing at it and looking for others to blame. Consider this also: Divorce is not a problem of morals as implicitly assumed. A little known fact is: Conservative Christians have the highest divorce rate in the USA; atheists have the lowest. Divorce is the natural consequence of economic independence of women, industrialization and higher mobility of populations---of modernity, in short, not of religion or morals. The solution is not to go back on these desirable conditions, but to find new solutions for such new problems. Moreover, you cannot go back even if you wanted to---modernity will come whether you like it or not. The only choice you have is whether to drift with it or welcome it---opposing it is not only wrong, but also futile and senseless. And modernizing at glacial speed misleads us into deceptive complacency.

We ban French TV saying it is against our culture. Malaysia bans our Bollywood films citing the same reason. We think it is our duty to fight a holy war against evil as the Gita preaches us. We forget that the other guy is also fighting his own kind of holy war against us as his own scripture preaches him. Scriptures always frame issues in terms of Dharma---Adharma. In fact the battles are always between my kind of Dharma versus your kind of Dharma; my values against your values; my God versus your God. We oversimplify the issues by calling the other person's Dharma as Adharma. Think: Ravana worshipped his God, Hitler was a devout Christian. If the question is whether the real problem is about morality, culture, or freedom, the answer is clear: None of the above. It is about conflicting faiths and the degree of modernization of those faiths.

The Hindu-Muslim conflict in India today is simply the most visible aspect of a larger contest between two competing ideologues that arose at two very dissimilar places and times in history. The conflict will not be resolved through a competition to break skulls or statues---they are incidentals. It will be resolved only through modernization of minds and beliefs. The one community that modernizes first and faster will win the race. Today there is pressure on the Muslim world to modernize itself. Where is the pressure on us, Hindus? Do we want to be left behind in the race? Think what will happen if they beat us again, as they did in the Middle Ages. Turkey, Israel and Japan did not allow religion to interfere with their march to modernity. It is no wonder that they are the most advanced nations in Asia today. Japan westernized feverishly after the Restoration of 1868 and won two wars soon after. The key here was modernization, not religion. The same happened to Turkey with Kamal Ata Turk. Even recent recruits to western style modernity like Taiwan, Singapore and South Korea have far outstripped the Middle East nations in spite of the huge advantage that the latter have in natural resources in oil.

Our Younger Generation

It is often futile to preach rationality to most old men of my generation. All the soaps and sodas of the world will not wash out the cobwebs of spirituality and faith that they have been conditioned to love. But the younger generation is different. Show them the rational alternative clearly and they will not fail to judge correctly. But do not beat about the bush. Tell this to them in unequivocal terms: "Life is not non-real, a dream or an illusion; it is a hard reality. Unlike a dream, it can be and must be changed, improved, modified; its battles can be won." They will understand. They have seen the world now. The world has become a global village.

Our young people today do not want to remain anti-modern. They are confused and they are not being given a real chance to move in the right direction, the direction of modern rational ideas. They are confused because they are constantly exposed to the rhetoric of bygone ages. They are today caught between two worlds, "one dead, the other powerless to be born." When a sense of direction is lost at a personal or a national level, it is not easy to recover. Such men or nations often become ungovernable. They are dangerous by their weakness, not by their strength. How you pull such a person or country away from anger, failure, frustration or danger has no easy formula.

I have supreme confidence in our young men and women I see today. They are less exposed to old dogma than we were; they have known other cultures; they can have a global outlook; they are capable of a healthy disrespect for old values, when they are properly motivated. If a violent upheaval does not intervene, our generation of old men will pass peacefully into oblivion. When our youth will decide to make a bonfire of the vanities of our past, they will light up the fires of our future. Then they will break all bonds and leap into a great future whether we let them or not. And a leap is exactly what India needs---a leap of reason, a leap away from blind faith, a leap into a confident tomorrow. India will be a great country again if only her past will let her.

As a matter of fact, our only hope for a change for the better rests on the next generation; and we old men have been showing them exactly the opposite direction so far. Nostalgia to return to that impossible period in the past is not going to do us any good. On the contrary, it is already doing us a lot of harm, converting us into self-righteous morons with split personalities and divided loyalties. We must break the vicious circle of a self-fulfilling deflation of expectations and achievements. While we have time to turn around, we do not have unlimited time.

Action: What should we Do? Sometimes we ask the right questions in the wrong order. Questions on what we should do about some evil must follow---not precede---questions about what exactly that evil is and how serious. "Ready, Aim, Shoot" is a far better sequence to follow than "Ready, Shoot, Aim". So the first thing to do is to be convinced fully about the evils presented in this book. The next step is to appreciate the gravity of those evils, because our response to evil always depends on the gravity we assign to it. For example, what I should do to counter communism or terrorism depends on how much I hate it, if at all. Since ideas rule the world and since we are not intolerant terrorists, the only way for us to make these ideas more and more acceptable is to propagate those ideas through all possible means. As president APJ Abul Kalam aptly put it, "The revolution required for this effort (of transforming India) must start in our minds."

This book is about changing beliefs, not about snap cures and short cuts to quick action. If I am motivated enough through right beliefs, I shall find what and how to do, what techniques to use and what specialists to consult. Numerous social, cultural and deep rooted ideological compulsions have resulted in the inability of our systems to act. Since our age-old values block our progress, the initial step is for intellectuals to come out openly and unequivocally in favor of a basic transformation in our value system-

--not beating around the bush, not mincing words, not coddling the conservatives, the traditionalists or nationalists, whatever their brand or disguise. As writer Norman Cousins said. "All things are possible once enough human beings realize that everything is at stake,"

The further lines of action are clear if we have followed the trend of our discussions so far. But to summarize in brief: 1. Forget the past glories. Forget the next world. "Act, act in the living present," as the poet said. 2. Challenge myths, presumptions: stand up, speak up. Abandon stupid traditions. Rationalize. Build and spread reason, not faith. Insist that public policy and private actions be based on social science, not on sermons. 3. Modernize genuinely, in ideas, not just in outwardly appearances. 4. Examine and scrap outdated core values. Affirm and establish new values like: Ambition is good, Money is not an evil, Old is not gold, Skepticism is better than blind faith in Gurus or scriptures, This world is more important than the next. 5. Insist that leaders hold fast to modern values. Ruthlessly question those who don't. 6. Be strong. Consider security, survival and decent living as primary values, not as secondary options. Establish them as values in their own right, not as fringe benefits of virtue or goodness, as in the past. We need to survive before we thrive. Ideological subjugation of Hindu society by its own leaders is the root cause of its long military subjugation by foreigners.

Can we do this? Can we change our value system? Yes, we can. It is not too late for us to get a value transplant, but the first step is to admit the need. When we realize we are in a hole, we will stop digging. For that, we need to discuss and spread the ideas we have put forward in this book.

Somebody needs to burst the bubble of our pundits' vanity in everything ancient and outdated. The only thing necessary for the triumph of irrationality is for rational men to do nothing. Modernism in India will come not if rational people wish it, but if they will it; not through sterile debate but through action. To be critical of religious dogma is not blasphemy. To be uncritical is not politeness. Neither is it humbleness nor courtesy. When humans struggle like worms in the streets, to overlook rampant superstition and degradation is neither detachment nor decency nor religion. To let dogma go unchallenged is timidity, hypocrisy, immorality and hence anti-religion in itself. So, speak out, write, act, do not be afraid of being demonized. Have the courage of your convictions. Never act as if you are ashamed of them.

A few random ideas in brief for practical steps: 1. Stop idol worship (Ch.20). Stop building more places of worship or pulling the existing ones down. 2. Reduce dependence on government, encourage volunteerism. 3. Don't tinker with the election system, revolutionize it. The state should finance all elections to check corruption at the roots and protect real democracy. 4. Restrict a few freedoms (cross directorships, vested interests) and enlarge others (free family planning, education). 5. Develop and implement a crash science initiative of research in alternative sources of energy like Solar power, Wind power and Bio-energy. A tropical country with India's intellectual resources and energy shortages needs to be a world leader, not a laggard, in these fields of the future. We need to galvanize the nation for both, a Manhattan Project for research and a Henry Ford plan for mass production, in order to do this today. 6. Encourage alcohol (not gas) based fuels for cars. 7. Encourage Professionalism in all fields. 8. Law is a modernized form of morality. Make it an agent of change, not of status quo. But it is futile to hope to prop up either law or morality without fixing the values at the root of their decay. So promote new values, not the outdated ones. A separate book could in fact be written to expand on each of the above ideas.

What do I mean by new values? Throughout this book, we have been talking about the old and the new. The values preached in our epics may be good or not so good today, depending on what and how we teach them, but we certainly need to add to them. Values taught by epics are just not enough today. Examples: 1. Apart from promoting elementary family values like brotherly love, how about promoting work-place values like efficiency, punctuality and co-operation? The age of the epics was a period of pastoral and agricultural communities. It had no workplaces as we know them today. So workplace values were naturally unknown, rather irrelevant, in those times. But today they are far more important than family values, especially when the family itself is changing, even disappearing, in the post-industrial age. 2. Protecting a married woman and her virtue is a good value, as taught by the epics, but how about promoting a little self respect, dignity, individuality and independence in her? These are new values, not ancient ones. Granting a husband the sole right to banish a pregnant innocent wife to a forest for whatever lofty reason is certainly not a value likely to be appreciated in modern times, even among highly virtuous kings. 3. Individual bravery and physical strength were good values in those under populated ages; but how about promoting team work and group co-ordination, that are of critical importance today in wars and in life? 4. Moral values clean the mind. Why not promote physical and community cleanliness and sanitation also as equally desirable? 5. In our scriptures, as a matter of routine, we *encounter* miracles. For a change, why not inspire people to *achieve* miracles? 6. We must borrow good values from other cultures. Ex: Why not emulate the Japanese culture regarding individual shame and accountability? Or the Islamic value of 10 percent donations?

Religion ruled the dark ages; reason must rule the computer age. If modern man cannot reasonably accept God and religion (Ch. 15), and he cannot abandon them at the same time (Ch.11), what is the way out? The only way out is to promote Rational Humanism. This includes: 1. Secularism or keeping individual religious beliefs private and deciding matters of public policy without a reference to any assumed truths. 2. Separation of ethics from its dependence on religion. 3. Accepting God as a desirable Value for those who cannot live without Him but denying Him as an objective Truth as agnostics and non-believers do (Ch.10). This is the only way to resolve passionate destructive conflicts that civilized man faces today. This is also the policy---called by whatever name---followed by most of the advanced civilized nations today, including England, France China and Japan.

The values we hold today withhold us. They have been clumsy and confusing; misplaced and misleading; and dangerously defective. Irrational modes of thought resulting from our outdated values are the common chemicals running through the body politic of our society. We need not only to dissect the body politic but also analyze the chemical enzymes controlling it. To find all of them---is the first important and vital step in pursuing a direction for a cure. And that is what I hope I have done, rather too bluntly at times, in this book. Someone may or may not agree with all the answers, but our society needs to keep asking the right questions.

How to build the rule of law or a competent civil service is so much more difficult a task than simply amending the constitution. Building an honest political cadre is much more difficult than preaching morality. Action is always more difficult than precept. My only hope is that our youth will consider whether and how far it is feasible to transform our values and our culture into a genuinely modern outfit in order to save our country and our religion. For, religion cannot save us. We need to save religion. While we can. If we can. If we want to. Can we do it?

25. TO SQUARE A CIRCLE
Can We Transform Our Religion and Values?

Dissatisfaction with Hinduism is old and widespread. But all attempts to reform it, without exception, have failed to make any lasting impact on the massive bedrock of Hindu tradition. Sikhism as well as Christianity obtained more converts from Hindus than from Muslims. So also did Buddhism in recent times. Why? If we do not stop the rot, in addition to the down trodden, intellectuals too will start going away from orthodox Hinduism. Today Hinduism needs transformation, not reformation.

The Vedic period attained pinnacles of philosophy. No society can continue to go on achieving that kind of excellence forever. We too failed to sustain our intellectual prosperity. When the pace slackened, originality in ideas got a back seat; consolidation of and conformity with established ideals gained prime importance; and ritual ruled supreme. Second rate poets and versifiers had a free rein, a virtual license, to amend, expand and twist original precepts to suit their own interpretations of the scriptures partly because Hinduism was too malleable right from the beginning. Rot set in on the roots of real religion. This process continued for several centuries.

In the sixth century B.C. Buddha and Mahavir made the first real attempt at correcting the excesses. Their serious challenge culminated in establishment of two independent religions. Their impact was nullified when Sankara (788—820A.D.) revived Vedanta. Buddhism was banished and Jainism was confined within a small fraction of the Indian population. After the Muslim conquest, reformist saints like Kabir and Nanak tried to reform and combine the best parts of both religions; Sufism was born; the great Moghal king Akbar tried a new religion--Din-e-Elahi. However, none made a real impact on Hindu society.

With English education in India, we came in touch with modern science and western philosophy. Many good and great people realized our weaknesses and tried to awaken Hindu society from its slumber. Reformers sprang up in some states but they were too few and far between to be effective. The inertia of a monolithic mega culture frustrated them all. Orthodox Hindu society had a fitting reply to reformers like Ram Mohan Roy, Dayanand Saraswati, and Vivekanand. It ignored the first, murdered the second and put the third on decorative bookshelves. This fact alone should be enough to shatter the sheer naiveté of our reformatory zeal. Today, even after 150 years of western education, we are unable to outgrow our ancient infantile beliefs. Good Hindus say: Hinduism is reformable. They said the same thing 2500 years, 1000 years and 100 years ago. What has changed? Ritual? Idols? Tradition? Dead-end belief? Nothing. Going from Rama to Shri Ramulu (Andhra patriot) to Rama Rao (Andhra Chief Minister) is no progress.

Today with global contacts, we do hear random pleas for modernization here and there. But they are cries in the wilderness---feeble, isolated, limited, defensive, too weak to make a difference. At rare times they seem to go far, but almost in every case, they do not go far enough. What Hinduism needs today is not one Martin Luther or one Calvin, but at least 16 Martin Luthers and 16 Calvins, one in each major language group of India. It is a far cry.

To give ourselves credit for imitation and borrowed reforms is the height of hypocrisy. We saw western countries at close quarters through our nonresident Indians and our foreign going brilliant younger generation. We are improving by imitation. But did the change come about from within? No. We could hardly stop it. But we did try. There is a world of a difference among a man who runs, a man who walks and a man who is pushed from behind to make him walk. When the world runs a marathon, Hindu society walks only when pushed, only when it becomes completely irrelevant and impossible to stand still in its outdated modes. We reform only when compelled by law or circumstances. Abolition of Sati, Untouchability, Child marriages---all reforms had to be pushed through by law, by foreigners or foreign

152

educated urbanized Indians. They were thrust upon an unwilling population and even today the evils continue---in this, the twenty first century after Christ. Their continuation through social sanctions is more vigorous than their abolition by law. Big marriages, big temples, big Yagnas---all continue as symbols of status, faith, ego---through societal sanction. Because of its incoherent non-rigid ethos, Hinduism is one of the rare religions that in theory are capable of reforming themselves, given the right kind of progressive leadership and vision. But alas, these have sadly been lacking so far.

From a ship, a man accidentally fell into the sea. His friend Bill saved him and carried him back to the deck, single-handed, braving the treacherous waves. They held a meeting to honor Bill. Everybody heaped praise on him for his courage and sacrifice. When it was his turn to speak, Bill said, "Thank you. But I demand to know one thing from you all: Who was that guy who pushed me from the deck in the first place?" We are pushed from behind and we feel proud. We are compelled and we claim credit. We are pushed, plodded, dragged into modernity and we proclaim how modern we are.

Can we transform our distorted value system from the roots, working through our outdated cultural ethos? The task is like squaring a circle or making an elephant fly. A camel will straighten out all his crooked limbs before that happens. It cannot really happen because we are at heart proud of the survival of our corroded culture throughout history--in spite of history.

When the world has been making quantum leaps into rational thought, rationalism has made little headway in India We urbanites discuss independence of women today. But Ibsen dramatized it ("A Doll's House"-1880) more than a century ago. We legislate abolition of untouchability and legalize equality of man today; but Buddha preached equality of caste, America put equality in its preamble and France based its revolution on it---centuries ago. Rationalism dawned in Europe three hundred years ago and it peeped into Indian skies a hundred years ago with people like Ram Mohan Roy and others. An influential leader like Jawaharlal Nehru was broadly modernistic in outlook and did not support religious taboos of any kind. Still we are the same. Did the leopard change his spots? A more relevant question is: Can this leopard change his spots? If the leopard cannot or will not change his spots, should we shoot him, pamper him, coax him forever or pray before him? If you don't like his spots, either you banish him or learn to live with him. Most people choose the latter course. But as mankind advances, the spots look more and more hideous, more and more out of tune with the changing world. Intelligent people start having second thoughts about the viability and wisdom of learning to live with him. We do not need a magnifying lens to see that his ugly spots are an inseparable part of himself, something he cannot change if he wished to. As the above reformers found years ago. How long will you wait to reform a favorite pet? You have to decide to consider other options, since reform has proved to be out of question.

Our wise men go on discussing the same issues year after year, decade after decade, seated comfortably in their armchairs, atop their ivory towers, splitting hairs while the noose gets tighter around the neck of their motherland. Our scholars cannot decide. When Rome was burning, Nero was fiddling. At least he knew what he wanted to do. When India is burning, our Neroes do not know what they want to do; so they are fledgling, hesitating, halting and bolting.

Small numbers of our intellectuals do realize this untenable position, although the pool of such scholars has the depth of a puddle and they have ideologically monochromatic minds. They fondly hope to reform society only through religion. Wishing to reform religion through religion is like trying to cure overmedication through more medication; or to cure obesity through more food. The failure of most of them to realize what harm spirituality has done to our progress suggests incapacity to see beyond the obvious facts of life. It is truly amazing how intelligent men can come so close to truth and yet manage to miss it. Their squeamishness to admit the irreparable harm spiritual obsession has done to our collective psyche suggests an unwillingness to confront the truth head on. Their silence in the face of religion's excesses suggests complicity. Their timidity is tempered by tradition and exceeded only by an over abundance of platitudes. We can drill deep into their minds without ever touching obvious common sense.

The meager efforts of some well meaning rationalists so far are too halting, too weak, too little and too late to make a difference. These benign intellectuals are killing mosquitoes buzzing over a severely wounded animal when a flight of eagles is pecking at its flesh. What they need to use is not an insecticide to kill the bugs but a gun to shoot down the birds of prey. It is better to be bold where hesitancy is a hindrance.

The Hindu civilization set out to sail the seas in a beautiful wooden boat in ancient times. It did rather well in the beginning. Over the arduous long journey, the wood started rotting; the boat developed cracks; the compass got disoriented. The boat with gaping holes in the bottom was unable even to keep afloat. Yet we noticed nothing, understood nothing, fixed nothing. All we did was pray for world peace with hands folded. To use another metaphor, the initial apples of the beautiful orchard of our Hindu civilization were sweet and succulent when fresh. Our aged fruits are now infested with worms. Bacterial disease on leaves can spread and kill a mighty tree. Our naiveté and nostalgia prevent us from acknowledging such a sad fact. Our misplaced faith in religion stops us from doing anything about it.

Our culture is obsolete. We created one of the best cultures in the world. We can recreate it. We must end what we cannot mend. Surgery is often good and inevitable. Though unpleasant, it is silly to shirk from surgery of an incurable festering wound. The question is: How long are we prepared to tolerate the decay? The decay is bad in itself. To live with it when the tissues start degenerating and start affecting the heart and the brain is worse. The sore spots in Hinduism are bad in themselves; to continue to live with them when they affect our capacity to think and even the will to survive is beyond reason. Today they hold us back from competing with the world on equal terms. We must break our bigotry of low expectations.

We spent centuries inhabiting a delusional mental landscape. Our nurture and culture, our pieties and priorities, our ideas and ideals---all these are circumscribed within a narrow circle that looks haloed but is in fact hollow; sounds flowery but is fuzzy; smells pious but is petrified; feels other-worldly but in fact is plain old orthodoxy itself. In the words of a Nobel Laureate (written in another context): This kind of mental state in our society "---- has become a kind of neurosis. Too much has to be ignored or angled; there is too much fantasy. This fantasy is not in the books alone; it affects people's lives." (V. S. Naipaul in 'Beyond Belief'---Random House, 1998). This is because religion is not simply a matter of private belief; it makes demands of the individual. People develop ideas, attitudes, priorities and values.

Moving to modernity is moving in the right direction. But moving with halting hesitancy is only half a loaf when a full loaf is needed fast---it is too weak to do the job. Half measures often produce full failures. Failure is deplorable but too slow a success is no less so. When a full dose of medicine is required rapidly, with as much speed as you can possibly muster, half a dose is as bad as no dose at all. Sometimes it is even worse, since it gives a fake impression of action when no effective action is taken. When you have darkness at noon you need a halogen lamp or a laser, not an oil lamp.

The waters of pure reason are struggling to break out of the surrounding solid mountains of orthodoxy in India, but how long will they take? As the anguished cry of Joan of Arc rings out from the stakes, in Shaw, "How long, O Lord, how long?" Can the scorched plains of the country wait for these rocks to wear out? What the mountains of orthodoxy and tradition deserve is not a wait for water to wear them out but dynamite to blow them to smithereens. When gold is too tarnished, washing soda or soap will not work; what is needed is nitric acid. If it is platinum we are trying to purify, we may even need aqua regia, the corrosive fluid to dissolve even the precious gold contaminant.

To adopt the words of an American revolutionary, today for India, "These are the times that try men's souls." We must think anew and act anew. We must reframe today's timid debate. We must unshackle our minds from ancient ideas and impractical values. If we cannot utilize our past as a prologue to a better future, it is better to bury the past and bid it a decent valedictory farewell. If we do not do this voluntarily, society may even need an external shock to jolt it into a painful revolution necessary to make a clean break. In a moth eaten house it is difficult to predict which part will collapse first and when. Sooner or later, hard reality catches up with us; an explosion occurs that jolts us from our stupor. Why should it take the threat of a crisis to do what needs to be done? We must act now. Physicists know Entropy---left to themselves, energy deteriorates. We all know the famous Murphy's Law. It states: "If something can go wrong, it will". Well, in our case, Murphy was an optimist.

26. THE MOMENT OF TRUTH
To Our Intellectuals

Purging our society of an all-embracing culture of irrationality is the crying need of the hour in India today. Who can do this but intellectuals? But so far our intellectuals have failed to do this. Why do our intellectuals stand by helplessly while the fabric of our great society is being destroyed by vested interests? Partly because they are indifferent. Partly because the problem is of gigantic proportions. Partly because they are themselves a part of the problem. If some of our acknowledged intellectuals themselves believe in what they write, they must be either childish or dishonest to themselves. Scholarly, thorough and detail oriented, they miss only one small thing--original intellect. The intellect that penetrates like an X-Ray, the intellect that blows away the chef and gets to the grain, the intellect that shines in original thought, not in tradition. Sometimes we do hear a couple of truly rational people moan. But it is mostly a charade, a mere simulation of outrage. We know this because the rants come from a point of departure that is already distinguishable from a philosophy that used to be called conservatism. For all their pretenses of modernity, their inner orthodoxy oozes out. Even while some mavericks fill the vacuum created by intellectual timidity, they miss the big picture. They swat solitary mosquitoes while the cesspools of culture breeding them remain untouched. They target small specs of dirt while huge dumps of trash fester unchecked in the minds of the masses. They nibble at the flanks while the hardcore rock of traditional orthodoxy remains as impregnable as ever. But our problems will not get smaller until our thinking gets bigger.

An American war veteran was boasting, "Well, we were no chicken. When the German bombs were bursting all around in London, were we hiding? No, sir, no way. We were firm, marching proudly, heads held high, our flag aloft." A listener, highly impressed, inquired where it was. "On the Fifth Avenue," he replied, "in New York." Our veterans in the war of social reformation don't march. They don't even stand up. Seated cozily on the couch in their ivory towers, they conduct hot debates in their meetings in Bombay, Calcutta and New Delhi---and nowadays in America. The listeners (when any), are duly impressed. The orators pet on their own and each others' backs. Even when they know they are barking up the wrong tree.

Our common people blame politicians for the problems of the country. Politicians blame the bureaucracy. The bureaucrats blame the politicians and the people both. Who will break the vicious circle? Who has the most brains to do it? We know that our people have a tryst with tradition that they can neither break nor outgrow. Politicians are a product of the same culture as the people; and reflect their psyche in a democracy. But the bureaucrats? The word has acquired a bad connotation but they are a part of the intelligentsia today. The most brilliant young university graduates in my time aspired for a career in the professions or in the civil services. They still do. They go through a stiff competitive nation-wide examination and the cream is selected. Then they are given modern management training. They run the country when politicians play musical chairs. If these are not intelligent people, who else is?

But today they play second fiddle to corrupt incompetent politicians. Is it too much to expect that they do better? I know there are many stock answers, pet peeves and explanations. And yet, again, is it too much to expect that the intellectual cream of the country should do much better? We can always find several reasons why we fail to do something. They may be perfectly valid reasons and yet, in spite of all those, intelligent motivated people can and do find ways to do what they want to do. These bureaucrats know much better than anybody else how to handle the public, how to deal with the political bosses and what needs to be done to solve the problems of the country. Can they not tackle the corrupt politicians and the naïve public corrupting them? They certainly can, if they themselves refuse to be a part of the problem they are trying to solve. Will they rise above pettiness, short-sighted selfishness, sycophancy and the blame game? Can they muster enough courage and tact? Since it has not happened so far in any organized or effective way in spite of a few brilliant exceptions, it is by and large true to say that our brilliant bureaucrats too have failed our country.

If one intelligent civil servant resists a wrong politician, he will be transferred, victimized. If ten civil servants show the gumption to resist, their careers may be adversely affected. If a hundred civil servants do not acquiesce in the wrong, what can the politicians do? Nothing, I guarantee. Is it too much to expect one or two percent of our most brilliant young men to rise to the occasion to save their motherland from all the senseless stupidities? I am not preaching rebellion or indiscipline here; I am advocating honest, firm, effective resistance that tolerates no non-sense from any quarters.

Poorly crafted legislation is the law of our land. Any rules the civil service makes, people will try to bend them to their own nefarious ends. Does that fact excuse the drafting of half-baked careless rules? It is always possible to draft intelligent rules of procedure that will anticipate most problems and will make it extremely unlikely that people can break them. It is a matter of who outwits whom---whether the lawmaker is more intelligent or the lawbreaker. Ex: Plots of land are allotted to elected politicians at dirt cheap prices. Every five years politicians change, sell the plots at huge profits to themselves at the cost of taxpayers. Is it too difficult to frame rules building proper safeguards to prevent such things? If politicians are not saints, can we not draft good rules to thwart bad men? In advanced countries, procedures are laid down with such thoroughness and anticipation that the highest political authority cannot misuse them. A president can be prosecuted or impeached if suspected to be lying. Rules can never be made air tight, but they can certainly be made least likely to leak. But we make rules that leave crevices. The bug of corruption seeps through it. Feeding and thriving on its own venom, it gradually swells to a size and strength overwhelming all laws.

Why do people elect criminals? Because criminals terrorize the locality. The simple way out is: Don't publish voting numbers for individual polling booths. Was it impossible to anticipate such problems and frame election rules accordingly? No. Why was it not done? Our most intelligent civil service could not or did not do it. Is anybody ever held responsible for drafting bad legislation in India? Do we have enough sense to establish procedures reasonably foolproof or largely free from loopholes?

I cited the civil service above as one example. Similar considerations apply to the other intelligentsia as well----teachers, professors, men of letters, judges, and other professionals. Examples are available for all these. We don't see courage. We see neither originality nor balance nor civic sense in their thinking or approach to problems. We don't see them act selfless, rational, independent or determined. Let me repeat with all the force I can summon: Our intellectuals have failed our country. Period.

To imitate the preamble to the constitution of the UNO, in Indian society today, "since irrational attitudes predominate in the minds of men, it is in the minds of men that the defenses of rationality must be constituted." And who can do this best but the really modern intellectual minds? The country has human talent, sometimes bordering on genius. Most of it gets lost, either wavering in indifference on the sidelines or trapped inside the muddy landscape of our orthodox culture; but never braving the whirlpools of action. My fervent plea to them: To act is better than to sit still and know. Debate issues; raise the bar of public discourse; do come out of your ivory towers. The country will be better served and you might escape dying of monotony or boredom.

For too long, rational men have been silent due to their own passivity or fear of offending men of misconceived faith. The real tragedy is that they had so much respect and knowledge with which to speak out. Yet the modernistic ideologue in India today is in essence a hope and a prayer. It hopes orthodoxy will dissolve by itself in time; and it prays for progress. It does not realize why it does not dissolve and it is surprised that the prayers are not answered. But to leapfrog over a gulf of centuries of retardation will take more than a prayer. It will take resolute action. Remember Newton's first Law of Motion: 'A body at rest continues to be at rest and a body in motion continues to be in motion unless otherwise acted upon by a force to change its state.' This is the classic scientific definition of inertia. It applies to the classic inertia of our Hindu society as well as to the current momentum of advanced nations. Our intelligent people have not exerted the force of their rational minds to change our state of inertia. So we continue to stand still and the advanced nations continue their momentum, ever widening the gulf.

The wailing of our cultural conservatives whenever any modernistic ideas are expressed is responsible for the dilution of those ideas and the consequent dumbing down of the masses. For the last millennium these people have been advocating a retreat to the past. Now the same gurus are advising another millennium of the same misguided medicine. These conservatives, hyperbolically patriotic and occasionally xenophobic, only offer a vague reactive opinion that our troubles are due to lax morality or cultural contamination. History reveals that cries of immorality and 'religion in danger' were commonly used tactics to stall progress. Societies that succumb to these cries retard their own progress. Our conservatives have dreams of pristine purity of our culture. It is politically correct for them to demonize the west and its concomitant modern culture. They are angling to criminalize modernity by enforcing a nostalgic redefinition of national pride. Reining in modern ideas arises as a battle cry from them. A hurricane of hype follows. In the ensuing firestorm, there is a substantial risk in disagreement. No amount of reason or fact can stop the public's panicked response. The scale of absurdity gets lost within the emotions of national and cultural pride. Preposterous propositions float around unchallenged. It tells you more than a little, and nothing encouraging, that we are conflicted over even the most common sense notions of modernity---like opposition to astrology and a woman's right to choose her future husband.

It is time to stop coddling these mythmakers. The times are yearning for a call to reason. Imagine the indifference of the intelligent people breaking out in a chorus of common sense against these merchants of myth and masters of cultural mumbo jumbo. The contribution our intellectuals can make is what the commoners want most but can't find on their own—direction, inspiration and rational outlook. Now, more than ever, our intellectuals must reclaim their irreplaceable role in society and share their indispensable gift of rational thought. For our intellectuals today a moral obligation to be intelligent is more imperative than a moral obligation to be plain old moral. It is also more important than the moral obligation to be politely and politically correct in respecting or tolerating the fantasies of faith-based naivete`. A real intellectual must have the courage not only of his own convictions but also the courage to face the die hard convictions of others. Just think: Should our natural politeness prevent us from piercing obvious stupidities propagated in the name of religion and faith? Remember: Silence is construed as half consent in common parlance and practice. Commoners follow the non-commoners.

Milton was wrong when he said, "They also serve who only stand and wait." For an intellectual in India today, to stand is to stagnate; and to wait is to await disaster for all. It is the surest way to a Paradise Lost with no hope of Regaining it. In fact, it is the surest way to hell. Reticence can be destructive, even lethal at times. If ideas rule the world and the pen is mightier than the sword, then only the intellectuals have the ability to change society and only they control the destiny of nations. India can be great again if its intelligentsia show the courage to overcome orthodoxy, the will to propel to modernity and the wisdom to manage both. That wisdom cannot come till outmoded faith rules supreme, till the intelligentsia can peel back the geological layers of outmoded ideas.

The Bible says: "If the salt loses its savor, wherewith shall it be salted?" I would like to say: If the intellectual will lose his power, wherewith shall he be empowered? Losing power is the inevitable consequence of refusing to use it.

No real change has ever been made by sticking to the middle ground. Change comes from the boundaries, not from the center; from innovators and peripheral thinkers, not from well-entrenched populist centrist ideologues and compromisers. And change always lags behind the changes we need to make. Society never changes as much or as fast as technology does. The real problem is that we bring something old---our static minds---to something new---our ever-changing world. In an ancient society, the majority can be wrong. And those who have the intellect to think right can be overcautious. A writer (Susan Anthony) opines: "Cautious, careful people, always casting about to preserve their reputation and social standing never bring about a reform. Those who are really in earnest must be willing to be anything or nothing in the world's estimation."

In most cases social reform has to be initiated or imposed either by a government or by a small group of committed reformers. If it is left to occur by itself in natural course, it may occur but it is too slow or too late. Liberation of slaves had to be imposed through a civil war, and yet it was not enough to establish racial equality in America. 100 years after Lincoln, George Wallace was elected governor of Alabama State in 1963 on a pledge of "segregation for ever." The same holds true for many other reforms like equality for women, social security, protection of environment and the like. We are so much accustomed to these nowadays that it is difficult to imagine the extent of the strong protest they encountered from the public when they were first introduced. If this is true for a country like America, it is all the more true for a traditional country like India.

The only people more dangerous than dumb bigots are smart educated ones. Many of our intellectuals today are rooted in a religion based orthodoxy that holds as incontrovertible truth whatever our ancients might or might not have believed or said or meant. And the more ancient the better. The reasoning is preposterous but it is justification enough to hold the entire Hindu society in a sort of mental handcuffs. Deep down under, these people are pretty superficial, so to say. They often take shallowness to new depths and elevate trivia to terrific heights. They are famous for being famous, unconnected to real ideas. William James says, "A great many people think they are thinking when they are merely rearranging their biases." Actually there are two kinds of intellectuals: People who think; and People who think they think.

Teaching a new language to a parrot does not really make a difference. Our intellectuals live off borrowed intellectual capital. They are holy cows---chewing, masticating, regurgitating, churning out the most ancient of ideas. We continue to churn out books on the Ramayana and the Mahabharat and commentaries on the Gita even today. The language varies, the emphasis may change, but with rare exceptions, it is the same old stuff in new bottles. Nothing new to say, no originality in ideas. Most indulge in semantic vandalism. Style trumps substance. Words win over ideas. Nobody ever attacks an idea even when it is manifestly wrong. A real intellectual can take on conventional wisdom and tear it apart when necessary. Our intellectuals take conventional wisdom and garnish it with flowery phrases, to prove how clever they are. Critical scrutiny is hardly visible, if ever. The mediocrity, the isolation, the dyed in the wool traditionality of our so called intellectuals is shocking, in spite of their brave attempts to quote western writers in order to impress the common man. The intellectual impotence that cannot breed originality is pitiable. The rootless modern elite have nothing of their own. They wear ideas on their shirt sleeves; their soul is not within them.

Many so called intellectuals today hide behind a curtain made up of impressive words criticizing gurus and traditions (especially when they are addressing Indians in America). On those rare occasions when the curtain is down, people find them practicing the reverse of what they preach. The common men are shocked, the uncommon become cynical and the cycle goes on. Many of our intellectuals and reformers today are like the comedian who said, "I am a thinker. Want proof? I play one on television." Yes, they do play the part, but that is about all one can say for them. Most of the time they seem to be skating on thin ice, unable to distinguish morals from metaphysics, hype from history and folklore from facts.

A journalist recently observed, "There is no Asian equivalent of say, Darwin, Max Planck (scientists), Freud (psychologist), or Picasso (artist). When it comes to ideas, the modern world is a western world. There is no equivalent of surrealism, logical positivism, or whatever list you care to make of 20th century innovations---be it plastic, antibiotics and the atom or the stream of consciousness novels."

To well educated Hindus, stupidities come cloaked in scholarship. So educated people, instead of questioning them, are impressed by them. Their scholarship is informed by orthodoxy. So instead of examining it they accept it as truth. The orthodoxy is rooted in cultural tradition. So instead of modernizing it, they are proud of it. The net result? The educated are proud of their stupidities. Even without realizing it. To less educated Hindus, stupidities come couched in platitudes. So instead of questioning them, they are attracted to them. The platitudes are rooted in simple pieties. So instead of examining them, they accept them. The pieties are a high sounding universal cultural tradition, so they are proud of them. The net result? The less educated too are proud of their stupidities and don't even know it.

The stupidities are thus securely and invisibly entrenched in a culture nurtured on beliefs that were born of religion and were supported through our ingrained orthodoxy. Rational thinking had no opportunity to break through this cycle at any stage. Our ancient irrational religion must therefore bear the ultimate responsibility for our backwardness. Because of our deep rooted orthodox religion, we are certainly much poorer than we otherwise would have been. They say we have population crisis, budgetary crunch, pollution problems, energy crisis, and so on. The unpleasant hard reality is that we are in the midst of an enormous rationality crisis. And the undeniable brilliance of a miniscule few cannot overcome the unspeakable irrationality of the huge masses.

To think the unthinkable is a mark of genius. When our intellectuals will come out of their grooves and start thinking the unthinkable, no power on earth will be able to stop India from becoming a great nation once again. Look at the history of science. Close to the transition into the twentieth century, Michelson-Morley posed a problem as big as the speed of light. No established theories would work. An unknown young man working in a patents office had the genius to think the unthinkable and Relativity revolutionized the world of physics. A photographic plate was found damaged in Roentgen's lab. Did he blame an evil spirit, a phantom or bad luck---or even a colleague? He had the imagination to think out of the groove and the world saw the birth of mysterious rays called X-Rays. To think the unthinkable, to go out of the beaten track, to outgrow your inherent predilections, is the royal road to success. It is the only way for India to advance.

It would be nice to have such a genius among us. But a beautiful rose does not grow in a desert. A suitable soil and climate are needed. Only a certain kind of culture will nurture a genius. It is futile to wait for a savior, as the Jews have been waiting and waiting for ages. However, it is essential, inevitable, almost imperative, to create a culture ready to receive and nurture one if he arrives, prepared to proceed even if he does not. If we create that, we will advance even with a second rate or average kind of leadership in the absence of giants. That is the kind of spirit India must create in its society if she aspires to a better future.

27. DECADENCE TO DAWN
And Beyond

Nobel Laureate V.S. Naipaul, a very perceptive writer of Indian origin, called India "a wounded civilization". He could not have been more correct. Dear V.S., I now have the latest news for you: The wounds are festering and would not heal. The wounded civilization is now dying. India's vaunted culture, her ancient civilization, is on its death-bed. The question now is: How costly shall we make the funeral?

You have two ways of looking at the issues presented throughout this book. EITHER: 1. You can simply ignore what you can brand as 'Hindu bashing' by somebody you will assume as a spoiled westerner like me to support his fleshy materialism. Well, I have been a devout Hindu, anguished by what has become of my great country and religion today. If you ignore the challenges presented in this book, you can very well continue merrily as usual in your ancient tradition as always. To remain asleep in the status quo is the most comfortable thing in the world. You will reap the added advantage of dispensing with the intellectual effort required to think about the perennial problems of India. OR: 2. You can think objectively with an open mind about the issues discussed, keeping aside the brain washing we all got from our culture since our childhood. You have these two options. If you act today you can save our dear India that belongs to us; if you do not, one day there will be no India for us to belong to. The future of your motherland is in balance and the choice is entirely yours.

Hindu enthusiasts today read the career obituary of their civilization as if it were a resume for a fresh job. They think they are remodeling the house when it is completely being gutted by an invisible fire inside. But only a few generations are granted the blessed role of leading a nation out of a deep quagmire. To adapt Roosevelt's words: "To some generations much is forgiven; of other generations, much is expected." This generation (of us Indians) has a rendezvous with destiny. Shall we fulfill that destiny or quit? The future of a billion people depends on it.

Our society nursing the notions of our ancient culture today is like a woman nursing a sick child she already knows will die. For Hindu society today, the moment of truth has arrived. Either we grab it or lose it. Either we shape our own future or let ourselves be slapped by nature's strong hand. Like that duped emperor in the story, either we can continue to strut on the world stage in our imagined divine invisible clothes of ultimate philosophical truths and even feel proud of them; or we can listen to the realistic cry of a child like me who had the innocence to declare that the king was in fact naked. How do you feel when one day you realize that most of what you had believed was based on distortions, partial presentations or illusions? You feel deluded, disillusioned, deceived by life---like Gora, the hero in Tagore's powerful novel. Like the ex-communist author Arthur Koestler in 'The God that failed.' Truth is bitter and exposure to brutal reality is not pleasant. But, we all must face it one day. And the sooner the better.

A Hollywood actress said, "I have been married three weeks now and I still love my husband. Isn't that amazing?" Well, not really. It is not half as amazing as what we have been doing. We have been married to our declining, decaying, doting culture for three thousand years and still love it.

We have had too long a tryst with tradition. Today we have a tryst with our destiny. A long night of scores of problems, a hundred sorrows, a thousand dejections and centuries of defeat can end at the dawn of the new millennium. We have the opportunity today to see the light at the end of the tunnel---if only we refuse to be sheathed in the shapes of the past and we decide to set our sights on the future. For this, we must give up our passion to perish and acquire a passion to prevail. We must replace our willingness to resign with a resolve to win. We must rise in rebellion against subjugation of our souls in the name of spirituality. For, our spirituality is a God that failed, a demon that destroyed us, a Satan that sapped our will to survive. Do we now need to insist that our society should commit suicide in a state of spiritual sanctity and ethical piety?

We have adopted western modes of life in all the outward manifestations. But not with our minds, not in ideas, not in the basic things that really matter. Westernization has come to us not because of our will but in spite of it. Yet westernization rules supreme today and it is the wave of the future. So stop fighting it. You cannot reverse it. You cannot stop the onslaught of history. Actually you need not stop westernization or modernization at all, you need it more and more in a real sense, with its emphasis on science, rationality, secularism, equality, freedom, creativity and respect for individualism.

We are at war with ourselves. Our values are at war with our desire for advancement. Our dream world is at war with our real world. We need to create an alternative to the overt religiosity that dominates our life and the worldly death that lurks below it. We need not fight a war to reverse the triumph of civilization over barbarism. We need to fight a war to modernize our civilization; not just the skin and the cosmetics but the heart and soul of our entire being. The battle for the heart and soul of our culture cannot be won in antiquity. It can only be won by stepping into modernity and striving to surpass it with a realistic vision for the future. Today we are like travelers in a boat rowing in the river of time. The river flows inexorably downstream but more than half of us are trying to row upstream, in irresolution and squeamishness, sights fixed on our distant past. It is not going to work. The waters have to run downstream, you cannot reverse the flow. All that we are achieving is halting progress, encouraging retardation and sowing confusion. Looking back is not going to help us. Looking forward will.

To summarize the ideas we discussed in the earlier chapters: The present day problems of India are superficial symptoms that have their roots in the traditional culture of our people. Our poverty is no accident. Neither is it our predetermined fate. There are sensible causes that caused it. Our backwardness and defeats are rooted not in material deficits but in intangible deficits----of the habits, mores, values and dispositions necessary for advancing in the modern world. Our beliefs are irrational; and our irrationality often bordering on absurdity is something we are too proud to acknowledge. The supreme task before us is to transform our negative culture into one of positivism, optimism and ambition. Our people are being limited. They need enrichment not only in food to nourish their bodies, but also in a fresh value system to challenge their minds. The old value system is a part of our culture that can be directly traced to our religion. Religion has created, condoned facilitated and promoted the irrationally charged environment prevalent in the country today. The religious ideas we inherited and encouraged for centuries past have inculcated in our masses a deep-rooted culture of negative beliefs and attitudes. We are in a veritable bind. But as usual we proffer pious sentiment instead of an overhaul that our value system needs. A major revolution in the entire belief system of the people of India is the crying need of the hour. We must not miss the historic chance to change course now. We need a whole new way of thinking. A shift in the tectonic plates of our values is vital for our survival as a civilization. Until the whirlpool of our old rhetoric is decisively and finally destroyed, the talented people of India cannot realize their true potential.

Over-emphasis on spirituality makes some of us feel that talking about knowledge absolves us from actually having to acquire it; emphasizing values absolves us from having to practice them. Facing a rock hard wall of reality in poverty, disease and destitution, we become inured; our little conscience gets anesthetized. Holy incense masks the scent of putrefying poverty all around. Only a society whose sensibilities have been anesthetized to the point of incurable insanity can continue to build big temples while its children die like dogs in the street----and gloat over its actions. Only a society whose intellectuals have deformed minds will encounter the tall talk of reforming religion with more religion when they know full well that religion has been deforming society. Only a society whose naivete has reached the point of silliness will continue to preach spirituality when it has a history of perpetual poverty, a millennium of defeat and subjugation under foreign rule.

Our sins are not responsible for our fall from grace. Our failures are not a 'Karmic' consequence of our sins. Nature did not discriminate against us in the award of native intelligence. It is not God's wish that we should suffer. Sure we have our share of quakes and floods, disasters and defeats, priests and politicians---like any other country. But we happened to be the most pious people that ever inhabited this planet. We don't let a leaf fall from a tree without ascribing it to the will of God. Our prayers ask for nothing less grandiose than world peace and universal brotherhood. Yet we suffered. It is not our sins that caused our backwardness. Neither can we blame our genes for our downfall. Stupid societies are not born but made. We were not born dumb---only our upbringing made us behave as such. Culture played a more important role than genetic factors. God has no capacity, talent or will to discriminate. Men have. This country did not allow its brilliant minds to flourish. More Indians won Nobel Prize in foreign countries than in India itself. Indians have achieved remarkable success----except in India itself. Indian society and India's cultural maze have trapped India's brilliant young people in the tangled web of inertia and frustration. It is neither sins nor genes---it is our culture and our nurture. It is our social environment and our wrong upbringing that put us in bonds. It is our beliefs and attitudes that chained our feet and shackled our souls. It is our orthodoxy and irrationality that clipped our wings and caused our backwardness.

Hindu society has been like a huge elephant. It will ignore all prompts and continue to stand still crushing all efforts to move it. Nothing can overcome its inertia. Elephants cannot fly. They can only walk. But walking is not enough in today's human marathons. The age-old inertia in Indian society may or may not be of our own making but we can make it of our own ending.

Still, if so many illustrious great men failed to change us, how can a small insignificant book like this succeed? I have no illusions. It is unpleasant to fail, but it is worse never to have tried. As poet Tennyson put it, "It is better to have loved and lost than never to have loved at all." And the effort is worthwhile, because times have changed. Victor Hugo said, "No power on earth can stop an idea whose time has come." Our great reformers were not wrong on the inevitability of change; but they lived when our society was not mature for change. Today we reap the benefits of widespread modern education as well as global travel and communications. The wheels of modernity are slow but they are turning. Today there is hope. That hope rests mainly on the youthful effervescence of India's young minds. They "have nothing to lose but their (cultural) chains. They have a world to win." And win they can, and they will, looking at what they are accomplishing today in the wide world----everywhere but in India itself.

Ours was a great country. Two millennia ago. Once upon a time. In the long long past. Then we stagnated. We headed in the wrong direction. Today at long last, after 800 years of foreign rule, has come the opportunity to make a course correction. Shall we seize it with both hands or let it slip away? The answer to that question will determine the future of a billion people, the future of one of the most ancient civilizations on earth. An author has said, "Men and societies will always do the right thing in the end---after they have exhausted all other options." We have exhausted all other options---political democracy, moralistic philosophy, cultural orthodoxy, theocratic dead-end belief. It is now time to do the right thing.

Many informed Indians understand the gravity of the problems we face today. Yet the problems themselves are not as perplexing as the questions they raise concerning our capacity to think wisely and act rationally. Will we tug pretty pieties over wanton practice? Will we resign ourselves to another millennium of endemic poverty and continue to debate inane questions without any action? Does this country of Raman, Ramanuj and Jagdish Bose have no brains to size up its own problems? Does this land of Pratap, Shivaji and Subhash have no spirit left to fight its way out? If not, it will perish---it must perish. Timidity has no temerity to battle its way out of the conundrums of its own creation. Stupidity has no sacred right to survive. Complacency cannot continue forever. Decay must end in death.

We can dream of a day when India will outgrow its obsession with the past and look forward to the future. We can also dream of a day when India will give up the mirage of a spiritual salvation and opt for the path of present day progress. We must reverse the emotional magnets beneath this world and the next. We must transform the ancient energy of our faith into the momentum of our march into modernity. We must assure ourselves that there is a world to win right here, before we dream to win any other world somewhere else. We must prove that the fires of hell that we endure on this earth can be extinguished with our own endeavor. We need to seek the liberation of our lives before we seek the liberation of our souls. And all this we can do without the mirage of myth and mythology.

Did I make my point? Or is it only a child's cry in the wilderness? Am I a lone fish swimming upstream? If you are reading this kind of book, you cannot but be an intelligent educated person and you will surely judge all these issues for yourself. If you desire more evidence than what is presented here, please remember this: On such a vast and intricate subject, any evidence presented will necessarily look sketchy because if you stop to study every tree, you will surely miss the wood. And the wood----the overall picture, the entire perspective----is what counts most in such matters. The argument may not be sufficiently detailed at times but the conclusions are clear: We need to change our value system completely in order to survive better or advance.

The history of every reformation, renaissance, or revolution begins in the heart of a single man or woman. You or I can be that man or woman with a spark. Every new idea starts with a hypothesis; and a journey of a thousand miles starts but with a single first step. I am just a tiny insignificant speck of a human. It is unlikely that I shall win the Nobel Prize for medicine for discovering a cure for India's ills. But it is quite likely that a few people may start thinking seriously about the issues I presented here. That alone would make my musings worthwhile. As author Franz Kafka put it, "A book should be an axe to shatter the frozen sea within us." And I do firmly believe that "not failure but low ambition is crime."

Bismarck (the German statesman) said, "Genius involves knowing when to stop in a war." Well, common sense involves knowing when to stop in such a war of values, ideas and ideals.

So good-bye, Dear Reader, and thank you.

BIBLIOGRAPHY

1. Asian Drama----Gunnar Myrdal (The 20 th Century Fund, NYK—1968)
2. A Study of History----Arnold Toynbee (Oxford Univ. Press—1947)
3. Beyond Belief---V.S.Naipaul (Random House, NYK—1998)
4. Collected Writings--Thomas Paine (Penguin---1976)
5. Culture Matters----Harrison and Huntington (Basic Books, NYK, 2000)
6. Development of Indian Culture----Laxmanshastri Joshi (Lokvangmaya Griha, Mumbai)
7. Guns, Germs and Steel---The Fate of Human Societies---Jared Diamond (Norton, NYK-1997)
8. Handbook of Psychotropic Herbs---Dr. Ethan Russo (Haworth Press, NYK--2001).
9. India 1999---A Reference Annual--- (Publications Division, Government of India)
10. India 2020----A.P.J. Abdul Kalam with Y.S. Rajan (Penguin India---1998)
11. India, A Wounded civilization---V.S. Naipaul (Random House, NYK, 1977)
12. Literary Occasions----V.S. Naipaul (A.A.Knopf, New York).
13. Sanskrit English Dictionary---V.S.Apte (Motilal Banarsidaas Publishers, Delhi--1993)
14. Seven Habits of Highly Effective People—Stephen Covey (Simon and Schuster—1989)
15. The Bell Curve---Herrnstein and Murray (Free Press, NYK-1994)
16. The Collapse of Complex Societies---- Joseph Tainter (Cambridge Univ. Press, UK, 1988)
17. The Complete Works of Swami Vivekananda (Advaita Ashrama, Calcutta)
18. The God part of Brain---Matthew Alper (Rogue Press, 2001)
19. The Third Chimpanzee----Jared Diamond (Harper Collins—1992)
20. The Transmitter to God---Dr. Rhawn Joseph (Univ. Press, California, 2001)
21. The Wealth and Poverty of Nations---David Landes (Norton, NYK—1998)
22. Tuesdays with Morrie---Mitch Albom (Doubleday, NYK—1997)
23. Underdevelopment is a state of mind--Lawrence Harrison (University Press of America, 1985)
24. Webster's New American Dictionary---Merriam-Webster (Smithmark, NYK--1995)
25. When self consciousness breaks---George Graham (MIT Press, 2000)
26. Why God won't go away-Brain science and biology of Belief-Andrew Newberg (Ballantine, NYK)

INDEX (A): NOTES ON LESS FAMILIAR NAMES

Arjuna	Mahabharat hero, the third son of Pandu, receiver of Gita
Bhishma	Mahabharat hero, idealized, elder statesman, fought for the evil Kauravas
Dayananda	Saraswati, reformer saint, established Arya Samaja,
Drona	Of Mahabharat fame, a Royal Teacher, fought for the evil Kauravas
Dwarika	Legendary town of gold where Lord Krishna ruled
Ekalavya	Low caste sharp shooter--Drona (above) demanded his thumb
Gandhari	Dutiful wife, covered her eyes for blind husband (Mahabharat)
Ganesha	Elephant headed Hindu God
Ghori	Mahmud, started the first Muslim rule in India (1198A.D.)
Gizni	Mahmud, looted India 17 times, broke idols (1024A.D.)
Hanuman	Hindu god, monkey devotee of Rama; could fly (in Ramayana)
Hitopadesha	Children's story book in Sanskrit—like Aesop's fables
Indra	King of gods in Hindu mythology, deity in the Rig Veda
Jagdish	Bose,J. C., Nobel prize winner in Science
Kabir	A poet-saint, tried to unite Hindu and Muslim religions
Kali	Mythological person, portends the currently running Age of Evil
Kalidasa	The greatest poet and dramatist in Sanskrit literature
Karna	Mahabharat character; friend of evil Kauravas; reputed as a donor
Manu	Writer of Manu Smruti, Hindu scriptural code of conduct
Narada	Mythological saint flying with a Veena in hand, devotee of Vishnu
Panipat	Famous battle-field near Delhi, scene of many historical battles
Parashuram	An incarnation of God in Hindu mythology, a virulent Bhahmin
Raman	Sir C.V., winner of Nobel Prize in Physics
Shambuk	Though he was low caste, he performed penance; so Rama killed him
Valmiki	A robber turned saint, Author of the epic Ramayana
Vedas	Most ancient Hindu scriptures (4), including the RigVeda
Vishnu	Hindu God, reincarnates himself periodically to destroy evil
Vivekananda	Modern reformer saint, widely traveled
Yudhisthira	Eldest of the five Mahabharat heroes, ever so truthful.

A FEW EXCERPTS FROM THIS BOOK

Preaching money as evil glorified poverty and encouraged hypocrisy. Unquestioning trust in Gurus discouraged independent thought and creativity. Hindu belief in rebirth promoted good ethics but harmful fatalism. It weakened society through lack of motivation, ambition and competition. (p.57)

People with sights fixed to the stars are more likely to stumble on the road. People who prefer saving the soul to saving the body are less likely to be physically very healthy. (p.57)

Culture can kill--ours did. Repeated exposure to bloated beliefs can be lethal—ours was. (p.57)

For us Hindus, the battles of Panipat were lost on the ghats (banks) of the Ganges. Our hopes lay wounded on the pathways to Heaven in the high Himalayas. Our will to fight was broken with severe blasts of spirituality from saintly scholars. (p.62)

We see stultifying intellectual conformism. I cannot understand why India did not produce a single priest like Galileo, when our long tradition of knowledgeable priesthood included thousands of brilliant minds. In modern times, why did we not produce a Walmart? An Ibsen? A Picasso? (p.65)

Hindu society committed three historical blunders of Himalayan proportions in the philosophical field (p.116)

If I were the Prime Minister of India, People would be my God; Constitution my Gita; and Duty my Guru and guide. I would seek Heaven in the heartland of India and Moksha in the prosperity of its mesmerized masses. Till then Brahma will be a blasphemy and Ishwara an epiphany. God can wait if He wants to. He can even go to Hell for all I care. (p.124)

The values we hold today withhold us. They have been clumsy and confusing; misplaced and misleading; and dangerously defective.----Religion cannot save us. We need to save religion. While we can. If we can. If we want to. Can we do it? (p.127)

Milton was wrong-----For an intellectual in India today, to stand is to stagnate; and to wait is to await disaster for all. It is the surest way to a Paradise Lost with no hope of Regaining it. In fact, it is the surest way to hell. (p.133)

We are at war with ourselves. Our values are at war with our desire for advancement. Our dream world is at war with our real world. (p.135)

Made in the USA
Lexington, KY
30 March 2015